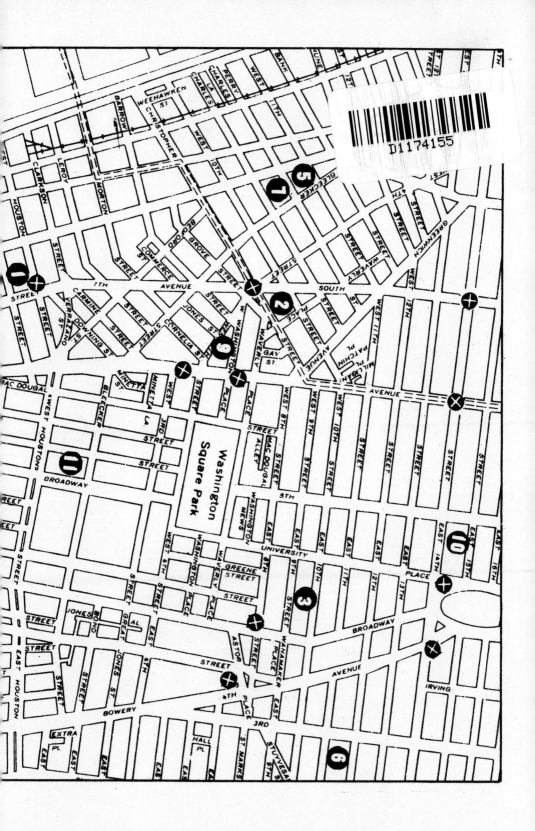

the Italians of Greenwich Village

THE SOCIAL STRUCTURE AND TRANSFORMATION OF AN ETHNIC COMMUNITY

the Italians of Greenwich Village

THE SOCIAL STRUCTURE AND TRANSFORMATION OF AN ETHNIC COMMUNITY

Donald Tricarico

First Edition
Copyright © 1984 by

The Center for Migration Studies
of New York, Inc.

Center for Migration Studies
209 Flagg Place
Staten Island, New York 10304

Library of Congress Cataloging in Publication Data

Tricaro, Donald.
The Italians of Greenwich Village

Bibliography, includes index.
1. Italian Americans—New York (N.Y.)—Social conditions. 2. Greenwich Village
(New York, N.Y.)— Social conditions. 3. New York (N.Y.)—Social conditions. I.
Title

F128.9.18T75 1984   305.8'51'07471   82- 74381
ISBN 0- 913256- 62- 5   ISBN 0- 913256- 64- 1 (pbk.)

To Michele

*t*able of contents

Preface

*P*rofessor Donald Tricarico lived, worked, and studied in Greenwich Village for a period of eight years from 1970 to 1978. When he first settled in the "traditional" South Italian enclave in lower Manhatten, the thought of studying it had not entered his mind. His decision to move there fulfilled in part, a desire to rediscover the neighborhood where his immigrant grandparents had settled when, before the turn of the century, they had migrated from Southern Italy to the South Village. Years later, his parents had moved to New Jersey, part of the great post- World War II migration that took so many of the immigrants' children out from America's urban ethnic ghettos to the open spaces and single family dwellings in the suburban "Greenbelt" developments. For Tricarico, then, the opportunity to return to the village where, like his parents and grandparents, he inhabited a "three room flat with a bathtub in the kitchen" was a return after two generations to his ethnic and family roots. In its four generations in America, the Tricarico family's search for a better life had taken it from Southern Italy to the South Village to New Jersey and back to the South Village.

Before returning to his ancestral roots, Tricarico had been enrolled at the Fordham University School of Business Administration, commuting daily from New Jersey to Manhattan. He had thought neither of becoming a sociologist nor of studying at the Graduate Faculty of the New School for Social Research. By the 1970s, the New School had become a fashionable post- graduate college setting for rebellious and radical youth attempting to disassociate themselves from America's cold war politics, the Nixon administration, and the stultifying conformity of suburban life. A chance encounter with another Village youth who told him the Graduate Faculty "was a good school" led him to undertake studies in that school's sociology program. Both of Tricarico's choices— place of residence and rejections of a career line presupposed in the suburban way of life. A return to the tenement flats of Sullivan or

Thompson Streets was hardly an affirmation of a middle class style of life, and a career in sociology was certainly no substitute for success on Wall Street or in the world of corporate business.

For many youth in that generation, the rejection of American society and its values was expressed politically. For others, however, it expressed itself as a search for an identity in American society that would not violate ethnic ties, but would allow a break with parental controls. Tricarico carried out his own version of the youth revolt by leaving the New Jersey suburbs and returning to the habitat associated with his ethnic origins. His choice of the New School for Social Research as a place to study could not have been predicted. At that time, many of its graduate students came from suburban middle class families — some of whom had entered graduate school in order to avoid the draft or fight the alleged corruption of university administrations — these youth associated the New School with socio- cultural heterodoxy and political radicalism, perceiving it as a kind of avant- garde intellectual center that straddled the boundaries of the East and West Village and lent academic support to the values of the youth revolt. Donald Tricarico did not fit the description of this body of New School students. He was neither radically politicized nor part of the hippie, flower- child counter-culture. His was a search for a personal identity; he hoped to find it through the residential and educational choices he made. At the time he had no idea that these choices would be the beginning of a long- term study of American culture as it might be seen through three generations of Italian- American experience in Greenwich Village.

After Tricarico had lived in the Village for four years and become familiar with much of its social and cultural life, he realized (in the process of preparing a paper for a New School seminar on Urban and Metropolitan Research) that his own experience could be combined with ethnographic and historical investigations to form the basis for a community study. It became apparent that what had begun as a return to his family's old neighborhood had become a comprehensive research project, already well under way. Tricarico committed himself to examine three generations of Italian American immigrant life in the South Village. His study focuses on its per-sistence and adaptive strategies in the face of interaction with the other groups that came to make up the neighborhood. For four years, from 1974 to 1978, Tricarico devoted almost all of his personal resources and energy to the in- depth and extensive col-lection of historical, census, demographic, geneological, economic and participant observation data. He read most of the literature that had been written on Italian Americans and studied the history of Southern Italy. He familiarized himself with ethnic and racial studies and their theories of assimilation, accommodation and ghettoization. Above all, he saw the South Village in the context of one- hundred years of trans-Atlantic and trans-cultural history, a history that embraced events in Italy, the South Village and its environs, and the processes of suburbanization in American civilization. Because he eschewed setting his Italian neighborhood as one more illustration of America's exaggerated melting pot culture, he perceived its theoretical significance less in terms of assimilation to a non-definable "American culture" than as an example of American culture in the process of creation. The Italians did not give up pizza, the Americans adopted it, but the pizza that all were eating was a new culinary creation, adapted for the American market and unknown as such in Italy and brandmarked as an American "ethnic" cuisine. Tricarico discovered that he was studying the very processes by which American culture has been formed, his study of the South Village is a study of American social and cultural history in microcosm.

As luck would have it the South Village was ideally situated as a research site. When Tricarico began his work, the West Village had already become a community of commercial atists, professors, illustrators, models and advertising executives for whom the village symbolized bohemianism. Max Eastman, Floyd Dell, Mabel Dodge, Big Bill Haywood and John Reed, who in the decade 1910-1920 had given Greenwich Village its original bohemian image, had been replaced by the new middle classes of the post-World War II American affluence. The latter took pride in their renovated town-houses and the cultural chic of "Village" life. Aware of this development Tricarico recognized that Caroline Ware's, *Greenwich Village,* 1920-1930, had depicted the era that followed that of his immigrant grandparents and preceded the return to the Village of highly assimilated middle classes who sought the ethnic charm of Italian bakeries, sausage shops, pork butchers, Zito's bread, espresso and arrugala. In Greenwich Village, these new middle classes incorporated Italian culture into their own lifestyles. To the East of the South Village lay the newly developing young artists community, SoHo, then being studied by Charles Simpson, another member of the New School's Urban Research Seminar. SoHo attracted a new generation of artistic and radical bohemians who associated the Village with self-expression, art and independence, but who could not afford the cost of brownstone housing in Greenwich Village. The youth of SoHo were college educated ex-suburbanites who sought their own salvation in the mecca of art and cultural freedom. Tricarico found that he could not study these generations of Italians in the South Village apart from the cultural, class and economic developments occurring in Greenwich Village, SoHo, Little Italy, Chinatown and Tribeca. The great virtue of his book is that it shows in detail the relationship among ethnic and urban cultures, middle class life-styles, intergenerational socio-cultural transactions, transformations of cultural values, and urban political parties and municipal governments.

The Italians of Greenwich Village can be compared to the studies of Italian communities, William F. Whyte's *Street Corner Society,* and Herbert Gan's *The Urban Villagers,* originally published in 1943 and 1962 respectively. However, neither Whyte nor Gans located their studies in an historical frame and neither had the advantage of inner access to the most private dimensions of life in the family and in the neighborhood, or to the Mafia's economic and social functions. Tricarico gives us an inside view of the community, informed by an intimate personal knowledge of Italian culture and combined with the intellectual attitude of a trained sociologist. He is able to "see" the three generations of Italian experience through social actors who lived it as a moving present. In *The Italians of Greenwich Village* one follows the lives and careers of grandmothers, brothers, priests, politicians, businessmen, Mafiosi, merchants, bureaucrats and corner boys as they move about in an ever- changing American society. As a result the reader is given a vivid portrait of a neighborhood changing as its people interact with a changing society. A book that is a case study thus becomes a general history of central tendencies of social change in American society as a whole, as these are refracted in and through Italian culture. To locate the sociological and historical significance of this book, one would have to compare it not only with *Street Corner Society* and *The Urban Villagers* but also with William Faulkner's fictional studies of Yoknapatawpha County and Chester Hime's sociological novels of Harlem: *Pinktoes, Cotton Comes to Harlem* and *The Third Generation.*

Arthur J. Vidich
Professor and Chairman, The Graduate Faculty
New School For Social Research

Acknowledgements

*t*here are a number of people who figured prominently in the work that went into this book. A good place to begin would be to thank Professor Arthur Vidich for his encouragement of the study from the time it was first proposed in his dissertation seminar and for his professional wisdom and friendship. Other New School scholars, especially Professor Stanford Lyman and fellow graduate student Charles Simpson, were invaluable sounding boards for a work in progress.

I would like to thank everyone at the Center for Migration Studies, including Lydio Tomasi and Maggie Sullivan for their commitment to publish the study. I have special regard for Silvano Tomasi for his early and continuing support. Eileen Reiter was undaunted as an editor who did her share to alleviate the anxieties of publication; I enjoyed our working relationship.

My thanks also to Tom Graham, my good friend and fishing companion, who lent his artistic talents to the book's cover.

I am grateful for a loving family—my mother and father, my sister and her family, and my grandmother. My South Village relatives were warmly supportive, in particular my Aunt Lee, who was as close to a research assistant as I had, and my Uncle Joe, who was my frequent companion in the neighborhood. My wife Michele shared what often seemed like an unwieldly and unending project at close range; she made things infinitely better by just being there.

Finally, I wish to express my thanks to everyone in the South Village who made living there an enjoyable experience. I hope I have portrayed your community as honestly as possible.

Donald Tricarico
February, 1984

Introduction

*t*he ethnic neighborhood is a salient feature of the American urban mosaic. The enclaves formed by European immigrants in industrial cities in the Northeast and Midwest in the late 19th and early 20th centuries were particularly notable—in 1910, European immigrants and their children comprised about 75 percent of the population of New York, Boston, Chicago, Detroit and Cleveland. Immigrant settlements took root on the residential fringe of central business and manufacturing districts. Their supply of cheap housing and population densities gave them the earmark of the classic urban slum. At the same time, ethnic concentration spawned urban villages where Old World practices were transplanted.

The dominant sociological approach to the study of the ethnic neighborhood (and ethnicity in general) has been from the related standpoints of assimilation and disorganization. Along these lines, the ethnic neighborhood is seen as a "staging ground" from which immigrants and their children entered the larger society as they became Americanized and improved their economic position. Although the ethnic community is regarded as a cultural retreat, the "incessant hammering" (Campisi, 1948) of American culture and the gradual upward movement of individuals precipitated the breakdown of ethnic institutions and the waning of ethnic identity (Sandberg, 1974; Crispino, 1980; Steinberg, 1981). With the drastic decline of immigration after World War I, it appeared that the ethnic neighborhood was withering away. The continuous process of invasion and succession within the city hastened the disintegration of the original settlement (Ward, 1971).

According to this model, the ethnic neighborhood is essentially an artifact of the immigrant experience. The emphasis on assimilation and disorganization tended to preclude a concern with, and an awareness of, the transformation or internal development of the ethnic community.

This scenario informs the rather limited study of the urban Italian neighborhood. Nelli's (1970) study of Italians in Chicago between 1880 and 1930 stresses "the tremendous amount of immigrant mobility" which was "the principal reason for the waning of community institutions" and the decline of core Italian settlements after World War I. Ware (1965) depicted the Italian community in New York's Greenwich Village in the 1920s as in a state of complete social and cultural disorganization primarily owing to the impact of "American ways" on the second generation. She specifically ruled out the restructuring of ethnic community.

Whereas Chicago's Italian neighborhoods may have been breaking up by World War I, another look at Greenwich Village suggests a different interpretation. Viewed in retrospect, one can now see that Ware lacked a perspective which might have enabled her to see structures that were only then beginning to emerge.

The history of Italians in the lower part of Greenwich Village extends back to the 1850s. The exiled Garibaldi was affiliated with the early Italian colony and reputedly made candles in a shop on Bleecker Street before returning to Italy (Foerster, 1919). A parish created in the South Village in 1866 became the first Italian congregation in New York City and the second in the United States. Primarily owing to the influx of impoverished Southern Italians, the Italian population of the Village swelled to about 50,000 prior to World War I. Only East Harlem and the nearby East Side (Mulberry Street) had larger concentrations.

Although out-mobility and immigrant quotas precipitated a steady decline in population following World War I, there were still 8,944 persons of Italian birth and parentage in core census tracts in 1960, and this did not include the third and fourth generations. Writing in 1963, Glazer and Moynihan commented on "the surprising endurance of the Italian neighborhood in the city", adding that "there is no more striking evidence of the strength of Italian communities than the tenements of the South Village". Moreover, the Italian South Village was not simply a residue of the original immigrant colony, *i.e.,* a "Little Italy" inhabited mainly by older members of the group who were left behind as the second generation moved up and away. Rather, the community underwent fundamental changes. Communal solidarity based on ties to persons from the same village or province (*i.e., paesani*) was recast along broader ethnic lines (*i.e.,* based on an identification as Italian or Italian American). Immigrant social frameworks like the mutual aid society atrophied and were replaced by new urban structures such as the district political club and the defended neighborhood.

Thus, instead of giving way to "disorganization", the Italian South Village was restructured by absorbing social, cultural and economic changes in the second generation.

Certain aspects of this communal transformation have been depicted with respect to other Italian neighborhoods. Whyte's (1943) participant-observation study of the North End of Boston during the Depression showed deep appreciation of the structurally stable Italian American community. Rejecting the prevalent understanding of the slum as a disorganized community, Whyte illustrated how the street corner gang and, to a lesser extent, "the rackets" and the political machine imparted an underlying structure to the lower class Italian district.

Suttles (1968) portrayed the Italian community in the Addams area of Chicago in the 1960s as an example of how lower class, slum populations impose a provincial moral order on the city. For Suttles, ethnicity was an important basis for "differential moral isolation"; provincial arrangements and understanding did not hold outside the Italian section. This led him to focus on generic slum institutions, such as "the Outfit" and male street corner groups, which were capable of enforcing local codes and defending a turf against outsiders.

Neither Whyte nor Suttles, however, connected essentially slum social institutions to ethnic social and cultural forms like Italian familism and the Mafia. To this extent, their work is more appropriate as slum studies than as ethnic community studies.

Perhaps the most authoritative work on the urban Italian American community is Gans' (1962) study of the West End of Boston in the late 1950s. Gans collapsed the meaningful social experience of West End Italians within the family-centered peer group; his study of the "urban village" is essentially a study of that institution which he saw as a typically working class formation. Italian peer group society precluded an involvement with the community; the latter was "relatively unimportant" and was discussed only from the standpoint of the peer group. Ethnicity was not a principle of communal solidarity. In fact, Gans maintained that there was "no identification with Italian culture and symbols".

In contrast with the West End, in looking at the South Village, it is possible to delineate an integrated ethnic community. The restructured ethnic community was comprised of social institutions that articulated with one another within a locality framework (*i.e.*, the neighborhood). It was characterized by a shared value system rooted in common ethnic traditions. Ethnicity was a criterion of communal membership. The neighborhood-based Italian American community reflected the adaptation of second generation Italians to the city at a particular historical juncture.

A number of historical reasons may be suggested to account for the restricted nature of ethnic community in the West End compared to the South Village. The West End experienced relatively rapid ethnic successions. It was dominated by the Irish until the turn of the century and by the Jews until 1930; the area was 75 percent Jewish in 1926. It was only after 1930 that it became largely Italian, and even then it contained sizeable pockets of Albanians, Ukranians and Greeks. Moreover, the West End was not the major settlement for Italians in Boston, but was essentially an "overspill" area for the North End after 1920.

By contrast, the South Village was predominantly Italian by World War I. There was also a much larger Italian population, numbering some 50,000 in 1910. Finally, the neighborhood remained relatively stable; there was not the succession of ethnic groups that Gans describes for the West End.

In the South Village, the size and concentration of the Italian population over several generations had consequences for the emergence and maintenance of ethnic communal patterns. The West End, on the other hand, did not support an Italian neighborhood. Gans points out that there was "relatively little interest in the West End as a physical or social unit"; Italians never used the term neighborhood in referring to the West End. There was a lack of identification with institutions like the local parish where the pastor, many of his priests and most of his lay leaders were Irish. In the South Village, the neighborhood and the institutional fabric associated with it were Italian from before World War I to the present period.

This book is a study of an urban ethnic community from the standpoint of adaptation and change. The South Village Italian community did not disintegrate from the impact of American culture and the cessation of large-scale immigration. An identifiable ethnic community persisted, although by no means as a vestige of the initial immigrant colony. Rather, the Italian South Village was restructured in the period following World War I. A new communal form reflected the adjustment of the second generation to the city at a particular historical juncture, combining traditional, social and cultural forms with lower class, urban institutions. The study will focus on the institutions that comprise the restructured ethnic community; the family group; the social neighborhood; the local parish; district political clubs; and the Mafia syndicate. It will trace the directions of change evidenced by community institutions into the present, especially in light of ongoing population decline and the succession of new groups related, in particular, to the emergence of an artists' community and the gentrification of the South Village area.

Research Methods

In keeping with the methods appropriate to community study, my research was carried out as a participant in local Italian life. I was a resident of the South Village Italian neighborhood from October 1970 to February 1978, although I had no thought of studying the community until 1974. Like many of the Italians living in the neighborhood, I inhabited a three room flat with a bathtub in the kitchen.

As with every community study, gaining access to the community posed the initial research problem; only by becoming a member of the community would it be possible to comprehend the provincial arrangements and values that comprised the ethnic neighborhood. I was fortunate in having relatives in the South Village who furnished a bridge to the community. Since people knew my relatives, I was not considered a stranger, a label that was attached to other young men and women who discovered the South Village in those years for its low rents and numerous emenities. A kinship tie opened up social networks in which my relatives were embedded. Thus, I became acquainted with cornerboy buddies of an uncle; in no time, my presence in bars and candy stores was accepted. I also attended wakes that my relatives had an obligation to attend. Several times, relatives put me in touch with people who were pleased to grant an interview. Utilizing this connection illustrates the preeminence of kinship as "social capital".

Being a resident of the South Village enabled me to observe first-hand the many facets of neighborhood life. I socialized with cornerboys, occasionally serving as a target for their sharp wit; exchanged pleasantries with the elderly women who spent hours on a playground bench taking the sun; and played basketball in local playgrounds and the parish gym. I knew merchants on a first name basis; purchases were couched in brief visits. I attended mass at the local church; was a substitute teacher at a parish grammar school, an opportunity arranged by an aunt who was the school secretary; visited people in their homes, attended community meetings like those held in the church basement to discuss the crime problem, and ventured into syndicate "horse rooms" where I knew bookies and loansharks on a neighborly basis. In all these encounters, I became privy to the gossip that flowed through the neighborhood like a river.

Participant-observation was supplemented by interviews and the use of existing data. Formal interviews were conducted to gather information on specific topics, usually with persons who had some civic importance and would take an holistic view such as parish priests, settlement workers, the officers of clubs and societies, politicians and businessmen. In each case, it was noted that the research was for a doctoral dissertation. Most people were cooperative, especially those who were obliging one of my relatives.

Several informants were tapped on a regular basis. In these cases, however, the interview format gave way to informal chats over beer or coffee. A second generation civic leader proved to be enormously valuable in shedding light on local political developments. He saw our discussions as an opportunity to gain recognition for civic efforts that neighborhood Italians did not sufficiently appreciate. There were other marginal individuals who were incisive observers.

Interviews and discussions were especially useful for unearthing neighborhood history. Old-timers vividly recalled the period before World War I; an elderly gent conducted a private tour in which he gave an historical account of specific locales. It was easy to get cornerboys to talk about something out of their past, such as swimming down at the piers or playing ball for the parish. Some people volunteered old photographs of intimate family scenes, cornerboy groups, settlement house classes, religious processions, etc. Nostalgia offered a brief retreat from a present that, for many, was disappointing.

Census materials and institutional publications were also consulted. Demographic materials provided a framework for the study of community organization, although the absence of federal census data on the third generation constituted a limitation. On the whole, there was a paucity of documentary materials. The only neighborhood institution maintaining records was the parish; one parish had marriage and baptism records dating back to 1856. The parish also published bulletins which were informative, although sometimes promotional. A helpful pastor produced a report commissioned by the order in 1924 (written in Italian) to assess the state of its parishes in the United States. At the main branch of the public library I discovered numerous pamphlets published by Protestant missions in the area before World War I in which they detailed their work on behalf of the Italian immigrants. While searching through an out-of-the-way file at the Hudson Street Library, I came upon community studies of Greenwich Village by the WPA (1939) and the New York University School of Education (1954) which contained material on the Italian neighborhood, each recommending urban renewal for the South Village.

Overall, this text seeks to present a fair analysis of the urban ethnic community within the fairly standard data constricts inherent to community studies.

The Immigrant Colony

*i*talian immigrants settled in a section of Greenwich Village in which nearly a quarter of the Negro population of the city lived in 1865. The so-called "Negro Plantations", or "Little Africa", adjoined the patrician Ninth Ward of Washington Square. James Weldon Johnson (1930:58) observed.

> When Washington Square was the center of fashionable life, large numbers of Negroes engaged in domestic service in the homes of the rich lived in a fringe of nests to the west and south of the Square.

In the late nineteenth century, the black South Village was noted for its squalid conditions. Besides its dire poverty, the district was also famous for its dubious moral character.

Toward the end of the nineteenth century, the old Negro Quarter was being rebuilt as a tenement district in order to house Italian immigrants recruited for the nearby sweatshops. In 1890, Riis observed that Italian immigrants were:

> ...overrunning the Old Africa of Thompson St., pushing the Negro rapidly uptown, against querulous but unavailing protests, occupying his home, his church, his trade and all, with merciless impartiality (p. 21).

In 1893, a Catholic Church serving a black congregation, St. Benedict the Moor, was purchased by an Italian religious order for Italian immigrants in the area. By World War I, only vestiges of the once formidable black community remained in pockets on Minetta Lane, Gay Street, and West Third Street.

Caroline Ware (1965:23) noted that blacks below Washington Square "were followed and finally supplanted by Italian immigrants, spreading over from their East Side center". However, it would seem that Italians merely completed the displacement of blacks, a process that had been initiated by other European groups. The Irish, in particular, entered the district earlier in the century and vied with blacks for jobs on nearby piers and in domestic service in the Yankee Ninth Ward. The Draft Riots during the Civil War threw this intergroup conflict into relief. In 1863, Irish mobs marched into the South Village to protest the draft lottery; Thompson Street was set afire, as was a tenement on Roosevelt and Sullivan Streets; a black was lynched on Sullivan Street. In all probability, then, blacks were already being routed when Italian immigrants began to settle in the South Village.

The Italian immigrants did confront a cohesive Irish community which remained intact until World War I. The Irish had roots in the Village that went back to the 1820s when they arrived to work as domestics or in the construction industry. However, the Irish had already retreated west before the Italians arrived. Baptism and marriage records at a church that was established for Italian immigrants in 1866 indicate that, toward the end of the nineteenth century, Irish parishoners lived in the better homes west of Sixth Avenue on King, Charlton, Vandam, Bethune, Greenwich and West Houston Streets. Few Italians lived in this section. Even though the Irish perceived the Italians as "the ones who took their neighborhood away from them", (Ware, 1965:128) the decline of the Irish community was primarily a result of a preference for the suburbs on the part of mobile second and third generation Irish, and a rise in real estate values brought on by the influx of middle class families after World War I.

However, despite physical segregation and intergroup conflict, the Irish exercised considerable influence on the Italians' adjustment to the district. The Irish retained power and prestige in key institutional spheres, in particular politics and the Church. The Italian immigrants viewed the Irish as "Americans", and as such, models for the second generation to emulate.

The six and seven story tenements erected south of Washington Square around the turn of the century established the Italian colony as a slum area. The typical tenement flat consisted of three railroad rooms situated on an airshaft; the largest room about 13 feet by 11 feet. Toilets in the backyard were shared by tenants; many second generation Italians still think the Italian word for toilet is "backhouse" (pronounced with an Italian inflection). Odencrantz (1919:197) noted that these "living quarters as a whole were distinctly below the American standard of a parlor, a dining room, and a kitchen distinct from a sleeping room". However, they seem to have been an improvement over the earlier apartments in which Italian immigrants lived.

All things considered, the Italian South Village compared favorably to other immigrant slums in the city. It did not have the population densities that made the lower East Side notorious. Riis (1900:53) reported a tenement inhabited by Italians on Elizabeth Street in 1900 that contained "forty-three families where there should have been sixteen". On the other hand, similar descriptions do not exist for the South Village. Odencrantz, who studied Italian women living in the heart of the old Negro Quarter, did not find the doubling and tripling up of families in tiny three room flats that Riis discovered on the East Side. Lord, Trenor and Barnes (1905:75-76) spoke about the Italian South Village in more positive terms:

> There has been even more notable change in the district running south of Washington Square to Canal St. and extending from Macdougal St. to West Broadway. Fifteen years ago this was one of the most notorious of the so called slum quarters of the city, very largely tenented by Negro and French families, and often glaring in its dissolute and riotous displays. Here the Italians began to settle about fourteen years ago, and their influx now dominates the section...the advance of the section has nevertheless been remarkable. Now whenever any real estate in the section comes into the market, it is eagerly bid for by Italian operators and builders. Hancock St. on both sides of Bleecker to Bedford now shows lines of tenements that would be a credit to any city... The value of the real estate in this section has increased, and the quarter is, in the main of excellent character.

Even Ware (1965:37) qualifies an earlier statement that the South Village had been transformed into a slum area with the arrival of Italian immigrants and the construction of new tenements. She notes that the Village was relatively stable since "there were none of the kaleidoscope succession of nationalities that have characterized some sections of Manhattan—only a gradual decline of the older relative to the new group". Moreover, in contrast to the East Side and other ethnic areas, the Italian Village has "neither a first settlement nor a second settlement, but something in between". Odencrantz (1919:37) similarly observed, "Into this neighborhood families have moved from the East Side as they became more prosperous, so that both poor families and those comfortably well off live on the same block".

The Village did not have the supply of poor-quality, low-rent houses found on the East Side and elsewhere in the city. In particular, it was not a deteriorated district of once wealthy residences. The section inhabited by old Yankee families remained intact throughout this time, serving as a check on industrialization and tenement construction. In 1916, the City Zoning Commission acted to guarantee the integrity of the American Ward. After World War I, artists, bohemians and the middle class were reclaiming immigrant sections; new apartment buildings were erected, and brownstone and Federal Period houses were renovated. This influx, in particular the artists who discovered the Village lofts and stables for their studios, foreshadowed the SoHo phenomenon of the 1970s, which perhaps signifies the possible completion of the bourgeoisification of the area.

3

Immigrant settlement in the South Village was influenced by the availability of manufacturing jobs. In 1906, "67 percent of all factory jobs in the city were below Fourteenth Street" (Kessner, 1977:150). The so-called "Venice of Industry" formed the eastern edge of the South Village Italian colony. The clothing industry was an especially important employer of Italian labor; in 1929 it still occupied 6,700,000 square feet of floor space in Village loft buildings (WPA, 1937). A 1905 sample of 4,169 Italian males living in the South Village and nearby east side Italian settlements found that 826 worked in the garment trades, —605 were tailors (Gutman, 1977: 529).[1] A large number of Italian women were also employed in clothing production. Odencrantz found that roughly half of Italian women at a local settlement house were "making men's, women's, and children's clothing" (1919:38). The proximity of factories made it possible for mothers to take in work and supplement family income.

The Social Structure
of the Immigrant Community

Italians arrived in this country in two interdependent population movements. The first consisted of lone working males. Between 1899 and 1910, 1,502,968 Southern Italian males came to this country compared to only 408,965 females (Glanz, 1971:12). Male sojourners intended their stay to be only temporary and were aloof from the American environment except for employment. The Old World orientation of this immigration is reflected in the $85 million remitted to Italy for the year 1907 (Foerster, 1919:374). The other movement was a migration of families. It was often a "delayed" migration whereby the immigrant male sent for his wife and children (and relatives) when he obtained a means of support and a place to live; until this time, he may have lived in a lodging house with other males or boarded with a family from the same town. A number of South Village residents had relatives who came over in this delayed fashion.

In either case, immigrant social organization was focused on other persons from the *paese.* The paese, which literally translates as "country", was the village or town from which the immigrant originated. The group life of immigrant *paesani,* or countrymen, was an

---

[1] Local Italian men were well represented in construction work. There were 841 unskilled construction workers in the 1905 sample (Gutman, 1977:529). Although Foerster (1919:353) maintained that other nationalities presented skilled work, 454 men were skilled building trades workers, including 101 carpenters, 52 bricklayers, and 43 stonecutters (Gutman, 1977:529).

4

outgrowth of the myriad local dialects and customs which characterized Italian peasant culture. This diversity was bred of geographical isolation and different historical experiences; therefore, contact with Greek culture had implications for the Calabrian and other Sicilian dialects (the widest cultural differences were between the Northern and Southern parts of the country). The paese generated a powerful sense of localism known as *companilismo,* which enjoined the peasant to confine his extra familial relationships to those living within the sound of the church bells (*campanile*). It found its consummate expression in marital endogamy.

These traditions were transplanted to the immigrant colony, although with a new urgency. Village "chains" brought paesans together in the city. In Greenwich Village, people from the same province often lived on the same block. A stretch of Sullivan Street was Genoese, while a part of Thompson Street was Sicilian. One Thompson Street tenement was inhabited by immigrants from the province of Avellino; a building across the street was occupied by immigrants from the province of Potenza. The latter has sent immigrants to the South Village for over one hundred years, and they still cluster in the same blocks and buildings.

The immigrants' settlement, then, was by no means a homogeneous "Italian" community. Rather, it was fragmented into lesser groups defined by place of origin (*i.e.,* the paese). The paesani subcommunity possessed a distinctive Old World dialect, folklore and religious cult. Relations between different groups were typically characterized by petty jealousies and animosities. As a result, casual social relations, as well as formal organizations, were often restricted to people from the same town or province.

The focal point of solidarity for the immigrant was the group of fellow townsmen. Immigrants who knew each other in the village often emigrated together and settled in the same neighborhood. The town was the symbol of their collective identity, and they remained in touch with it through the ebb and flow of migration. For some towns in the province of Potenza (Basilicata), this movement of population has rendered the South Village a virtual colony, a relationship that has continued into the present. There is still the custom of returning to the paese to choose a wife, and a few men did; in other cases, a match was made through agents (*i.e.,* relatives or *campari*) in the town. A powerful tie to the paese is through kin who either decided not to emigrate or returned to Italy. The immigrants also retained a devotion for this village patron, and celebrated a *festa* in conjunction with the festa held in the paese. One example of the strong relationship still felt to the town of origin is an immigrant from Montemurro who proudly named his grocery after the patron saint of his village, San Rocco; the backroom of the store serves as a clubhouse for paesani who wax nostalgic about the fig harvest and

5

the view of the town from the cemetery and picture postcards of the town are thumbtacked to the walls.

In this country, similarities of dialect and customs and relative proximity (seen from overseas) engendered fraternization and a common identification among immigrants from towns that were part of the same province or region. For example, immigrants from the rural towns of Moliterno and Montemurro came to regard themselves, at least for some purposes, as paesani. Both towns were within the province of Potenza and the region of Basilicata Despite local prejudices, there was a great deal in common, especially in light of contrasts with other groups of "strangers" (*i.e.*, non-Italians and Italians from more remote parts of Italy). Similarly, immigrants from the provinces of Catania and Palermo recognized each other as Sicilians, and were so regarded by other Italians. These provincial and regional unities gave rise to a formal and informal group life.

The South Village Italian colony contained a wide array of village, provincial and regional groups. In 1919 Odencrantz observed that, "On the West Side, extending roughly from West Broadway to the Hudson River and Canal to West Fourth, is the district most varied in its Italian population" (p. 12). Ware (1965) observed that the Village "community differed from other Italian areas in the city in that it contained a large number of provincial groups within a smaller radius...in contrast to the East Side where solidly Sicilian and Neopolitan schools served adjacent territories" (p. 156). Marriage records from one of the Italian churches in the Village gave an indication of this diversity. Among the provincial towns mentioned as places of baptism for individuals married in 1908 were Avellino, Bari, Barletta, Castellmare Del Golfo, Cosenza, Catania, Napoli, Potenza, Salerno, and Trapani.

Superimposed on the village, provincial and regional diversity of the immigrant colony was the fundamental distinction between Northern and Southern Italians (between 1899 and 1910, about six times as many Southerners emigrated as Northerners). This caste-like bifurcation of the immigrant community was given a cultural and racial basis. Northern Italians were believed to be more advanced, comparable to Northern Europeans; on the other hand, Southern Italians had an inferior and backward "Mediterranean" culture (Covello, 1967). In the South Village, Odencrantz noted that Northern Italians "showed a better understanding of democratic institutions", while remarking on "the traditional indolence of the Southern peoples" (pp. 168 and 171).

Within the immigrant colony an internal stratification emerged ranking Northerners as *alt'Italiani* (high Italians) and Southerners as *bass'Italiani* (low Italians). An invidious distinction was extended to dialects and other cultural forms, so that Italians from the South

6

spoke "low Italian". Status differences and inequality posed a major obstacle to fraternization between the two groups. Southerners accused Northerners of being 'cold" and *superbe* (snobbish). Parish records for the years before World War I indicate that intermarriage was rare.

In Greenwich Village, this status order was reinforced by the earlier arrival of Northern Italians, primarily from Genoa. They tended to come in slowly as an overflow from the East Side, whereas Southerners arrived *en masse*. Ostensibly referring to this Northern Italian settlement, a *Harper's Monthly* article (1881) noted that the Italian parish on Sullivan Street was "attended by a superior class of Italians, all apparently prosperous and at peace with their environment" (Adam, 1881). When the mass of Southerners began arriving toward the end of the 19th century, Northerners had already established themselves and scorned the new arrivals, the 'low' Italians, not wishing to be associated with them, yet dominating the affairs of the entire Italian community.

Differences between Northern and Southern Italians possessed a spatial dimension. In the twenties, Ware found seven blocks that were "almost entirely North Italian" and five that were "exclusively" Southern Italian. There were institutional cleavages as well. Saloons, cafes, bakeries, undertaking establishments, etc., tended to cultivate clientele from either North or South. The two Italian parishes in the South Village tended to draw parishioners from one or the other group, although this was partly because of settlement patterns.

Mutual Aid Societies

Paesani sustained an informal social life within the immigrant enclave. They tended to cluster together in the same buildings and blocks, socialize in cafes and form alliances through intermarriage and godparentage. As friends and neighbors, they did sundry favors for one another. Shops owned by *paesani* were patronized. Immigrants helped paesani find employment. Italians from Bari, for example, followed one another into the ice and coal business.

A noteworthy development among paesani was the formation of mutual benefit associations which helped newly arrived immigrants to cope with sickness, loneliness and death and held social functions. In Greenwich Village, it was estimated that fifty percent of Italian men belonged to a society of paesani in 1910. When this study was undertaken, none of the societies were still in existance; therefore, little evidence could be gleaned about specific societies.

Societies performed critical social and psychological functions. Fenton (1975) observes that:

Within the society, men could speak dialect without misun-
derstanding one another, discuss common problems, organize
activities and make plans to erect statues (p. 52).

The societies were also religious associations, many named for the
patron saint of villages. For many, the major purpose of the association was to sponsor the festa of the saint or madonna. They
were to coincide with, as well as replicate as far as possible, the
festa taking place in the paese. A share of the money affixed to the
statue of the saint or madonna carried in the street procession was
remitted to the village shrine in Italy.

The paesani societies were the basic structures of mutual aid
outside the family, rooted in tradition of *campanilismo.* The Italian
colony was characterized by the absence of structures based on
wider loyalties. One such organization, however, was the Italian
Benevolent Institute, which was located on Houston Street in the
South Village. It was founded in 1882 by delegates from a number
of mutual aid societies, although it received large subsidies from the
King of Italy. It was described as a "place of refuge for the destitute",
however, it appears to have mainly served as a labor exchange.
Although touted as a community-wide organization, it seems to
have been no substitute for the myriad societies of paesani.

The Immigrant Family

Except for the significant numbers of male sojourners living with
paesani in lodging houses, immigrants transplanted traditional
family patterns. Although it was not the all-embracing institution it
was in the peasant village, where the unity of the family was secured
by custom and common rights in the land, the family was the regulating principle of immigrant experience. It was at the center of a
paesani community which, in turn, sustained a supportive milieu for
common family traditions.

The first generation Italian family was very much intact. The
1905 sample points out that 93 percent of 2,945 households had
"husband or father present"; less than 3 percent of all households
were "male-absent" and headed by women under forty years of age.
The data indicated that 60 percent of all households were nuclear,
while 23 percent were extended. Kin ties, then, persisted between
two generations; where relatives were not included in the same
household, they were often living nearby in the same neighborhood.
Relatively few Italian households were augmented with paying boar-
ders (Gutman, 1977:525).

The family retained a traditional posture. The immigrant couple
and the community were imbued with the virtue of having a large

8

number of children. The 1905 sample shows that 64 percent of married couples between 30 and 39, and 61 percent between 40 and 49, had three or more children under eighteen (Gutman, 1977: 530). The Richmond Hill House study of 1,095 women found that there were 6.2 persons belonging to the average worker's family.

In particular, family traditions did not crumble in the face of industrialism. Female employment patterns, for example, were constrained by cultural expectations upholding a traditional status. Women supplemented family earnings in a way that minimized the disruption of family solidarity and, more specifically, their roles as wife, mother, homemaker, daughter, etc., while men traditionally addressed the outside world as breadwinners.

In the Richmond Hill House sample of female wage earners only 13 percent were married, suggesting that other responsibilities took preference for married women. For the most part, it was the young single women who went to work in factories; two-thirds of the women were under 21 and only 6 percent were over 35. Practically all of the women who were single (87%) lived at home with their parents.

For the Italian women, then, it appears that work was a way station leading to marriage, children, running a household and integrating a wider kinship network. With formal schooling behind her, a young girl went to work to contribute to the family's material welfare. Since Italian women worked in garment factories, there was a chance to acquire traditional skills that would later be valuable in managing a household. In most cases, marriage put an end to a wage earning career, it installed a woman in her own household, sustained by the wages of a hard working husband. In some cases married women supplemented the family income by doing piece work at home. In 1911, one-third of Italian women in New York City were earning wages at home (Pleck, 1978:495). However, this activity was comfortably integrated within their general role as managers of the domestic economy. Their principal economic contribution was a resourcefulness rooted in a peasant culture. Immigrant women possessed a know-how, handed down by mothers, grandmothers and aunts, which made the small earnings of their husbands go farther; this was an indispensable attribute in a wife. They made their own bread and macaroni and rendered their own lard. They were guided by the principle of using everything. Thus, the necks and gizzards of freshly killed poultry made a hearty soup. The butcher provided cuts of meat that American housewives had little interest in, like the skin of the pig which was used to flavor a variety of dishes. Women also made and mended clothing, curtains and bedspreads. The men made a contribution to this domestic economy, too. Each autumn, they pressed grapes into wine from a family recipe. They also conducted forays into the wilds of Staten

Island and New Jersey for mushrooms, dandelions and other greens which their wives prepared in the traditional manner.

The immigrant community was composed of family units, each possessing a little tradition dovetailing with a common culture. Individual paesani were recognized as belonging to constitutent families, and classified in terms of their family background and reputation, which accompanied them in steerage. Paesani comprised a moral community, which, through constant surveillance and criticism, assured an adherence to the traditional folkways governing family life. Special relationships were found between families where intermarriage and godparentage (*comparaggio*) were concerned (paesani were preferred by custom in both of these cases).

The Immigrant Church

An important institutional development for the immigrant enclave was the Catholic parish. In contrast to the mutual aid societies which were generated by the immigrants themselves, the parish was introduced from the outside through the efforts of the Archdiocese which, at the time, was predominantly Irish, and through Italian religious orders. Moreover, it was set up as a common ground for immigrants of different *paesani* backgrounds.

The development of an immigrant parish has to be seen in terms of the general difficulty of incorporating Italians within American Catholicism, that is, the so-called "Italian Problem". Even though the overwhelming majority of immigrants from Italy were Catholic, they did not readily take to the Catholic Church in America, and vice versa.

The religio-cultural backgrounds of Italian immigrants were alien to the institutional Catholicism of American Catholics, in particular, the dominant Irish community and hierarchy. *Contadini* beliefs and practices did not correspond to the doctrines and liturgy of the official religion. Although profoundly religious, Italian peasants subscribed to "a religion of fear" that had more in common with the ancient Roman and Hellenic pagan cults. Vecoli (1969) describes their religion as "a folk religion, a fusion of Christian and pre-Christian elements, of animism, polytheism, and sorcery with the sacraments of the Church". These religious strains clashed violently with the pious Catholicism of Irish (and to a lesser extent German) Americans. In 1888, it was noted in *The Catholic World* that "the Catholic Church in America is to the mass of the Italians almost like a new religion". From the immigrants' standpoint,

> *Those Italiani who ventured into Irish or German churches found them as alien as Protestant chapels. The coldly rational*

atmosphere, the discipline, the attentive congregation, were foreign to the Italians who were used to behaving in church as they would in their own homes (Vecoli, 1969: 230).

The American church was openly hostile to the immigrants. The feste of the madonna and the saints were considered irreligious. The Jesuit journal *America* reported in 1914 that Italian religiosity lacked piety "no matter how numerous be the Italian processions, no matter how heavy the candles, no matter how many lights they carry". The immigrants were also castigated for their meager support of the Church. At the parish level, the immigrants were often

turned away or seated in the rear with Negroes. Sometimes they heard themselves denounced as 'Dagos' from the pulpit and were told they were not wanted (Vecoli: 1969:23a).

In the parochial schools run by Irish teaching sisters, Italian children were often seated in the last row of the classroom and exposed to humiliating treatment.

There were two Italian parishes in the South Village. One was begun in 1866, well in advance of the mass immigration from Italy; the other in 1892 as Italians were inundating the Village area. However, the origins of each show some interesting contrasts and, at least in the first case, some contradiction with its basic premise.

The first Italian parish was preceded by a mission located on Canal Street, sponsored by Archbishop Hughes of New York in 1859. The Archbishop appointed Father Sanguinetti to minister to the needs of the growing Italian population of lower Manhattan. At the time, there was only one other Italian priest in the entire city, stationed at an Irish parish in Greenwich Village (Marraro, 1949).

The mission closed after only one year. An early parish publication claims that operations were terminated for "reasons unknown". A later publication contends that the chapel foundered because it was too far from the main Italian settlement. It added that the "meager chapel" was not emotionally suited to Italians who were "accustomed to a grand edifice in which to worship", and because the immigrants required a church that was "geographically centered" and able to "express the social content of the *piazza*".

Notwithstanding the interpretation proffered by the parish, the closing of the mission appears due to a less romantic set of reasons. Sanguinetti supposedly ran afoul of the lay committee in charge of the collection over the issue of mission finances. The committee physically assaulted him in the church. Back in Rome to petition relief from the Vatican, he was instructed by the Papal Consul to relinquish his chapel. It is believed that, at the bottom, Sanguinetti

11

was sabotaged by diocesan opposition to religious practices considered too Italian (S.M. Tomasi, 1975).

With the mission closed, Italians were given a church of their own in 1866. At the invitation of Cardinal McCloskey, Italian Franciscans founded a parish that would accommodate the burgeoning number of immigrants in the area. Toward this end, the Franciscans procured a vacant Methodist Church on Sullivan Street. A Neopolitan priest was appointed as its first pastor. Marriage and baptism records kept at the mission on Canal Street were transferred to the new parish.

The parish was established as a "national parish", the first created for Italians in New York City. However, Cardinal McCloskey designated it as a "territorial" parish as well. As a result, it included a substantial Irish population residing nearby. It is ironic that the first official act performed at the first Italian national parish in New York was the baptism of an Irish baby. A plaque in the hallway of the parish grammar school commemorates Irish parishioners who played an important role in its foundation.

A mixed ethnic congregation had two purposes. On the one hand, Italians were too poor; a parish publication noted that "the small Italian community would be insufficient to support an adequate church". On the other hand, the Catholic hierarchy was opposed to a separate Italian congregation on the grounds that it would delay their incorporation within the Church, as well as inhibit their Americanization.

Church records show that the Irish figured prominently in the newly established Italian national parish. In 1869, for example, there were 92 marriages at the church in which both spouses were Irish. In that same year there were only 10 Italian couples married at the church. Through 1899, the number of marriages between persons of Irish descent remained fairly constant; there were 100 in 1879, 82 in 1889 and 84 in 1899. However, as Italian immigration to the Village, and the proportion of Italian females to males, increased, the number of Italian marriages recorded had reached 153 by 1899.

The first Italian parish, then, seems to have been largely Irish at its inception and constrained by the policies of an Irish Archdiocese. This seems to have created a number of problems for Italian immigrants. Although primarily established for Italians, they occupied the basement while the Irish congregation attended mass in the main part of the church. The feste of the saints and the madonna, a central aspect of the immigrants' communal solidarity, were not sanctioned by the church. The feste were celebrated outside parish frameworks by the societies. The problems experienced by Italians may have caused some families to switch to the new parish when it was built in 1892.

12

The second Italian parish was not founded as a mixed congregation. It was organized on a language basis, without regard to territorial boundaries and thus open to Italian immigrants regardless of where they lived. The parish, which was run by the Scalabrini order, was actually an outgrowth of a mission started in 1891 by the San Raphael Society. The mission continued its work after the parish had been established. From its headquarters on Waverly Place, the Society assisted immigrants with the usual problems. In 1911, it gave refuge to 900 women and 171 men, in 1912, it assisted 1,192 and 1,406, respectively. It also attempted to encounter the exploitation of immigrant labor by the padrone. The society was subsidized by the Bank of Napoli, Italian shipping lines (Lloyd, White Star, Fabri, Italian); half of its funding was derived from the King of Italy.

In 1900, the parish took over a church that had previously served a black congregation, although it was originally built in 1816 for the Third Universalist Congregation. The parish seems to have been dominated by Northern Italians whose principal settlement was in the vicinity of the church; in particular, it benefited from the influence of the Scalabrini order. An ethnically homogeneous congregation, the parish is reputed to have maintained a more Italian character. For example, the parochial school employed an Italian order rather than the Irish sisters used at the other parish. Nevertheless, Irish Christian Brothers were retained to teach Sunday catechism, perhaps as a concession to the Archdiocese, and the religious feste were equally proscribed, partly because of the opposition of Northern Italians. In 1900, the parish had a membership of about 10,000 persons.

The Nature of the Immigrant Community

The initial adjustment of Italian immigrants to the city occurred within the paesani group (i.e., fellow-townsmen, supplemented by immigrants from the same province and region). Paesani hailed from the same locale, spoke the same dialect and adhered to the same traditions. Solidarity with paesani was expressed in informal friendship and neighborhood cliques, and in associations that furnished material assistance in time of need (i.e., sickness and death) and celebrated a common religious life. The most important institution of Italian culture, the family, was rooted in this supportive milieu, preserving traditional patterns.

The communal solidarity that emerged among Italian immigrants appears to have had little or no precedent in the peasant experience. For the Southern Italian peasant, in particular, the family was the only social concept. Everyone outside the family was considered a stranger, and regarded with indifference or hostility (Covello, 1967).

In light of peasant cultural backgrounds, it would appear that community and group consciousness among Southern Italians developed in the United States. Mutual aid societies, for example, do not seem to have existed in Southern Italy, although similar organizations were formed by Northern Italian artisans and bourgeoisie in the 1890s. It may be argued, then, that the immigrant context facilitated a transcendence of the inclusive social world of the family. A breakthrough to a wider solidarity was partly a response to "the absence of sufficient family members to provide resources necessary to meet all emergencies" (Nelli, 1973:91). Paesani furnished a ground of interpersonal relationships and meanings in which traditional peasant social forms, including the family itself, were sustained. This attained a special importance in an environment that was culturally alien and assigned the immigrant to the bottom of the social ladder. The immigrant could not afford to be indifferent or hostile to fellow townsmen and other paesani. The cultural shelter comprised by paesani made it possible to live with the strangeness, anonymity and impersonality of the city.

This communal breakthrough had definite limits. Paesani distinctions, based on different dialects and traditions, tended to circumscribe a group for communal purposes. Moreover, they gave rise to suspicion and animosity between groups, especially Northern and Southern Italians. In the South Village, then, the diversity of village, provincial and regional groups imparted a multicellular structure to the wider Italian colony. Each paesani community engendered its own set of immigrant institutions facilitating adjustment to the city including a network of families and a mutual aid society that was also a religious cult. It was sometimes ecologically distinct as well. Although the parish was introduced on a more inclusive basis (*i.e.*, nationality), it does not seem to have been a replacement for paesani frameworks and loyalties, especially in light of the "Italian problem". The *feste* of the madonna and saints, then, continued to be sponsored by the societies, independent of the Italian parish.

The Restructuring of
The Ethnic Community

W orld War I marked a turning point for Italian immigrant communities. The onset of hostilities interrupted the ebb and flow of immigrants. Nativist sentiment following the Armistice gave rise to immigrant quotas so that Italian immigration between 1921 and 1930 was one-fourth of what it was between 1901 and 1910 (S.M. Tomasi, 1975:16). Without replacements, core Italian settlements began to thin out and contract (Nelli, 1970).

As in other Italian districts, the Italian population in the South Village declined markedly following World War I. In two adjacent census tracts, population declined from 16,766 in 1915 to 9,611 in 1930 (although there was a slight increase in the population of one census tract between 1915 and 1920); the sharpest decline occurring between 1920 and 1930 (Laidlaw, 1933: 41-43). However, the South Village Italian community was not disintegrating. A sizeable Italian population remained in the neighborhood well beyond the period of large-scale immigration. Moreover, while there was an erosion of social frameworks expressing the solidarity of immigrant paesani, such as mutual benefit societies, new structures crystalized which reflected the communal adaptation of second generation Italians who remained in the South Village.

The Persistence of the Italian Population

Although the Italian population of the Village began to decline after the war, it was gradual enough to sustain an ethnic community organization into the present period. In 1960, there were still 8,944 persons of Italian descent in census tracts that contained a large Italian population before World War I; this did not include Italian Americans whose parents were native born and the approximately ten percent of the population who had "not reported". This persistence is significant, especially in light of typical patterns of mobility and succession operating through the immigrant slum (Ward, 1971).

One reason for this persistence concerns a complex of economic factors. Into the second generation, Italians remained near the bottom of the city's occupational structure. In 1950, when two-thirds of all second generation Italian males in New York City were blue-collar workers (Glazer and Moynihan, 1963:206; D'Alessandre, 1935), South Village residents were still concentrated in lower level jobs. In one census tract, 1,029 out of 1,289 males could be classified in such occupations:

clerical and kindred	169
craftsmen, foremen and kindred	179
operatives and kindred	332
service workers	199
laborers	150

Female workers showed a similar distribution. In the same census tract, 483 out of 619 women who worked were employed in clerical positions or as operatives (300 were classified in the latter category).

These workers probably found it difficult to become economically mobile. In 1960, the median income of all families in this census tract was $4,190. Working class incomes kept families in the South Village where rents remained low and there was close proximity to employment. In 1940, 70 percent of tenant occupied units in the census tract rented for less than $40 per month. In 1950, the median rent was $23.83.

The typical tenement flat was small and had many inconveniences. In two South Village tracts, 44 percent of all dwelling units were listed as having no private bath in 1950. In 1960, one-eighth of the dwelling units in these census tracts lacked plumbing facilities and almost one-fourth shared toilets. At the same time, however, the South Village was able to acccommodate real improvements in living standards. Many landlords renovated old buildings, installing toilets, steam heat and hot water. With modest material gains, families moved to more spacious, airy and attractive apartments; fewer children made dwelling units more commodious. Those who were better off bought private houses on the "better" block in the neighborhood. Lower densities and less industry made the neighborhood more pleasant, as did proximity to Washington Square Park and the middle class village. Families, then, were by no means impelled to leave the neighborhood as their circumstances improved. By taking advantage of low rents, it was possible to afford amenities which otherwise would have been out of reach, such as buying better cuts of meat and going on vacations or to accumulate savings for a house or business.

Besides economic factors, Italians remained in the South Village because they were culturally tied to the ethnic community. A major reason for staying in the neighborhood has been to be near parents and other kin. To this extent, the ethnic community had a "retentive power" over its members (Firey, 1947:212).

The persistence of the Italian South Village has to be seen in the context of urban ecology. For the most part, the South Village did not have to contend with serious "invasions". It has been immune from significant incursions by new immigrant groups a factor that has precipitated flight in other neighborhoods. Industry was not expanding; in fact, there was a steady decline in the number of industrial establishments in the village area after 1900 (Ware, 1965:450). The reclamation of the Village by the middle class following World War I primarily affected blocks to the north and west. Moreover, the preponderance of tenements and factory buildings in the South Village defied easy conversion. Slum clearance was not proposed with any seriousness due in part to the opposition of a firmly entrenched Italian community. In effect, the South Village remained a "zone of transition" until the value of loft conversions in the declining factory district adjacent to the neighborhood was fully exploited after 1971. By this time, the Italian population numbered only a few thousand. Thus, the Italians were not "pushed" out of the South Village, but "pulled" by the logic of upward mobility and assimilation.

Communal Reorganization

The war and the introduction of immigrant quotas not only precipitated a decline in the number of Italians living in the South Village, they also altered the demographic composition of the local Italian community. Between 1920 and 1930, the foreign born population of four South Village census tracts was reduced by seven percent. In addition, there was a steady increase in the proportion of women and children under fourteen (Laidlaw, 1933:21).

This demographic shift reflects the ascendance of families and native born. It would follow that the institutions that structured the immigrant experience would be less relevant and in eclipse, including the institutions comprising the world of the "migratory" male sojourners (i.e., boarding houses, relief agencies, the padrone). The temporary character of this immigration, as well as the inherent marginality and uprootedness, imparted an instability to the Italian colony before World War I (Ware, 1965:154).

A notable casualty of the demographic shifts after the war was the mutual aid society, which was formed by paesani for the purpose of self-help and the maintenance of local traditions, including dialect.

17

However, with members scattered and the second generation e-volving new interests, the societies were no longer active. It was estimated that whereas half the men in the community belonged to a society before the war, only ten to fifteen percent were members in 1930; in some cases, headquarters and meeting places were moved uptown or to Brooklyn (Ware, 1965:157-160).

In general, paesani considerations were much less of a factor in the second generation. They were by no means as constraining in the choice of a spouse. Parish records indicate that provincial endogamy was the rule of the South Village before 1916; where place of baptism was given, it was clearly the case that most people hailed from the same province as their spouse. However, the second generation employed different criteria. Even Northern and Southern Italians, having grown up in the same neighborhood, intermarried in the second generation.

Similarly, paesani differences were not as inhibiting of peer group relations. A greater degree of fraternization may have taken place among Southerners than between the latter and Northern Italians in light of initial settlement patterns, times of arrival and the overall predominance of Southern Italians within the population. Still, many Northern Italians grew to be friends with those from Southern Italy.

Paesani differences were sublimated within emerging neighborhood institutions. The ethnic parish for example, accommodated a range of paesani heritages. The only interethnic distinction it reflected was between native and foreign born Italians—a new distinction based on differences in acculturation. Therefore, masses were said in English and Italian, and there were English and Italian branches of parish societies, although relative to nearby Irish, German and Lithuanian churches it was an Italian parish. District political clubs also subsumed paesani distinction vis-a-vis the old guard Irish who sought to maintain their hegemony in the district.

Distinctions among paesani were not entirely extinguished. As the American environment levelled out differences among groups (e.g., dialect), paesani identification was relegated to an historical significance. The second generation was aware of its paesani background, knew some dialect and respectfully acknowledged their parents' paesans. Paesani distinctions were the source of friendly competition within family and peer groups. Harsh words were reserved for other nationalities. Even the invidious distinctions between Northern and Southern Italians were blunted, overshadowed by sharper differences with non-Italians who lumped them together.

In the second generation, a wider identification emerged (i.e., as "Italians") which served as a basis for an adaptation to the city. This was especially the case in Greenwich Village where the fundamental social division was the ethnic one. Therefore, the second generation lived in an Italian neighborhood, belonged to an Italian parish, was served by an Italian district leader and so forth; neighborhood Italians saw other groups living in a parallel fashion, yielding a map of the city with ethnicity as a regulating principle. An ethnic identification extended beyond the neighborhood level and was evidenced in a symbolic approbation of Italian American prizefighters (Rocky Marciano), baseball players ("Joe D") and entertainers (Frank Sinatra). Their photographs adorned neighborhood clubs, taverns and candy stores; their legends have been recounted (and embellished) on many a street corner. They were second generation Italians who made it in American society. Sinatra achieved the greatest prominence because of his wide acclaim which he won without relinquishing a distinctive ethnic identity and neighborhood style.

A shared ethnic identification was informed by common cultural elements which diverged from the core culture into the second generation. These included distinctive dietary preferences as well as a style of religious observance (*e.g.*, the second generation retained a special devotion to St. Joseph, whose feast day is celebrated with a traditional pastry named after the saint). Perhaps most important were common family traditions which could be distinguished from those of non-Italians. Therefore, neighborhood Italians could conclude that permissive methods of childrearing and loose family ties made "the Americans" specifically "not like us" (there was an evaluative implication here as well).

Following World War I, then, there was an erosion of immigrant frameworks in the South Village which accompanied a decline in population. Rather than signalling disorganization, however, there was a restructuring of ethnic community among those who remained—in particular, the second generation who were more acclimated to the urban setting but had not become part of the mainstream. At its center was the traditional family group, which included extended kin and godparents. An underlying solidarity was sustained among Italian families living in the neighborhood, replacing paesani as the supportive matrix for ethnic family patterns. An ethnic community was also based on a social neighborhood of peer relationships and voluntary associations. Localized interaction delimited an ethnic "turf" where "strangers" were *personae non gratis* and formal authority was usurped. An Italian neighborhood possessed an institutional superstructure comprised of a parish organization, political clubs and a Mafia syndicate. These institutions had implications for local leadership and control, formal group membership and the allocation of scarce resources; they also mediated ties to a world outside the ethnic neighborhood.

A Family Neighborhood

*i*n her research on the Greenwich Village Italian community in the 1920s, Ware (1965) argued that "Americanizing pressures" undermined traditional family patterns. However, although it was not the "inclusive social world" of the peasant village (Covello, 1967), the family group was the center of a restructured ethnic community after World War I. In this sense, the South Village was, in the words of the residents themselves, "a family neighborhood".

Notwithstanding the purported effects of Americanization, the family seems to have attained an even greater importance for Italian community organization after World War I. The immigrant colony had contained a disproportionate number of single males who sought to accumulate savings and return to the paese. These sojourners lived as lodgers and depended on paesani, immigrant banks and employment bureaus, and relief agencies like the San Raphael Society. However, with the relative decline in the number of male soujourners, the institutional structure of the Italian community increasingly reflected the needs and rhythms of families.

The ascendance of families is reflected in the notable increase in the baptisms at the old Italian parish beginning in the period just prior to World War I. Where there had been fewer than 500 baptisms a year recorded between 1898 and 1901, 896 children were christened in 1912 alone. There was only a slight decline in 1916 as 861 baptisms were recorded. As in previous years, the overwhelming majority of the children baptized were Italian. The parish register shows that the parents of 777 children had Italian surnames; in 13 cases one parent was Italian (with a few exceptions, the remaining children were Irish).

The church in these years thronged with parents and godparents on a Sunday afternoon waiting to present the newborn to the Italian priest. Over the years, the number of baptisms tailed off only gradually:

1919-1924	3,452
1925-1933	3,041
1934-1940	1,046

This decline reflects the limits on family size reached by the key population group, as well as ongoing outmigration. Between 1941 and 1949, 1,041 baptisms were registered, most of them occurring in the post-war years. Parish records indicate that most parents of the children baptized in the post-World War II period were themselves baptized locally.

Family groups dominated the local landscape. This impression was conveyed by several middle-aged cornerboys who, without much effort, were able to enumerate 81 children living in a tenement on Spring Street in the early 1930s (there were twenty apartment units, each with three rooms).

The Orbit of Family Life

To be sure, the urban-industrial setting effected significant changes in the Italian family. Patriarchal aspects were modified in the direction of family limitation and more equalitarian relationships, although women traditionally exerted considerable influnce within the family (Covello, 1967:212). However, the essential structure of the traditional Italian family remained intact and many customary functions were retained. Therefore, Italians living in the South Village after World War I have to be seen, before all else, as members of family groups and actuated by considerations of family well-being.

The family defined fundamental roles for individual members. Into the second generation, the Italian husband and father was the family head and provider. Although some men made more money than others and may have been distinguished by specialized skills, what mattered most was that one "worked hard". Besides being a diligent worker, he was expected to be upright in his social habits. Therefore, his street corner activities were to be kept within bounds of good-natured socializing, i.e., a casual joust with the fellows or a token bet on a horse. The more Americanized father seems to have been a less distant and severe figure than his immigrant counterpart or predecessor. One woman recalled her native born father as an "easygoing" man who let his wife do "all the talking" and allowed his youngest daughter to rifle his jacket pockets for nickels when he came home from work. He took his sons to ball games and became involved in their youthful sports careers before World War II. On the other hand, one man noted that his immigrant father's "word was law". He recalled that whomever was not present when "Papa" sat down for supper did not eat, since the door to their flat was summarily locked. Still, he was a "good man" who "lived for his family".

Prepared by her immigrant mother in all the essentials, the second generation Italian woman was the consummate household manager. With wage earning experience, the married Italian woman now operated the domestic economy using only the small salary her husband brought home. She was a thrifty cook and kept the house spotless. Her husband expected this much while her mother and mother-in-law guaranteed it. She also had a primary responsibility for the everyday business of raising children. The Italian mother took pains to instill the proper manners in "her" children, as her husband was wont to observe. She got them off to school and to mass on Sunday, and followed their progress at the settlement house where American social workers checked their scalps for lice and served up American culture. The faithful execution of this domestic role was a factor in determining the family's status in the community. Whereas household responsibilities tended to preclude outside employment, widows often returned to work.

Although the targets of settlements and the public schools, and swayed by peer groups and the mass media, youngsters growing up after World War I were likewise integrated within a family unit. Females looked after younger siblings and assisted in labor intensive household tasks, such as handwashing clothes and bed linen. One woman still remembers her mother's spring cleaning with a mild shudder. Another recalls assisting in the kitchen from an early age, although her mother never relinquished her symbolic position at the stove.

Despite being more immersed in a street corner subculture, young males had family duties as well. One man whose parents were native born observed that he and his brother had chores to perform until they went into the army during World War II. When the family had a wood stove, they were charged with fetching scraps of wood from packing crates discarded by local warehouses. Back home, they chopped the wood for the stove that heated their apartment. Another chore was to scour the railroad tracks near the piers for bits of coal. Of course, wherever their daily searches might lead, they had to be home for supper; the traditional Sunday afternoon meal, followed by visits from relatives, really cramped peer group activity.

Older children were compelled to work to help out financially. Families did not have the resources to absorb tuition costs or the loss of another salary. Moreover, there was an ingrained skepticism of formal education—a Southern Italian proverb cautions against making children better than their parents (Covello, 1967). As an example, one woman who won academic awards in high school did not attend college for financial reasons and because it conflicted

22

with traditional sex roles. Instead, she took a job as a bookkeeper and helped support the household until she married.

While "the family came first", it was, in turn, the individual's preeminent source of support and comfort. The family was always there; you never knew "when you might need your family", and it was "such a cruel world". It sought to envelope and fortify the individual against reality. The family also imparted a sense of dignity to lower class slum life. It accorded the individual intrinsic value as a member of the family, regardless of occupational status or education. In turn, one took pride in the family. Notwithstanding its material circumstances, the family could have "respect" in the eyes of the Italian community on moral grounds. This can be illustrated by the following remarks of two second generation Italian women, both of whom were in their seventies:

> We were poor, but we raised a family just the same (not like today). Nobody ever had anything to say about us.

> We had enough to eat, and our mothers kept us nice and neat. The teacher always praised my mother because of the way she kept us when we went to school...And let me tell you, we grew up nine children on Thompson Street. It's what you want to make of yourself; I have very respectable boys.

No matter how poor, each family possessed a set of traditions which gave it a special unity and identity in the community. The custom of naming children after relatives was an expression of this solidarity. It also reflected an appreciation for the hierarchical structure of the family. Family cohesion was expressed in the manner in which food was prepared. Certain dishes, especially tomato sauce for pasta, conveyed this sense of family solidarity and singularity; it was traitorous to like someone else's sauce. The pizza exchanged between families at Easter time also had this symbolic significance. Each family's pizza contained a variation of the customary ingredients and had a unique shape, often having the family's name baked into the crust or spelled out with strips of dough. Solidarity was expressed in other areas as well. One woman noted that it was "a tradition" in her family to vote Republican. This began with her grandmother, whose *paesan* was a Republican district leader. Every time she voted, she was being loyal to her family.

Family traditions actually put the individual into focus and defined him or her. Behavioral as well as physical traits were explained against a kinship background. As traits became manifest, kin set about deliberating exactly who the individual "took after", invariably claiming for their side of the family the admirable qualities and relinquishing responsibility for the more dubious, when not blaming them on the other side. When a precedent was found in the family, the individual lost his distinctivness and continuity was established

("He's all his grandfather, God bless him"). The individual learned to see himself, and was seen by others, in terms of a long line of forebears. Where no precedent was discovered, the individual was chided for being an anomaly.

Family history was recounted orally and amply documented in photographs and memorabilia displayed in the home. It constituted a frame for ordering a past and viewing the larger pattern of historical events (*i.e.,* "Papa got sick when Truman was president"). The family calendar of birthdays, wedding anniversaries and other occasions set aside for family celebrations were the dates around which a meaningful future was projected; this was especially true for the women as "integrators" of the kinship network.

The cohesive family was not necessarily harmonious. Family members did not always get along; in some cases, jealousy and bickering caused long-standing and sometimes irreparable rifts. While seeking to extend protection, the family was capable of smothering the individual (A. Parsons, 1969:135). One woman recalled that her parents instilled a fear in her toward the outside world. On her honeymoon in 1947, she received telephone calls from her father who related, through his sobbing, how much "everybody" missed her. Even though she was staying in a hotel on Twelfth Street, which was within walking distance, he persuaded her to shorten her honeymoon. The newlyweds had an apartment waiting in the same building as her parents.

The Wider Family Group

The nuclear family was firmly ensconced in a close knit kinship network. Related households came to America together, or else followed one another in family "chains", and settled in the same neighborhoods. Relatives furnished a structure of social and material support; more established kin were especially helpful to recent arrivals. Immigrants who did not have family to turn to often had to rely on charitable institutions like the San Raphael Society, which sent many of the destitute back to Italy.

In the second generation, new cells were grafted on to the family group as those born or raised locally branched out into their own households. The family was given further depth and range. Through intermarriage and godparentage, the family was sinking roots into the Italian neighborhoods.

New households were enmeshed in a kinship group by virtue of strong attachments to the family of origin (*i.e.,* blood ties). Mother-daughter ties were especially powerful. This was manifest in living near "Mama" after marriage and constant accessibility. Attachments to siblings approached mother-daughter ties in intensity, especially those involving sisters. For the women, kinship counterbalanced a

24

male street corner life, although the two worlds were not mutually exclusive. In any event, ties to the family of origin delimited an intimate and active sphere of kinship relations beyond the conjugal unit.

The South Village has been characterized by the stability of family groups. One woman's parents came from Italy as children around 1900 and were married in 1919; she herself was married in 1946 and raised two daughters in the neighborhood. Another family has been in the neighborhood through five generations. Its oldest member immigrated in 1905 at age 18, whereupon she married a man from the same paese. A daughter, born in 1910, and a granddaughter born in 1930, also live in the neighborhood. The latter's son, born in 1951, lives in the neighborhood with his wife and their son, who was born in 1976. Four generations were baptized at one of the neighborhood parishes. While this is rare, although one man in his twenties claimed to be a fifth generation Northern Italian, it is not uncommon for families to have remained over three generations. Family groups like these comprised the "solid core of community" in the South Village.

The structure of the wider kinship unit may be illustrated by a close look at a particular family group. It may be taken as representative of those families around whom ethnic communal patterns crystallized.

The family's roots in the South Village and the United States go back to the early 1880s. Its first generation was represented in the persons of Giuseppe and Carmela. Giuseppe was twelve years old when the family immigrated in 1882. Carmela arrived with her family one year earlier when she was two years old. The respective families were paesans since they were from the same province, although they were from different villages. Giuseppe and Carmela were married in 1894 when a "match" was made by fellow paesans; he was twenty-four and she was fifteen. A short while after they were married, Carmela's father married Giuseppe's mother (both had been widowed since arriving in this country). The elderly couple returned to Italy. However, Carmela's two sisters and one brother and Giuseppe's two sisters and two brothers remained in the South Village. These siblings were likewise married by this time.

Giuseppe and Carmela had their first child in 1898, a daughter, although two children had earlier died in childbirth. Three more daughters were born: in 1904, 1906 and 1909. Meanwhile, Giuseppe's brother and sisters had eleven children between them; the other brother and his wife were childless. Carmela's family was smaller; two sisters had three children between them, while her only brother and his wife were childless. After World War I, Carmela's oldest sister and her family moved near Albany. Another moved to Linden, New Jersey. One of Giuseppe's brothers relocated to the Bronx.

Giuseppe and Carmela remained in the South Village where the family began extending its range. Their oldest daughter was married in 1914 at age sixteen. The two families were paesans and Carmela's sister instigated a match. The groom was twenty-seven and born in the neighborhood.

The three other girls were married: in 1923, 1926 and 1933. Their husbands were also Italian, born and raised in the South Village. However, none of these marriages were matches. The families were not even paesans; in fact, one of the daughters married a Northern Italian.

By the time Giuseppe died in 1935, his three oldest daughters had presented him with eight grandchildren. The oldest grandchild was seventeen, while the youngest was two. Within three years of his death his youngest daughter gave birth to two girls. In the years prior to World War II, the four second generation households were living within a few blocks of one another. The widowed Carmela kept her own apartment, across the street from her oldest daughter.

Carmela's daughters had their respective in-laws living in the South Village as well. Each of their husbands had siblings who were married and raising families. However, these in-laws started to move away by the late thirties. They went to places like Jersey City, Staten Island and Astoria (Queens); one son-in-law's mother and unmarried brother moved to San Francisco.

Carmela's ten grandchildren grew up in the neighborhood. Delayed by the war, the oldest was the first to marry in 1946. By 1956, all but the two youngest were married. Six grandchildren married second or third generation Italians from the neighborhood. One married a second generation Italian from another section. In 1956, then, the family descended from Giuseppe and Carmela consisted of thirteen households living in the South Village (Carmela, four daughters, eight grandchildren). More distant kin and in-laws rounded out this localized kinship group. It began to extend even further with the birth of Carmela's great-grandchildren.

The focal point of localized kinship structure was the family of origin. At this level, interaction was most frequent, obligations the most pressing. Solidarity was secured in the physical proximity of related households. Families that were relatively prosperous purchased small houses in the neighborhood. In the forties, a house on Sixth Avenue was shared by two brothers and their respective families, as well as their parents and two unmarried sisters (constituting three separate households). In another case, a three-unit dwelling was divided among a second generation couple, their married daughter's family, and the wife's elderly mother (in a small top floor apartment).

Close kin comprised a small social world. They "dropped in" on one another for coffee in the afternoon or evening. The women were the most active members of this kinship network. Mother and daughter typically saw each other every day; during daily visits they caught up on matters that transpired in the interim. The larger group gathered at appointed times. Family get-togethers attained special importance on birthdays, wedding anniversaries, etc. Special occasions are often recalled in snapshots of family members crowded around the table, arms on each other's shoulders, blowing out candles on cakes, and so on.

Kin also made up a system of support at several levels. In particular, they furnished assistance in times of crisis, lending money, babysitting, helping to raise motherless children, etc.

Close kin complemented the nuclear family in the control of individual members. Relatives were free with their advice; they did not hesitate to keep family members in line. This control function may be illustrated in the response of one family group to the arrest of one of its members, a nineteen-year-old who "hung around with a bad crowd" (even though "he was a good boy"), for narcotics use in the early fifties. Instead of rebuking him or shifting responsibility elsewhere, the wider family closed ranks to solve the problem themselves. An uncle with contacts settled legal complications. A prosperous uncle contributed to the cost of private medical care; one of the aunt's recommended a good doctor. A cousin got him a job driving a truck. Perhaps more importantly, brothers, sisters, aunts, cousins and grandparents "kept an eye on him night and day" to make sure that he stayed away from his cohorts. Even after he married and had a child, the family continued to monitor his conduct. The family group, then, comprised a network of interpersonal supports. For all intents and purposes, there was no substitute.

Making a living was often a wider family effort, and had probably been more aspired to than actually realized. Kin jointly pooled their capital and labor.

There were other kin who were not part of a close knit family group centered on the family of origin (i.e., siblings and their families plus siblings' parents). Cousins, who were included in a common family circle in their youth, tended to form separate branches as they married and had children. Interaction was less frequent. Obligations were fewer and were generally restricted to ceremonial functions such as weddings and wakes. These were the gatherings of the entire clan. They even brought relatives who had moved away back to the neighborhood.

The family group also included persons who were not related by blood or marriage. This occurred when the institution of godparentage created a fictive kinship bond, mediated by various religious rituals. Respected and close friends stood up for one another at the baptism of a child, a confirmation or a wedding. Already friends and neighbors, godparenthood "validated the relationship by bringing the person into the orbit of family life, and thus make him a genuine relative" (Covello, 1967:184). Actually, entire families became intertwined in this fashion.

Compari functioned as relatives and were capable of a closer relationship than genuine kin. In keeping with tradition, relationships also had a formal aspect, reflecting the instrumental significance of friendship in peasant cultures. Even in the second generation, it required that formal terms of address be employed (*compare, commare*). There was a ritual exchange of gifts on the feast day of St. John the Baptist, the patron saint of godparenthood. Compari were also expected to prepare a meal for the family of the deceased following the funeral.

Because it endowed alliances between non-kin with aspects of kinship, godparenthood widened the sphere of persons among whom a special moral claim was felt. For this reason, it was desirable to become aligned as ritual kin with a prosperous family. A local politician noted that his family was frequently "honored" by requests from people in the neighborhood to serve as compari.

Even when they did not become compari, however, close friends were grafted on to the family. Friendship was not just a companionate relation between individuals on the street corner, the work place or at school. Friends came into the home, met the wider family, had coffee and cake, appeared in photographs that went into the family album and were intimately exposed to the rhythms of family. In every sense of the word, they were "friends of the family". The families of close friends knew one another, and of one another, and exchanged "respects" at appropriate times (*e.g.,* wakes, weddings).

The ethnic neighborhood was the spatial locus of family group life. In many cases, the neighborhood was saturated with kin; relatives sustained a familiar landscape. One's mother lived in this building, an aunt in that. A brother and his wife lived on West Broadway, while a married sister lived across the street from the church. A brother-in-law hung out on a certain street corner, while a nephew belonged to a social/athletic club on Prince Street. The parents of a girl whom a cousin had married owned a grocery store up the block. Localized kinship imparted a reassuring stability to life in the city. The people one trusted most were nearby. This was a priority for Italians who felt vulnerable in urban life.

The Solidarity of the Family-Centered Network

The nuclear family was ensconced in a widening circle of moral

28

relationships to close and more distant kin, godparents, friends, neighbors and their respective families. It was the center from which binding obligations radiated out with diminished intensity. Therefore, only with close kin was there the expectation to lend money, visit on Sundays, soothe in the event of an illness or exchange birthday presents. Certain occasions activated the entire family- centered network in the display of solidarity, reflecting the degree of relationship. These were typically life-crises rituals that served as opportunities for individuals, as representatives of family groups, to exchange appropriate measures of respect.

More than any other event, death mobilized the surrounding community in a demonstration of solidarity. Death was the most flagrant violation of family cohesion, even more than the "individuation" accompanying upward mobility and acculturation. Therefore, it evoked an obligation to respectfully acknowledge the family's loss. Death rites afforded the institutional channel for the reciprocal discharge of obligations. In the Italian neighborhood, they were first-rate communal affairs, bringing everyone out in their contrast with the mundane (P. Williams, 1933- 2000).

The execution of obligations followed a definite pattern. It was dictated by the closeness of the relationship and, more pointedly, the magnitude of "respect" exchanged in corresponding situations for which a precedent existed. For instance, if a close friend acknowledged the death of one's husband by sending flowers and riding out to the cemetery, a similar respect should be reciprocated Acknowledging the event with just a mass card and attending the wake would constitute a failure to reciprocate properly. Once an obligation was recognized, it had to be reciprocated in like measure to avoid insult and an ensuing rift. These considerations covered which and how many members of the family should actively participate, as well as the form that the respect assumed.

Reckoning the extent of its obligations was a serious business; the family must not lose face. Families often kept ledgers which recorded the name of the family paying a respect, the individuals involved and the nature of the respect. A list compiled by one neighborhood family (second and third generation) detailed the respects paid by its social network "In Memory of Pop" (1953). It notes that 117 families sent mass cards. For the most part, these were more distant relatives, friends and neighbors. Twenty-six families sent flowers. A more expensive gesture, this was undertaken by the inner circle of relatives and friends of the family. There were 33 financial contributions made, again, by this inner circle. Finally 19 sympathy messages were forwarded by family friends and relatives who lived elsewhere.

In addition to this accounting, there was a guest register listing persons who merely attended the wake. These were casual friends,

29

acquaintances, fellow workers and neighbors; they wished to express their sympathy and respect for the family short of a material obligation. Nevertheless, these obligations were consequential and had to be reciprocated. The guest register, which signified the further reaches of the family's moral world, and the ledger were consulted when an obligation presented itself in the future.

There was a similar accounting for weddings; although this has become more significant as families become more affluent enough to afford catered affairs in lieu of the "football weddings" of a generation ago (which were open to anyone who wished to attend). Invitations and gifts were weighed down by considerations of respect and prestige. An invitation had to be reciprocated; a gift was supposed to reflect the magnitude of one received. In the manner of the death ledger, the money gifts were tabulated by the family in a book for future reference. In both cases, the sum total of "respects" paid the family signified the breadth of its family-centered network and the amount of honor it possessed in the community.

Family and Community

Kinship was a central social and moral category in the Italian neighborhood, having a significance comparable to occupational status in the larger society. Family name and history identified the individual; a kinship affiliation placed the latter in an intelligible tissue of social relations. A link to a neighborhood family was a precondition for further knowledge about character; the individual was the mere tip of the iceberg. From a communal standpoint, it was possible to get a bearing on a great number of people (Suttles, 1968:101). Family histories were accessible in a community where everyone seemed to mind everyone else's business, especially if it was in the slightest way scandalous. Persons inhabiting the same life-world were thereby rendered familiar and, because of the moral implications of family life, trustworthy.

Kinship more than identified the individual. It also mediated contacts to the neighborhood (Young and Wilmott, 1957:81). Rather than seal people off from non-kin, it promoted relationships to a network of local individuals and families. It opened up a community where knowing people was a critical resource. Since kinship was localized over a period of years and even generations, one invariably knew one's relatives' friends, neighbors, in-laws and even work-mates. In a person-oriented setting, one also "knew of" a great many people on the basis of hearsay. For example, one might learn from an aunt by marriage that the latter's cousin was having "trouble" with her son.

Kinship was the basis of a moral consensus. South Village Italians

30

expressed a tacit belief in the preeminence of familism, whereas American culture often seemed inimical to family solidarity. Conceptions of the "good life" were framed in terms of familism and family. Within the Italian neighborhood, role patterns worked out in a family context furnished ideal guidelines for individual conduct. Welded together by a general regard for the family, solidarity was expressed in the collective adherence to the rules governing family life. Common family traditions were a blueprint for a moral order, enjoining individuals to "do the right thing"; they were the social glue of ethnic community since other nationalities were "not like us". Although one's own family came first—an injunction that was culturally prescribed—solidarity was premised on empathy with other Italians who had a similar family life. There were moral implications in the recognition of another as someone's son, father, daughter, etc. (*i.e.,* as someone who could be readily perceived in terms of a kinship status). The individual without a kinship connection (the individual whose conduct was not integrated within a family context) was suspect and unnatural. In particular, Italians have regarded the nonfamily life-styles of bohemians, artists and students with a mixture of inscrutability and pity ("Don't they have families?").

In the Italian neighborhood, a good neighbor was, above all, a good family man or woman. Adherence to common family traditions was the quintessential moral life. There was, as a result, considerable preoccupation with the honorific implications of conduct. The individual had to comport himself or herself in a manner that would bring credit to the family. A good man was one who worked hard to support a wife and family. A good woman kept a "spotless" home and made sure that her children were mannerly. A man who gambled his salary away was a "bum", as was the woman who stayed out and neglected her family. Above all, one must avoid giving others the opportunity "to talk". At this level, there was a measure of status competition between families.

Neighbors were tireless critics of deviations from the code of familism. Gossip censured individuals for their failure to comport themselves properly in the enactment of family roles. In characteristic fashion, individual transgressions were regarded as a misfortune for the family; the errant individual let his or her family down.

In general, then, neighbors cooperated with one another to assure that the cultural blueprint outlined by familism was being followed. Merely strolling in the neighborhood brought one in contact with people who asked after the welfare of the family. This supplied a constant reminder of one's rootedness in a kinship structure, and an awareness of responsibilities attendant to a specified kinship status.

Conclusion

Despite the "incessant hammering" (Campisi, 1948) of American society, the family was the principal social capital of neighborhood Italians who did not have access to mainstream institutions and identities. Into the second generation, it comprised a meaningful and compelling social world that determined major role responsibilities. The exchange of mutual respects and a general regard for Italian familism gave rise to an underlying solidarity of neighborhood families. Thus, the family fostered the development of community which, in turn, served as a buffer against Americanizing pressures.

The preeminence of the family has apparently led students of Italian American group life to minimize or overlook the existence of communal organization. Muraskin (1974:1484) has suggested that the study of Italian Americans has been biased by the Banfield thesis of amoral familism (1958). Although they imparted a distinctive cast, ethnic family patterns did not preclude communal solidarity in the South Village (interestingly enough, the South Village contained a large number of immigrants from the very province studied by Banfield in the 1950s). There was an element of status competition among local families, although this "antagonistic cooperation" produced a measure of communal solidarity in its own right (Lopata, 1973; Lyman, 1974).Moveover, there were not the harsh material conditions that made Montegrano families "potential enemies" (Banfield, 1958:110-111). In an alien cultural environment, other Italians assumed an importance for sustaining an ambience conducive to ethnic traditions (e.g., support for the axiom that the family comes first). Furthermore, the family and familism did not exhaust possibilities for ethnic group life. There were other occasions for interaction and solidarity within the neighborhood.

The Social Neighborhood

*U*rban life furnished myriad contact points with neighbors, that is, neighbors with a common cultural and ethnic background since in Greenwich Village ethnic concentration defined the boundaries of social neighborhoods (Ware, 1965). In a tenement district, residents confronted one another at virtually every turn. The occupants of a tenement walk- up were on especially intimate terms. They shared rooftops for sundry household tasks and leisure in warm weather; cellars were utilized for storage and perhaps winemaking; hallways and stairs provided common passage; toilets were located in hallways and shared among families; the airshafts which narrowly separated the old "dumbbell" tenements were used to hang brooms and mops since there was little free space inside flats. Housewives sharing an airshaft arrived at informal rules for hanging wash, lest garments on the higher floors drip water on those below, and shaking dustmops in the airshaft when someone had clothes on the line. The airshaft also provided an effective means of communicating with parties bordering on it, as long as privacy was not a consideration.

Since private resources were limited, there were informal networks of mutual assistance. Neighbors often shopped for one another, sometimes lending small amounts of money, and watched each other's children. Neighbors also met needs for information, via gossip chains, that maintained a connection to the community and reaffirmed moral standards (Keller, 1968:45; Vidich and Bensman, 1960:43- 46.

In general, the boundaries separating the dwelling unit from the neighborhood were rather permeable. Many of the activities that take place in the homes of middle class families here occurred outside the home. For example, the lack of hot water and bathing facilities led Italians to patronize public baths. Also, housewives often brought bread and pizza to be baked in commercial ovens because they did not have the facilities at home. Indicative of the relationship between the dwelling unit and the neighborhood life, is the observation that doors and windows were always open. It was important to keep passageways open for ventilation since the inner rooms bordered on the airshaft. At the same time it kept people in touch with neighbors and the neighborhood. From an open window, it was possible to keep track of children or hear someone calling from the street.

Since the tenement flat was too congested for much else besides sleeping and eating, especially in the case of large families, the street became a social stage. Groups of men collected on street corners and in candy stores. Children played ball against the stoops and turned back yards and alleyways into hiding places. Housewives turned shops and doorways into meeting places. A popular social ritual that included both men and women was going for the *Daily News* after supper. People began milling around their favorite candy store up to an hour before the truck was scheduled to pass, enough time to socialize and exchange gossip. The street was also the backdrop for the parish feast, funeral processions and block parties like the ones Italians celebrated when their men returned from World War II. Watching such goings-on in the street from a window perch was a form of entertainment.

Localism was a distinguishing feature of neighborhood life. It was possible to confine social interaction to the neighborhood to a considerable extent. In particular, the Italian neighborhood was capable of satisfying interpersonal needs. This localism was embodied in a peculiar personality type, the "territorial local" (M. Fried, 1973:104). Locals were unable to sever themselves from the comforting routine and ambience of neighborhood life for any length of time. They tended to stay put, even so far as to have become fixtures on a particular street corner or bar stool. Measured against their small neighborhood world, distances appeared great and irksome to cover. Neighborhood housewives shopped in local grocery stores rather than trek to supermarkets several blocks away where the prices were lower. Journeys out of the neighborhood, especially out of the city, elicited special preparation, commotion and anxiety. Back in the neighborhood, the local could relax, recounting the most mundane experience as an adventure and imploring friends to fill him or her in on what had happened while he or she was away.

Neighborhood Peer Groups

A social neighborhood was distinguished by relationships between individuals as members of age and sex cohorts. This was significant since the traditional Italian family was an inclusive social world (L. Covello, 1967:149). Persons outside the family orbit were "strangers"; extrafamilial contacts were formalized and marked by instrumental considerations. The concept of friendship did not exist in southern Italian culture (Covello, 1967:171), nor was there a word for "classmate" in the peasant dialects (Covello, 1967:260).

Urban-industrial conditions modified traditional attitudes toward certain non-kin. The family was no longer able to envelop the individual. In particular, Italian youths growing up in crowded urban slums forged close ties to peers who were going through the same experience of cultural assimilation. It may be argued that "the bonds formed in street gangs marked the first extrafamilial socialization for Italian youngsters" (F.G. Ianni, 1971:88; 1974). In the second generation, peers became "significant others"; peer group relationships persisting into adulthood delimited a social sphere outside the family, although not entirely independent of the latter, especially for females. In contrast to kinship, individuals came together on the basis of equality and companionship, although kin could also be peers.

Peer group interaction more than lifted second generation Italians out of narrow familistic confines. It also promoted the transcendence of invidious *paesani* distinctions. Village and provincial jealousies were not the impediment to fraternization they were for the immigrant generation. Lines were more likely to be drawn between ethnic groups inhabiting adjacent neighborhoods; friendship was problematic when it came to the "Irish boys" from Eleventh Street.

Peer group relationships represented a wider fraternization that was a necessary ingredient for community building. In contrast to kinship, they possessed a fundamentally public character. Whereas the family could still strive for a private existence (*i.e.,* a house and garden in the suburbs), peer group life was manifest on the street corner, in club memberships and in organizational affiliations. Friendship cliques, segmentally ordered by sex and age, comprised an informal network of extrafamilial relationships throughout the neighborhood. They were the basis for membership in parish societies, political clubs, settlement houses and criminal syndicates (although, especially in politics and the syndicate, membership tended to be defined by instrumental considerations). At the same time, these institutions were vehicles for peer group fraternization.

Male Group Life

Males were allowed greater freedom to engage in extrafamilial activities. This was the case in Italy where a male peer group pat-

35

tern was spun around the cafe and the piazza (*dolce far niente*). By contrast, females were encumbered by considerations of household and kin, as well as by traditional concerns for sexual modesty.

The consummate expression and prototype of male bonding was the street corner group. In this pattern, adolescents and adults alike affixed themselves to a particular street corner or commercial establishment, such as a bar or candy store. Members of the group "hung out" for a major part of the day; individuals passed in and out, but a basic group structure remained with certain individuals present at regularly appointed hours.

Particular locales were bound up with cornerboy membership and activities. They assumed the properties of a private address. where one paid a call. In contrast to females, male peer grouping was almost exclusively conducted outside the home. The corner or club were the places where one could be found when not at work or at home. Indeed, men were "at home" in these private locales where everyone knew them by their nicknames. Cornerboys brought folding chairs outside in warm weather and grilled sausages on Saturday afternoons. On Sunday mornings, when the women were at church or frying meatballs, men "made the rounds" in their finery, visiting friends in clubs and on corners throughout the neighborhood.

If the location was a commercial establishment, cornerboy conviviality was superimposed on business transactions. At one candy store, folding the supplement sections of the Sunday newspapers was ritually attended with buns and coffee; cornerboys also helped behind the counter with the morning rush. Butcher shops, bakeries and other stores also supported contingents of cornerboys; typically, folding chairs were available to enhance fraternization. Neighborhood taverns were foremost centers of male sociability which discouraged patrons from outside the neighborhood; the stranger met with stares and was otherwise treated in a perfunctory manner.

Cornerboys cultivated the art of small talk, which invested the most banal event with significance (of course, life was not especially exciting for men who had menial jobs and whose social horizons were limited to the neighborhood). The most trifling issue became the subject of a great debate, with everyone taking sides, such as the tastiest recipe for preparing mussels, or the best route to a cemetery in Queens. The aim of these encounters was not to reach a decisive resolution, but to furnish a platform for cornerboy expressiveness and personal disclosure, and to sustain a level of pure sociability comparable to the "toasting" sessions in the lower class black subculture. There was a strong leveling aspect to street corner life; the qualities that mattered were "smarts", wit and gregariousness. One group of cornerboys included a lawyer who was forever being teased about a lack of "common sense". In the candy store, he

36

was just one of the boys, waiting his turn to tell a story and talking sports.

A good part of street corner life involved playing the numbers and betting on horse races. Men congregated on sidewalks deliberating the merits of a certain jockey or waiting for the daily "number" to "come out". Each digit of the number was phoned in one at a time to the syndicate club running gambling operations and relayed along the grapevine into bars, grocery stores and butcher shops.

The male peer group achieved even greater distinctiveness with the formation of social/athletic clubs. Ware observed that the clubs "were of comparatively recent origin among the Italians, largely because the second generation only reached club forming age in the 1920's" (1965:355). As a result, she accorded them no importance for local group life. However, the clubs attained a popularity for the second generation, providing a context for sociability comparable to the immigrant societies. They were an index of a more stable neighborhood, and generally reflected the acclimatization of Italian Americans to lower class urban life.

In the thirties and forties, there were quite a number of clubs in the South Village, and a membership of thirty or more was not uncommon. Each social/athletic club possessed an official charter, granted by the state, and a storefront clubroom featuring its name stencilled on the front door or window. A club charter and clubhouse were passed down, establishing a tie between two generations of cornerboys; older cornerboys sponsored charters and generally supervised the activities of younger club members.

The private club afforded dues paying members a chance for a richer social life. It furnished an outlet for interaction too intimate for the street corner. At the same time, the club articulated with the community. Club dances were advertised throughout the neighborhood. One club whose charter was held by a local district leader had a membership exceeding one hundred in 1934. In its heyday, it held an annual dinner dance, attended by several hundred people, in an uptown hotel. Elaborate programs from these affairs listed prominent politicians and businessmen in attendance. As the nomenclature indicates, athletics were an integral part of the club format. Clubs engaged one another, as well as parish and settlement house teams and clubs from other neighborhoods, in baseball and basketball games.

Male peer groups were an aspect of the underlying neighborhood-family system, not ensconced in an isolated male sphere. For most men, family membership defined a principal identity and role. Peer group membership and the corner were secondary. Spending time with the boys was not incompatible with family responsibilities, especially in a class-culture where women were intimate with their mothers and sisters, and the home was a female preserve. To an extent, male street corner life was a safety valve or refuge from the rigors of the domestic regime; even gambling was not a threat to the family as long as most men made small wagers that were primarily a part of a social routine in which the entire neighborhood took part, including the women.

In the main, male peer group activity was regulated by the exigencies of family life. The male head of the household above all, was a breadwinner. Therefore, the street corners and bars would empty on a Sunday afternoon when families sat down to dinner. In a similar vein, the delivery of the evening newspaper signified the return home for most men; neighborhood bars and clubrooms tended to close by eleven o'clock. After all, there was work the next day.

Cornerboys, then, were "good family men" and, therefore, respectable. This was true even for "action-seekers", for whom life was episodic and often extra-legal (Gans, 1962:28-32). In their cases, however, kinship loyalties were often manifest in close ties to family of origin.

Street corner cliques were informal manifestations of peer group sociability. They probably constituted the preponderant part of social interaction outside the family for the majority of neighborhood men. However, extrafamilial memberships were also furnished by formal organizations which had their roots outside the neighborhood and were at least partly oriented to nonlocal concerns. Relative to street corner groups and social/athletic clubs, they possessed an instrumental, instead of a purely expressive, significance. Membership was intended to secure some practical material or social advantage. Their formal organizational character tended to enhance their members' status in the community. A prestige claim inhered in links to structures outside the Italian neighborhood.

Whereas formal organizations in general gave rise to a status level above street corner life, some proffered more prestige than others. The most prestigious organization in the South Village was the target shooting club. Target shooting was an avocation of Italian country gentlemen, and the club distinguished itself with the use of live instead of clay pigeons. Since this was forbidden by the state of New York, members practiced their sport in Pennsylvania. The club's prestige was based on a number of other factors. Its interests aligned it with the upper crust of the Italian community in the city; one of its favorite projects was the Casa Italiana at Columbia University, a repository of high Italian culture. On the other hand, it remained aloof from the local Italian community. Moreover, it did not admit Southern Italians until 1921. Most neighborhood Italians knew little or nothing about the club and its membership. Its distance from the community was reflected in the contrast of its sumptuous quarters with the tenements and storefronts that were the focal point of most people's lives.

A cut below the target shooting club in membership, dues schedule and prestige was a club for Italian businessmen and politicians. Although there was some overlap in membership with the former, the club did not have a connection to the Italian elite nor an air of exclusivity. Although its quarters was an elegant brownstone just off Washington Square, it was not as remote from neighborhood life. It was accessible to ambitious neighborhood businessmen with little formal education (*e.g.,* the hard working proprietor of a parking garage), as well as to second generation Italians who attended college and/or had white-collar occupations. They joined to further career interests (*i.e.,* establish contacts) and to mix with a "better class" of Italians. An affiliation gave them a status advantage over other neighborhood residents, signifying that they were on the way up. The club did maintain a formal connection to the neighborhood through a small stipend presented to needy graduates of parish grammar schools. Members also had some visibility in civic affairs and parish societies.

Closer to street corner life were voluntary associations like the American Legion, Knights of Columbus and the various parish organizations. They furnished opportunities for men interested in performing some service, although without subordinating the sociability attendant on informal gatherings and the pressures of upward mobility. Members held charity drives and sponsored recreational programs for neighborhood youngsters. They also marched in parades on holidays. The service dimension did confer distinction. Within the framework of a service organization, however, the men "hung out". The American Legion, the Knights and the parish maintained clubrooms for members to socialize, although the wives were included for Saturday night dances and buffets.

Female Group Life

Southern Italian mores channeled the energies of women and girls into the home. However, second generation neighborhood women were not rigidly confined within the circle of domestic relations. Like their male counterparts, they participated in an extrafamilial sphere that included interaction with peers, although this tended to be deliniated by traditional role expectations that defined a woman's place relative to the home and family group (*i.e.,* childrearing, housecleaning, integrating the wider kinship network). As a result, a female peer group pattern only approached that worked out by the males in terms of its institutional distinctiveness.

A female peer group pattern was spun around domestic responsibilities. Fraternization was engendered by the common tasks of childrearing and household management. In particular, the supervision of children supplied contact points in which peer relationships flowered. It was in this spirit that women joined mothers' clubs at the parish and social settlements and belonged to associations of parents and teachers at the schools their children attended.

The mothers' clubs organized by the Protestant social workers were a significant development, especially among the second generation (Ware, 1965:176). The women who joined clubs at the settlement did so in the course of supervising their children's activities outside the home. As mothers of neighborhood children, they patronized clinics and received instruction about health practices; one settlement showed films that were accompanied by lectures delivered by doctors and social workers. The women looked in on their children in the settlement, assisted social workers on outings and even accompanied children to a summer camp sponsored by the settlement house. While this was progressive, club membership does not seem to have "removed the traditional basis for their prestige" as Ware maintained (1965:175). A woman's self-image and position was still determined relative to household and kin; it was perhaps no coincidence that these women were joining mothers' clubs. These Italian women were not about to relinquish control over their children to social workers who were Protestant, American and middle class.

The mothers' clubs did break new ground among the second generation. Besides educating the women in childrearing techniques and health practices, they assumed a social and recreational importance for the women. One settlement sponsored arts and crafts and a regular social group, while another held daily "businesswomen's lunches". A club sponsored by the Children's Aid Society held political debates and endorsed local candidates. In the forties, the club had a membership of 800 women, including the wives of some prominent businessmen, politicians and Mafiosi. The club was directed by an educated second generation Italian woman, a social worker who did not live in the neighborhood. She appears to have been a compelling fixture, as well as something of a feminist who was an adversary of incompetent neighborhood politicians.

Traditionally, religion has been available to women as an outlet for wider social expression. The older women, in particular, went to mass and took part, with the rest of the community, in religious processions. However, a parish organization expanded their participation beyond the traditional religious events (i.e., securing indulgence by attending novenas and masses). In the second generation, women belonged to parish societies, sold chances for the parish raffle and worked tirelessly for the feast. They also geared a peer group around their childrens' activities at the parish grammar school. Parish bingo games were also a center of female peer group interaction.

Female peer group life also articulated with the street. The close supervision of children brought mothers together in playgrounds and schoolyards. For example, one group of women met in a luncheonette for coffee before meeting their children in the afternoon after school. Others congregated on playground benches; their own mothers were often nearby, occupying a bench with their friends. However, these peer group formations never quite crystallized in a classic street corner pattern. It was not that the street was unsafe; cornerboys and the Mafia had seen to that. In the final analysis, the home was their preserve, and there were always so many things to do "upstairs". Moreover, women were close to their mothers and sisters, and even to cousins and aunts. Friendships focused on a few close friends who visited one another's homes and exchanged frequent phone calls.

Consequently, women regarded the street with more of a purpose. Unable or disinclined to "hang out", they would rendevous only briefly. A peer group pattern revolved around daily shopping; most shops had folding chairs where women could pause and converse, and perhaps have a cup of coffee. Some women frequented luncheonettes in the afternoon while waiting for the number to come out. In the evening, they would gather in candy stores, perhaps in a house dress and slippers, waiting for the arrival of the newspaper truck. However, they were by no means as conspicuous and assertive as the men with their street corners, clubrooms and bars, although women did stay in close touch with the street from their window sills.

A Protective Enclosure

The more or less bounded Italian neighborhood (in the sense that a particular territory was understood by residents and others to be inhabited by a population that was predominently Italian and thrown into relief by adjacent areas identified as Irish, industrial, bohemian or middle class) was more than a site for group life. It was also a "safe moral world" (Suttles, 1968) that kept the city at arm's length. While the city may have been threatening and noted for crime, the neighborhood was a different world. Although there were exceptions, people were trustworthy and crime was infrequent. Doors and windows were left open, and there was no fear of the streets, even at night. Neighbors were watchful and solicitous and closely monitored the movements of strangers. A careful scrutiny of outsiders and a toughness with interlopers earned the South Village Italian neighborhood a reputation that residents believed frightened predators away (this reputation was their first line of defense). A substantial part of neighborhood life was organized for defense against strangers. The feeling that property and person

41

were secure was perhaps the most valued feature of neighborhood life.

The importance of the protective enclosure also derived from the fact that the neighborhood was an extension of the home, a setting for primary group life. The boundaries between the apartment and the neighborhood were blurred. Doors and windows were open to the street. Children slept on the fire escape in summer and women mended clothing out on the stoop. Housewives shopped in cotton house dresses. Men lounged on benches in front of social clubs. Public space, then, was converted into a "home territory" (Lyman and Scott, 1970).

Business establishments were similarly privatized. Neighborhood shops were settings for fraternization; commercial transactions took place within this framework. They supported a contingent of regulars who socialized inside the store; folding chairs were usually provided by shopkeepers, who enjoyed the company and participated in the conversation. A candy store was a virtual clubroom to one group of cornerboys. The proprietor entrusted them with a key when he went on vacation so they could still hang out, confusing patrons who thought the store was open for business. Shops were also for babysitting grandchildren and visits from relatives.

Since neighborhood streets and facilities were a setting for primary group life, it was important to restrict, or at least regulate, the access of persons who were unfamiliar and possibly untrustworthy. Where private lives were enacted in public space, there was a feeling of vulnerability *vis-a-vis* people who were unfamiliar and "not like us". Italians worried that "beatniks" or blacks would "say something" to their women and children, or that a stranger might take advantage of an open door or window. Store owners had to be sure that the people who came into their shops, where security precautions were minimal, were not there to rob them. The effective management of space was a functional adaptation to the complexities and uncertainties of the city.

The intensive use of local space was itself a defense against predators (Jacobs, 1961). Furthermore, elements within the community specifically exercised an informal control function. Male street corner groups were the self-appointed enforcers of local order. They were responsible for defining and maintaining the integrity of the enclosure; cornerboys, then, were about more than "doing nothing in company" (Ware, 1965:339). Male groups of varying ages comprised a local militia who made sure the streets were safe. The most militant in this function were the teenage "gangs" (in a rather loose sense) who defended their turf against other ethnic groups and isolated interlopers. The gangs armed themselves with baseball bats—the neighborhood musket. Social/athletic clubs served as depots for bats and other weapons, which were sometimes hidden under storefront windows for easy access. Within these groups, discussion frequently turned to topics like whether minority groups would "invade" the neighborhood and how defenses could be fortified.

Troublemakers, defined as anyone who started trouble, were dealt with brusquely. Justice was swift and direct. For example, several middle-aged cornerboys once chased a burglar, with bats flailing, pursuing their quarry through alleyways and yards. There was broad support for the use of force against troublemakers when it was "the only way" to deal with such matters.

The right to exclude outsiders, or at least regulate their movements, and dispense justice was legitimated by an historical claim to the neighborhood. Outsiders and "guests"—the latter lived or worked in the neighborhood, but were not identified as part of the Italian community, such as artists—were expected to defer to Italians and otherwise "mind their own business". Local sovereignty was communicated in both subtle and forceful ways, including territorial markings like ethnic banners and graffiti, hanging out and the close scrutiny and harassment of strangers. A proprietary attitude toward the neighborhood was conveyed by the merchants who swept the sidewalks in front of their shops and the cornerboys who opened fire hydrants to clear street gutters.

Male street corner groups were complemented in securing the enclosure by virtually every member of the community. It was a paramount civic duty like voting in a general election or conserving energy. Even housewives monitored the movement of strangers from their kitchen windows. More than a few times, women alerted men on the corner or in the clubroom about a suspicious presence on the block.

The Mafia reinforced this control function. The Italian neighborhood was a field for syndicate activities; extra-legal activities were coordinated from local clubs and bookies serviced accounts on the street corners. Therefore, it was necessary to restrict access to persons who were not trustworthy. There was a special concern that strangers might turn out to be undercover policemen. The syndicate also exercised control over troublemakers, and generally sought to keep the neighborhood quiet in order to deflect attention from its activities and personnel. Toward this end, it backed up cornerboys with something more formidable—the reputation for total violence. This reputation was a valuable resource for a defended neighborhood.

The enclosure was made secure with little direct involvement on the part of the precinct police, who had official jurisdiction at the local level. One reason for this was the indifference of law enforcement authorities to lower class, ethnic communities. At the same time, precinct police tended to recognize the sovereignty of neighborhood groups, and even integrated with local controls. The police, then, were said to have been "on the pad" of local racketeers. Moreover, they supported the law and order philosophy underlying the defended neighborhood; they had nothing but admiration for the low crime rate in the area, and perhaps envied the direct method of dealing with troublemakers employed by cornerboys and the Mafia. At the very least, local controls made their jobs easier. However, middle class Villagers criticized precinct police for the leeway given Italians in policing the neighborhood.

Since the neighborhood was a protective enclosure, it possessed the sheltering properties associated with the home. Neighborhood streets were not "inherently dangerous, tempting and freely accessible only to men" (A. Parsons, 1969:22). Provincial controls established a safe moral order. Cornerboys, in particular, kept an eye on strangers, reproached adolescents for using foul language, chastised young women for staying out too late and escorted ladies to their doors after bingo games. However, other areas could be forbidden and amoral. In the twenties and thirties, Italians did not enter the Irish section of the Village lightly. The factory district, which bordered the South Village at West Broadway, comprised a morally indeterminate region, a no-man's land that was reserved for purposes that were irregular or illicit. Young Italian men traditionally regarded bars in other parts of the city as appropriate settings for sexual adventures and rowdyism. In contrast to the neighborhood, communal surveillance was not extended to these regions. However, there was greater danger, both morally and physically.

A protective enclosure was predicated on the assumption that people from the neighborhood were relatively trustworthy. This seems to have been due to the fact that they were known or familiar, although their moral status also rested on a common ethnic background. Yet, there was still a need for internal controls. Young male gangs constituted a potential problem for the neighborhood. They were largely held in check, however, by adult street corner groups who socialized them into a street corner world and by the Mafia syndicate which had a vested interest in local order. Teenage agression was channeled against other neighborhoods and occasional troublemakers in the spirit of turf defense. There was also close surveillance of "bad apples" who were immediately suspected when something went awry. Although this neutralized them to a considerable extent, transgressions were committed, activating local mechanisms of control.

The neighborhood may be considered an enclosure in another sense. Besides insulating Italians from physical danger, it was a cultural retreat that sheltered them from the invidious comparisons

44

inherent in systems of ethnic stratification (Sennett and Cobb , 1972:10-31). As long as group life was confined to other Italians, the individual was not reminded of his or her low class and ethnic status. In fact, Italians responded with their own ethnocentrism, regarding non-Italian and their customs with disdain. In the neighborhood, then, there was strong approval for Italian traditions and ethnicity. Moreover, in the neighborhood, it could be assumed that "no one was better than anyone else". Therefore, no one was entitled to "put on airs". Neighborhood Italians affected a moral equality premised on a common culture, ethnicity and social status.

Conclusion

The neighborhood delimited a framework and ethnic community within the city. The exigencies of tenement life gave rise to networks of sociability and dependency among neighbors with common ethnic and social backgrounds. Peer group relationships, in particular, fleshed out a communal structure centered on the family. The more or less bounded Italian neighborhood—other neighborhoods were similarly preempted—assumed the properties of a "home territory" where locals had a sense of control and felt safe against the city. This locality community is a characteristic feature of working class populations in the city (Fried, 1973; Suttles, 1968). In the South Village, a social/defended neighborhood materialized fully in the second generation; immigrant group life was focused on paesani and referred back to the paese and the social structure of the Village.

The neighborhood was the locus for institutions that had community-wide significance. The parish, district political clubs and a Mafia syndicate comprised another level of ethnic community organization that articulated with family and peer groups. These institutional settings will be discussed in the following chapters.

The Neighborhood Parish

*A*lthough a parish was established for Italian immigrants in the South Village in 1866, it seems to have been dominated by Irish laymen (perhaps up to World War I) and reflected diocesan policies set down by an Irish Catholic hierarchy. The perpetuation of village feasts by the immigrant societies is an indication that Italians remained essentially marginal to local religious frameworks. However, integration within a parish organization was substantially achieved in the second generation.

The tensions inherent in the duplex parish founded in 1866 were mainly resolved by shifting population patterns. After World War I, Irish parishioners constituted a dwindling minority. Moveover, there was an increasing number of Italian families, especially women and children, who were more likely to affiliate with the church and participate in parish activities. By the second generation, acculturation had made Italians more receptive to the American Church (Russo, 1970:198-213).

A development that brought the Church closer to Italians in the South Village was the activities of Protestant settlement houses, neighborhood centers and missions. Protestant churches in the Village area had long been losing their congregations through upward mobility. The buildings occupied by both Italian parishes originally housed Protestant denominations in the first half of the nineteenth century. However, in an effort at survival, Protestant churches responded with institutional programs geared to the needs of the poor Italian population. In light of the "Italian Problem" within the Church, which led Italians to be considered as only "nominal Catholics", and the dearth of welfare assistance available to the immigrants, Protestants were relatively sanguine about their work in the Italian colony (Mangano, 1915).

There were a number of Protestant missions in the South Village. The Charlton Street Memorial Church was founded in 1877 by the City Mission Society. The Judson Memorial Church, a Baptist denomination, "inaugurated a work among the Italians" in September

1896. It perceived the need for missionary service in the "disintegration" of social controls within the Italian colony, particularly those associated with Catholicism (Jones, 1938).

According to a second generation Italian born in 1901, the sight of Protestant missionaries preaching on street corners was quite common when he was a boy. The missions distributed food, clothing and other "material inducements to bring the Italians into their chapels and schools" (Vecoli, 1969:202; Ware, 1965:301). The calendar of the week's events at the Judson Church shows that a free dispensary was operated every day at 12:30 in the afternoon; a kindergarten was the only other daily service. In 1931, the church set up a health center to "Americanize the health and life habits of this foreign-born element so that their children might become future American citizens physically and industrially efficient" (Judson Health Center, Annual Report, 1927).

The Protestant churches' concern for the Italian poor was shared by a plethora of welfare agencies and settlements, numbering around two hundred in Greenwich Village in 1930 (Ware, 1965:371). Although their explicit goal was not to convert Italians to Protestantism, they did seek to effect a "civic betterment" as contained in the philosophy underlying the social gospel movement (Ware, 1965: 373). Moreover, they were funded by the philanthropy of wealthy Protestant families and staffed by Protestant social workers. At a Spring Street settlement, subsidized by the Bates family, children were innoculated against disease as part of the day nursery program and sent on summer vacations to the country; photographs of the kindergarten class at the settlement in 1920 show Italian youngsters in sailor suits waving American flags under the stern glance of a social worker named Miss Carter.

Prior to the efforts of the missions and settlement houses, the Catholic Church did little for the social and material benefit of its flock. The Irish churches in Greenwich Village had scorned institutional programs of the kind aimed at Italians as "purely extraneous activities" (Ware, 1965:308). However, the Italian churches were apparently compelled to introduce similar programs in light of Protestant activities (Vecoli, 1969:205). They sought to bring Italians "within the fold and to compete with the social agencies and the Protestant missions of the locality" (Ware, 1965:312). This appears to have been the rationale for the construction of a day nursery by the older parish in 1915. On the occasion of its seventy-fifth anniversary in 1941, it was noted that:

> On account of the less fortunate condition of many families within the limits of the parish, many wives, to help meet the expenses of a large family were obliged to work in factories, and not knowing to whom they may confide their little ones, there being no such Catholic institution within their reach, they had recourse to Protestant Day Nurseries, with what danger to these innocents one may imagine.

47

In addition, parishioners had access to welfare functions performed by The American Protectory of the Sons of Columbus Legion, organized by the Italian Franciscan Fathers who staffed the parish. A principal reason for the organization was to oppose the "sectarian charity work" directed at needy Italians, and that was "carrying them away from the Catholic Church to Protestantism and atheism" (Tomasi, 1975:132). The other Italian parish was bound up with welfare and other institutional programs from the start. A 1963 parish anniversary bulletin refers to the San Raphael Society as a mission "established...for the same purpose as the parish, to aid Italian immigration". It further notes that when a new Italian pastor was appointed in 1901, "one of his first projects was to transform the basement into a suitable meeting place" for parish programs and societies.

Parish Frameworks

In the decades following World War I, the parish became the center of social life. It furnished a setting where infants were baptized, children attended school, women made novenas and persons of varying ages joined societies. Virtually everyone in the community was likely to come in contact with the parish for some religious, social or recreational purpose. It articulated with family and peer group life and with other communal institutions like the political clubs and the Mafia.

The importance of the parish for neighborhood Italians was reflected in the increasing use of the parish church for rites of passage like christenings and marriages, which were high points of family life. In the three years from 1912 to 1914, 2,644 children were baptized at the old Italian church (only a handful were not Italian). In 1916, there were 188 marriages between persons with Italian surnames. A parish historian at the younger church wrote that "on one Sunday alone" in 1918, "there were 31 baptisms and 17 weddings". Outstripping even these formidable numbers, a Franciscan journal reported in 1924 that "each Sunday as many as 50 babies are baptized and 20 marriages celebrated at the old church" (Operai Degli Francescani in America, 1927).

The parish was the focus of religious worship. The Franciscan journal maintains that daily mass (Messa Quotidiana) averaged 1200 people. Besides the mass, which was held in English and Italian, there were special religious services. In particular, there were devotions to the Madonna and saints which were intended to petition some favor. An especially popular novena was the service for St. Jude, the patron saint of hopeless cases. The old church held a devotion for its namesake, a popular Italian saint, every Tuesday; on that day, a perpetual novena was performed five times. A special devotion was conducted for the parish patron twice a year, one of which led up to his feast day in June. Beginning in 1951, the celebration centered around a parish feast, which included a religious procession and other devotions. The religious side of parish life was dominated by neighborhood women. The elderly were especially fervent. A third generation woman maintained that the latter were wont to attend as many services as possible, even a funeral mass for someone they did not know, to garner a surplus of indulgences; in their travels through the neighborhood, they would purposely pass the church so they could bless themselves with the sign of the cross. Although the men "didn't go in for church much", many had their own private devotions, as reflected in miraculous medals worn around the neck or pinned to the sun visor of an automobile.

In addition to the properly spiritual dimension, the parish offered an opportunity for organizational memberships in societies and clubs, as well as in institutional programs of various kinds. Under the direction of priests and laymen, these organizations took root among the second generation after World War I. Both parishes made facilities available for parishioners. The older church erected a settlement hall in 1915 which was initially intended as a day nursery that could accommodate over one hundred children. However, it also served as a place for meetings and recitals. The basement of the hall was used as a social and recreational center. In the thirties, the younger church acquired new facilities for its social and recreational programs.

Membership in parish organizations was largely on the basis of sex and age. For example, adult men and women belonged to the Fathers' Club and Mothers' Club respectively, although some societies included both sexes, such as the Alumni Club. For the young people of the parish, there were Boy Scouts and Girl Scouts, Little League, a chapter of the Catholic Youth Organization and open recreational programs. The Children of Mary Sodality, for example, was a religious and social organization for the young women of the parish. The only exception to this differentiation along age and sex lines was an organization to accommodate Italian-speaking parishioners. One parish had the *Azione Cattolica* for young Italian immigrants. The other mentions only one organization geared to Italian-speaking persons, the parish chapter of the Third Order of St. Francis, which was divided into an English and an Italian branch.

At the older parish, several societies originated during the predominantly Irish phase. A Saint Vincent DePaul Society, which provided limited relief to the indigent of the parish, was founded in 1869. The Children of Mary Sodality and the Holy Name Society also had their roots in this period. The only other organization that can be connected to the Irish-dominated parish is the Dramatic Society, which remained an Irish project after the parish became predominantly Italian.

By the 1930s, however, Italians succeeded the Irish in these societies. The officers and membership of the St. Vincent DePaul Society and the Holy Name Society and later the Dramatic Society, were largely Italian.

Besides inheriting these societies, other organizations were formed in the 1930s. In 1941, a parish yearbook listed ten different organizations and societies. While there are no figures for total membership in that year, the Franciscan journal maintained that 4,730 people belonged to parish organizations in 1924.

One of these organizations was a club established in 1935 named after the parish patron saint. Although it was intended to promote spiritual well-being, the club also provided social activities for the men of the parish. Club facilities, which included billiard and card tables, were set aside in the parish settlement hall. A membership of only fifty men in 1941 suggests that most men preferred the corner or playing cards in a social club to a formal affiliation with this parish society, although some men may have used these facilities without being members.

In addition to the day nursery established for parish children a mothers' club which was primarily social in scope was started for neighborhood women in 1930. In 1941, however, there were only sixty members and meetings were held only twice a month. Low membership may reflect a preference for the settlements and the continued salience of domestic responsibilities, although membership was said to have been greater after the war.

The Alumni Association of the parish grammar school came into its own in the 1930s when it was reorganizaed and a new constitution was adopted. The Association awarded memorial medals and scholarships to neighborhood youth. Alumni returned from distant points for the annual communion breakfast and award ceremony (completing grammar school was something of an honor when many people in the neighborhood did not make it to the eighth grade).

A Journalists and Printers Group comprised a unique parish organization. Formed in 1931, it published a parish newspaper out of the church basement. The editor and the two pressmen were second generation Italian; the former graduated from City College and was quite active in parish and local civic affairs. However, the paper supposedly ceased publication when an old-school Italian pastor objected to "its unorthodox style as a parish bulletin" (the former editor proudly insisted that it was more properly a community paper, which may be viewed as the forerunner of a Greenwich Village weekly that he subsequently joined).

The parish social calendar included noteworthy events for the entire neighborhood. Parish dances, motion picture showings, card parties and bingo games all brought out a crowd on a given evening.

On bingo night, scores of women traveled to the church hall for a good time and the chance to make a "small hit". There were also the periodic theatrical productions. Some affairs, like parish picnics in the country and basketball games against a rival parish team in the gymnasium, were attended by family groups. From the fifties onward, the parish feast became the preeminent neighborhood event. Many former parishioners came back to attend the celebration and renew old ties to the parish, parishioners and the patron saint. Young people, in particular, focused their activities on the parish. In a tenement neighborhood which did not have a playground until 1954, the parish gymnasium and settlement hall were vital resources. Adult volunteers organized league play against other parishes and settlement houses. Young people wore jackets with the parish name emblazoned on the back.

The parochial school was an integral part of parish organization. The older parish established a grammar school in 1872 that was housed in a renovated factory until a new school was constructed in 1912. Although a parish publication asserted that the school was in response to "the rising influx of Italian immigrants and their families", it seems that the school was not well attended by Italian children until after World War I. In the first place, tuition and fees were probably a deterrent, especially in an ethnic culture that assigned a low value to formal education. In addition, the school seems to have been identified with the Irish. Irish laymen were instrumental in the school's construction, a fact that is noted in a commemorative plaque in the school lobby. Further, Irish teaching sisters were employed as instructors. The combination of these factors seems to have been responsible for Italians sending their children to nearby public schools.

Matters, however, were different after the war. The parish school gradually became the neighborhood school, as the church likewise became the symbol for the Italian community. The closing of P.S. 38 in 1930 probably had something to do with this, since there was no longer an elementary school in the immediate vicinity. Moreover, by the late thirties, tuition was no longer required for attendance. The concept of a Catholic education had probably also become more agreeable to second generation parents. As a result, the enrollment of Italian youngsters increased steadily after 1930. In the thirties the grammar school and the two year commercial high school at the older parish had a combined enrollment exceeding one thousand students. The younger parish did not build an elementary school until 1930, although it was well-attended once opened. During World War II, attendance increased from four to seven hundred students. In contrast to the older parish the teaching sisters belonged to an Italian order.

51

Financial Support

Poverty, thrift and traditional restrictions outside the kinship group combined to handicap the early Italian parish regarding funds (Vecoli, 1969:236- 237). The meager contributions of Italian immigrants constituted a salient dimension of the Church's "Italian Problem". However, both churches in the South Village came to depend on Italian parishioners despite their vaunted stinginess in religious matters.

It is reasonable to assume that Italians contributed to the neighborhood church as their economic situations improved. A Franciscan publication announced that the older church "was built and maintained exclusively with the small offerings of the Italian workers", although it is likely that the Archdiocese was more instrumental in obtaining the church building and property in 1866 at a price of $53,000. Nevertheless, parishioners acknowledged their financial responsibility over the years. In 1941, there were over one thousand small donations from individuals and families in honor of the church's seventy-fifth anniversary (the average gift under five dollars). Politicians, businessmen and Mafiosi were more generous benefactors of the parish, and their contributions were conspicuously evident.

At the younger parish, parishioners made possible the financing and construction of a new church when the extension of Sixth Avenue necessitated the demolition of the previous structure in 1925. Responsibility for the project was mainly assumed by local businessmen of Northern Italian extraction who made sizeable contributions of money. A building fund was established and according to the parish historian *ogni famiglia dette la sua offerte.* The $104,200 raised in this manner was "without precedent in the annals of national churches in the Archdiocese of New York". At the dedication ceremonies in 1928, Cardinal Hayes of the New York Archdiocese noted that the effort "speaks of the advance the Italian people have made"

Besides monetary contributions, parishioners donated their time and services to raise funds and run parish activities in conjunction with the priests. Laymen operated weekly bingo games. They helped plan the parish feast and worked in church booths without pay. Parishioners ran card parties and sold chances on parish raffles for prizes donated by local merchants. Women helped around the rectory and school, although some were members of a paid staff. Men coached sports teams, kept the gymnasium open on week nights and served as ushers at Sunday morning mass. Politicians also did their share for the parish. They were able to secure gambling and liquor licenses for the feast without having to go through the inevitable red tape; one year a prominent politician was able to obtain permission for the extension of the feast because of inclement weather. Even Mafiosi performed their share of favors and were renowned as generous patrons.

The Parish Priests

Corresponding to the institutional significance of the parish was the social role of the parish priest. Priests were community leaders, a fact that assumed importance since the educated tended to move away and political and syndicate leaders were concerned with more private advantage. Their distinctness rested on their religious status, as well as their superior educational background, both of which gained them recognition outside the Italian community. They then had control over resources by virtue of their institutional affiliation which could be put at the disposal of the community (*e.g.,* the gymnasium for recreation, the church basement for meetings and dances, prime concessions and locations during the parish feast).

The pastor's secular position as the manager of parish operations made him the peer of other community leaders. Pastors were an important source of legitimation of sundry communal projects, including those initiated by other leaders, and were customarily enlisted to appear at civic meetings. They were on informal terms with politicians and Mafiosi, cooperating on a number of practical matters.

An illustration of their leadership role is the manner in which the pastor and other parish priests "went to bat" for parishioners who ran into trouble with the authorities (a service performed by Mafiosi and district politicians as well). In particular, they served as character references on the basis of their wider reputability.

Priests and brothers were often great favorites with the people of the parish. The basis of their popularity was a close and affectionate involvement with neighborhood life. The younger priests, for example, had a commitment to the youth of the parish through their sponsorship of recreational programs. The elderly also received special attention, and were often visited at home where communion was dispensed. Some of the priests were known for their intimacy with cornerboys. One was said to have stirred the men from their street corners and clubrooms on Sunday morning. Another is reputed to have "hit the big bookies up" on one occasion in order to buy uniforms for a parish baseball team.

Conclusion

Italians became solidly attached to the neighborhood parish in the second generation. The local Italian parish gave expression to common religiocultural backgrounds, sublimating the myriad paesani cults within a neighborhood cult of the parish patron (S. Tomasi, 1975:124). The single neighborhood feast symbolized this ethnic communal breakthrough. The societies and institutional programs, the parochial school and the leadership role of the parish priests made the parish a focal point of neighborhood life. As such, it attained a significance comparable to parishes of other Catholic ethnic groups including the Irish.

There were a number of reasons for these developments. In the first place, the initial strains generated by ethnic conflict were sufficiently overcome as the parish became predominently Italian and the religious acculturation of the second generation moved them closer to the standards set by Irish Catholics (Russo, 1970). The parish also made key resources available to the local Italian population, not the least of which were its physical facilities and institutional programs. Although the settlement houses controlled similar resources and were quite popular, an attachment to the parish was reinforced by a religious affiliation and family traditions, which buttressed a commitment to Catholicism and counteracted Protestant prosletyzing. Moreover, the parish was not as specialized as the settlements, integrating with the neighborhood on a number of levels, and was in closer agreement with the social and cultural backgrounds of the ethnic population.

Although the ethnic parish was an important alternative to non-Italian churches which were culturally remote and often held Italians in contempt, it invariably oriented parishioners toward mainstream Catholicism and the core culture (S. Tomasi, 1975:124).

While established for Italian immigrants, the older parish was shaped by policies delineated by the predominantly Irish archdiocesan hierarchy. It was dominated by Irish laymen who were incorporated from the start on a territorial basis. The parish school was operated by Irish teaching sisters. Even when the parish became overwhelmingly Italian, it still would not support the traditional feste (i.e., the waxen images, the brass bands and fireworks, the women walking barefoot in fulfillment of vows); a feast was not adopted until the parish decided that it would be a means of realizing needed income, and even then it was purged of its peasant aspects. For the most part, then, the second generation was incorporated within a parish that was basically American (Irish) Catholic.

The parish made ongoing adjustments to American conditions. Progressively fewer masses were said in Italian, although this was also a function of the decline in Italian immigration over the years. Mass times were changed. Clearly, the establishment of a two year commercial high school for girls at the older parish was in tune with a changing labor market (i.e., opportunities for clerical work) and the desire of second generation women for something better than factory work.

Two priests associated with the younger parish have suggested that the younger parish remained more faithful to Italian religious and cultural traditions (*i.e.,* less assimilation). The apparent reasons for this were its historical association with an Italian missionary order and its status as a national church. Nevertheless, it evolved a similar parish structure and became equally Americanized. It likewise eschewed an involvement with the feste, although apparently because Northern Italians were as eager as the Irish, if not more so, to suppress Southern Italian peasant customs since they risked being lumped together with their low status countrymen (Ware, 1965:312). Ware was impressed by the extent to which it "sought to identify itself with the American scene", as reflected in the new school building and sophisticated hall, replete with stage and tiled showers in the locker room, and which evidenced a "modernity in thoroughly materialistic American terms" (p. 314). Even though Italian sisters taught in the elementary school, Irish Christian Brothers explained the catechism on Sunday mornings.

Both Italian parishes, then, were abandoning "those characteristic Italian religious practices which marked them in the eyes of the younger generation as 'foreign' " (Ware, 1965:312). Still, neither parish was able to keep pace with their parishioners' upward mobility and acculturation in the long run, although this is more properly the dilemma of the ethnic neighborhood in general. Inevitably, parishioners moved away to "better" neighborhoods, attaching themselves to new parishes. Some Italians transcended the parish even while staying in the South Village, attending services at one of the Irish churches in the Village or the Catholic chapel associated with New York University. Several families who belonged to an Irish parish also enrolled their children in the parochial school which was referred to as an "academy" by neighborhood Italians. They regarded this is a sign of status enchancement, lauding it over parents whose children attended the Italian school. Notwithstanding ethnic conflict, the Irish were a model for Italian religious acculturation and the latter, in turn, was an index of social mobility.

District Politics

*i*talians were relatively slow to make inroads on the urban political system. Significant gains were not realized until the 1930s. One reason for this was the entrenched position of old-guard Irish politicians in the Democratic Party and Tammany Hall. In the interest of preserving their hegemony in the district, the Irish opposed and frustrated the inclusion of Italians within the political system, although for a time Irish politicians coopted ambitious Italians to keep their countrymen in line.

Another factor was a political culture informed by an inveterate mistrust of official authority. In Southern Italy, the peasantry was excluded from political participation and subjugated by the nobility, the Church (a major landowner) and a succession of conquerors. National Unification (1870) did not succeed in incorporating the lower orders within the mainstream (the Republican movement was not widely supported in the South). In fact, the new Republican government subordinated the interests of the Southern peasantry to the industrial and agricultural development of the North; as far as the South was concerned, the *Risorgimento* mainly substituted another predatory power (Iorizzo and Mondello, 1971). In a society where government was oppressive and ineffectual, the family furnished a refuge of support based on primordial ties. Exclusive reliance on the family, in turn, served to inhibit solidarity with wider political units (*e.g.,* party, state) and an adherence to abstract political principles (Banfield, 1958:96). Outside the family, the peasant became annexed to a powerful padrone (*e.g.,* a local land owner, Mafioso or government official) who performed special favors in return for personal loyalty. The competition of peasant families for feudal privileges also preempted class solidarity.

In the immigrant colony the family again served as the basic unit of support. Systems of patronage were reproduced around prominent paesani who arrived earlier, spoke some English and had some capital and influential friends. Labor organizers, racketeers and immigrant bankers became the new padrones. However, Southern Italian political culture did undergo something of a change with the formation of mutual aid societies.

These developments tended to insulate Italian immigrants from the urban political system. In 1911, there were only 15,000 Italian voters among the half million Italians in New York City (Pecorini, 1974:94). This electoral apathy had a telling effect on the number of Italians on the city payroll and in governnment office for years to come.

Following World War I, however, the second generation began taking urban politics more seriously. Unlike the immigrants, they were not immersed in mutual benefit societies. More importantly, they desired the jobs and other resources they had seen accrue to the Irish (Ware, 1965:281-282). As the Irish moved to better areas, Italians posed a growing threat to succeed them in local precincts.

Politics at the district level was premised on the distribution of material benefits to the ethnic lower class in return for loyalty to the district leader. Indifferent to issues and ideologies, the lower class perceived their political role (*e.g.,* their vote) relative to "the things the machine can offer in exchange" (Banfield and Wilson, 1966:117). The district clubs, as part of a machine organization attended to practical needs such as finding jobs and distributing food baskets. Italians, moreover, possessed a cultural background that was receptive to machine politics with its system of patronage and the leader who could "get things done" because he was "connected".

The district leader was the link between the neighborhood and the club. He was directly involved in the allocation of favors or inducements. His forte was the ability to "bridge social systems with a face-to-face personal contact" (Banfield and Wilson, 1966:290). In particular, he was able to broker, or mediate, institutional sectors (*i.e.,* government) for the benefit of a consistuency lacking the resources to do it themselves. In the South Village, the leader, as well as the club, was an integral part of the local community. Politicians had families in the neighborhood and grew up on the block. In fact, relatives, friends and neighbors constituted the core of their support. The district club also had ties to street corner groups and social clubs, the parish and the Mafia syndicate.

Greenwich Village was the preserve of local Tammany clubs run by Irish politicians. The leadership of the first assembly district was the virtual hegemony of the Finn family, which presided over Village politics for three generations in the persons of "Old Battery Dan", "Battery Dan Jr." and "Bashful Dan"(Connable and Silberfarb, 1967:303- 4). The clubs with the assistance of Tammany Hall, resisted the threat to local political arrangements posed by the influx of Italians into the district. Toward this end, district lines were gerrymandered in 1917, severing South Village precincts that had become Italian from the rest of the Village. Redistricting created a "new boundary through the West Side in an irregular line which roughly coincided with the boundary between Irish and Italian settlements" (Ware, 1965:280). The bulk of the Italian population in the South Village was combined in a new electoral district with Italians on the East Side (the second assembly district).

For the time being, redistricting preserved the Village for Irish control. A challenge to the regular clubs had been mounted under the leadership of an Italian paper supply manufacturer who founded a reform club in the early twenties (Connable and Silberfarb, 1967:313). However, the club made little or no headway against the Finn family, which had firm support inside Tammany Hall. It remained for politically ambitious Italians to work for the regular organization, securing the loyalty of their countrymen in return for a political appointment or other considerations.

It was not until 1943 that an Italian was elected to the district leadership. In that year Carmine DeSapio defeated "Bashful Dan" Finn breaking the Irish clan tradition. DeSapio was a second generation Italian who was born in the South Village. He had previously worked for the Finn club as a runner and precinct captain. For his efforts, he received a minor government appointment. Although socialized into machine politics by the Finns, he broke with them to run for district leadership out of an insurgent club in 1939. However, that office eluded the Italian challenger for four years owing to the ability of the incumbent leadership to muster support from Tammany Hall, the Democratic Party organization of New York County, which refused to recognize DeSapio despite electoral victories. He was finally installed a district leader in 1943 with the help of Irish voters who were disillusioned with the regular club. His election signaled a shift in the distribution of power and benefits in favor of the Italian community. An important base of support for his club was the *noveau riche* Italian families who had moved into the elegant Federal Period houses on Vandam and Charlton Streets, known as "Striver's Row". Included among this group was the erstwhile reform challenger and manufacturer.

The South Village was "Carmine's neighborhood" for eighteen years and then some since his influence could be felt after he left office. Open meetings were held at his club two nights a week, with neighborhood people arriving with requests for favors. At the outset, he had popular support. One former aide contended that he was a politician who was "for" the Italian community (and "against" the Irish). Italians were recruited for club membership and rewarded with material benefits, such as post office or Department of Sanitation jobs. The club schooled a generation of neighborhood Italians for a political role at the neighborhood level.

58

DeSapio was the consummate neighborhood padrone. Besides doing favors for individuals, his beneficence was extended to the wider community. The club sponsored a summer camp for neighborhood children. It made conspicuous contributions to the local parish, taking out full-page advertisements in parish anniversary bulletins and donating money or raffle prizes. Italians regarded the "padrone" with the proper deference.

Of course, DeSapio's power far transcended the district. In 1949, he was elected leader of Tammany Hall. Subsequently, he served as a Democratic National committeeperson. In 1956, his portrait appeared on the cover of *Time* magazine as "America's Most Celebrated Boss". He has been described as "far and away the most important politician New York Democrats produced in the post-war era" (Glazer and Moynihan, 1965:215). However, he became lax in his district responsiblities and fell out of favor with his Italian constituents.

Italians gained control of the district that had been put together out of South Village blocks and the East Side somewhat earlier. The manner in which it was done was rather dubious. In 1931, two years before LaGuardia was elected as a reform mayor on the Republican ticket, Al Marinelli was elected district leader. Marinelli had the distinction of being the first and only Italian district leader inside Tammany Hall. He was backed by a notorious Mafioso, "Lucky" Luciano, who was "suspicious of the Irish" and sought "more direct power" (Bell, 1961:144). While sitting in his office near City Hall one day, the incumbent Irish leader was allegedly informed by Luciano's men that he was "through". The ensuing election, in which Marinelli emerged the victor, was "marked by torn ballots and broken laws" (Connable and Silberfarb, 1967:311). Marinelli's tenure, however, was short-lived. He was evicted from office in 1939 by Governor Thomas Dewey who sought to purge state politics of underworld influences (Bell, 1961:145).

Marinelli's successor was an Italian who was better known as the proprietor of a Village cabaret. His son was elected to the state assembly in 1941 and then to the district leadership. Through the years, he was a classic machine politician, working behind the scenes and earning the title "boss" from opponents. He was not formally educated nor an eloquent speaker. However, he was adept at securing special favors for constituents; his long tenure in the assembly undoubtedly made him privy to considerable patronage. Neighborhood Italians voted for him out of habit, ratifying a choice made by special interests in the district and the party. He never bothered to campaign, especially since there was never serious competition provided by the Republican club, which ran candidates just to "make it look good". Most Italians tended to accept this arrangement.

In a Democratic city, Republican clubs seem to have been some

59

what more accessible to Italians. This was due, in part, to the dominance of the Irish in the Democratic clubs. South Village Italians were possibly drawn to the second assembly district's Republican club as its fortunes improved. The fact that it experienced some success in a Democratic city and district could be attributed to the leader's brother, who was a famous bootlegger and was reputed to have had "every cop in the city in his back pocket". Another factor was the election of LaGuardia in 1933. While he was in office, the club reached its zenith; it was during this time that the leader was able to "make" two judges. Still, the club never challenged local Democratic hegemony. For the most part, its approach to patronage was based on cooperation with the Democrats.

In keeping with machine practices, Republican district leaders performed various favors or services for individuals in the neighborhood. A number of South Village residents still hold jobs in municipal government that they obtained through the club. The leader was also able to "fix" traffic tickets and excuse constituents from jury duty. Leaders received neighborhood people in the cluttered back room of a clubhouse that was also a place for cornerboys to hang out.

Neighborhood politicians traditionally served as mediators of societal institutions (i.e., the world beyond the Italian neighborhood). In particular, they intervened in crisis situations on behalf of constituents, a role that also distinguished Mafiosi and parish priests as community leaders. Politicans operated by "fixing things" with the agents of the larger society, deploying strategic inside contacts. Effective leaders knew a host of people who could get things done. Neighborhood Italians reduced politics to the cultivation of personal contacts, as summed up in the axiom "It's not what you know, but who you know".

Politicians frequently came to the aid of individuals who were frustrated by, or in conflict with, the legal system. Their function in these instances was to "pull strings" and serve as character references. Fairly common services included "fixing" traffic tickets and obtaining exemptions from jury duty, although they intervened in more serious matters.

Politicians did not limit their services to individuals. They also intervened in situations perceived as threatening to the "common good" of the community. They expressed and coordinated communal response to threats to sedimented neighborhood patterns, threats seen as emanating from outside the community.

One such threat concerned proposed slum clearance in the 1950s which would have uprooted the Italian community. The urban renewal of the South Village had high level support from the likes of Robert Moses and New York University, which sought high-rise housing as part of its campus expansion program. Even though

60

proponents claimed to be liberating Italians from a slum district, there was strong opposition from Italians who turned to community leaders to thwart the project. Italian politicians and civic leaders formed "The Lower West Side Civic League", a coalition of social/athletic clubs, parish organizations, fraternal societies and street corner groups, to coordinate opposition to renewal. Its director was an up and coming civic leader who was affiliated with Carmine DeSapio's local Democratic club. Strategy mainly consisted in behind-the-scenes pressure brought to bear on "the right people" in city and state government. There was also an element of collective protest not normally associated with clubroom politics. The League filed petitions denouncing N.Y.U. with the community planning board and staged a mass protest. The event began with a religious service at the parish church. Following a benediction for the "good intentions" of the protest, demonstrators left in buses that were chartered by the League for City Hall. Although four high-rise buildings were erected in a predominently industrial area, the greater part of the South Village was spared from urban renewal.

Politicians also intervened in the conflict with bohemia in the fifties. Italians complained that the proliferation of coffee houses in the area of Macdougal and Houston Streets was infringing on their residential neighborhood by spewing loud music into the streets late at night and attracting an undesirable element. A number of incidents resulted. Neighborhood leaders called meetings that were well attended by the community to discuss the problem and vent popular anger. Politicians supposedly got the city to promise a stricter regulation of bohemian establishments.

Conclusion

Village Italians were integrated within the urban political system at the ward and district levels of machine government. As with other aspects of their acculturation, this occurred in the context of the ethnic neighborhood. The neighborhood was the territorial unit to which district lines tended to conform. Loyalties to politicans had an ethnic basis.

As with the parish, district political frameworks were largely inherited from the Irish, although Italians already understood the language of patronage. Ware observed that the second generation had so successfully adapted to the machine form of government that they "took on the techniques, the assumptions and the manner of the Tammany Irish until they became indistinguishable from them" (1965:285)—and this was written before the likes of Carmine DeSapio. It is doubtful, however, whether the clubs ever became as "central to the life of the community" as they were for the Village

Irish (Ware, 1965:268). By the time Italians were gaining control of machine frameworks, New Deal reforms were being instituted with respect to civil service appointments, public welfare and the relative importance of congressmen and senators to district leaders (Whyte, 1943; Gabriel and Savage, 1976). Moreover, there were alternate structures of power and resource distribution in the Italian neighborhood, which were partly a response to Irish control over Tammany Hall. In particular, the Mafia performed many of the functions associated with the machine and exercised considerable influence within the political sphere itself. Frank Costello, for example, was touted as "the power behind Tammany" in the 1940s (Bayor, 1978:43). Furthermore, there was still the family network and going outside the family was a measure of last resort. On balance, most neighborhood Italians expected and received little from politics and politicians because "everybody takes care of their own". Politicians were seen as motivated by self-interest and favors were believed to accrue mainly within an inner circle of club members and special interests.

For the most part, the communal responsibilities of South Village politicians were limited to crisis intervention. However, while the neighborhood looked to them to restore the taken-for-granted character of local life, they rarely provided the initiative for something that would add to the common good, and sometimes even opposed communal interests.

The Mafia Syndicate

a Mafia syndicate played a major role in the South Village Italian community (the term "Mafia" follows the usage employed by neighborhood Italians; there was a widely known membership affiliated with an organization identified by this term). As with other Italian enclaves, the South Village served as a headquarters for syndicate personnel and operations. This had implications for the local economy and civic life.

The Economic Significance of the Mafia

"Black Hand" activities surfaced in the Italian immigrant colony, which was a "frontier settlement" in the sense that the police were largely indifferent and an atmosphere of lawlessness prevailed (Ianni, 1972:59). Immigrant gangsters turned to "robbery and extortion, frequently accompanied by murder" (D'Amato, 1974:174). They involved "threats of death and bodily harm, vendettas and block feuds (particularly between Neapolitans and Sicilians)" (Ianni, 1972:55). Black Hand gangs secured monopolies over certain goods and services. In East Harlem, for example, Ignazio the Wolf and his brother-in-law, Ciro Terranova, imposed a *camorra* (tax) on meat, fish, vegetables, and fruit sold out of Washington Market before World War I (Selvaggi, 1978:52). However, it is important to note that these activities were not organized on any large scale and that they were the work of small gangs without operational ties to the Mafia in Sicily or another secret society, the Camorra in Naples (Ianni, 1971:87).

Black Hand crime was focused on relatively low profit operations within the immigrant colony; until the 1920s, large-scale organized crime was the preserve of Irish and Jewish gangsters (Bell, 1961). However, this was decisively altered by the Volstead Act. Prohibition became "the source for power and profit which allowed an American Mafia to form" (Ianni, 1972:46). Moreover, a new pattern of organization was forged among the second generation through street gang alliances in the Italian slum to exploit this opportunity (Ianni, 1972:63).

In the 1920s, Greenwich Village supported a flourishing liquor trade. The Village bustled with cabarets, or speakeasies, that were patronized by middle class Villagers and an uptown clientele. These were operated and supplied by Italian racketeers (Ware, 1954: 53-55). Wine and liquor were made under the cover of the Italian community—beverages traditionally produced for the consumption of the immigrant family, although enterprising immigrants sold a gallon or two to paesani. In the urban slum, the fermenting and pressing of grapes took place in the basements of tenement buildings. Cordials were easily made from fruit, alcohol, rock candy and sugar and were reserved for special family affairs. With Prohibition, ambitious Italians expanded their production to supply the needs of local distributors. Bootlegging became a major industry in the Italian neighborhood (Ware, 1965:55-62). Wine and liquor were sold clandestinely in local restaurants. Alcoholic beverages were also sold out of candystores and social clubs, a practice that survived the end of Prohibition and was especially popular among cornerboys on Sundays before the bars were allowed to open. Bootlegging spawned a stratum of *nouveau riche* Italian families in business, politics and the professions.

With the repeal of Prohibition, Mafia operations within the Italian neighborhood shifted to the provision of other goods and services. Probably the heart of its local rackets was gambling (other sources of profit, like prostitution and labor racketeering, did not directly affect the neighborhood). Gambling operations involved the placing of bets on the horses, numbers (keyed to the daily handling of a local racetrack) and sports in season. Working class Italians, looking to make "a big hit" or simply indulging in a social pastime, were avid customers, as were workers in nearby factories and truck terminals. Gambling was part of the fabric of neighborhood life, with housewives and grandmothers putting a few cents on a "lucky" number or a "hot tip".

Gambling operations had numerous ramifications for the wider Italian neighborhood. For one thing, it created jobs at several levels. In particular, it gave rise to the archetypal neighborhood character, the bookie. The bookie was a ubiquitous presence on the street. Each specialized in one type of betting and serviced accounts within a territory assigned by the higher-ups in the syndicate. Circulating through the neighborhood for much of the day, he was an important part of local control and was an integral part of the local grapevine that tied the neighborhood together.

Syndicate gambling operations utilized legitimate businesses as "drops" for the day's receipts. These commercial establishments were perfect cover for this facet of the gambling racket; at the end of the day, receipts were collected by another syndicate employee. This service provided an extra income to the proprietors, who may have had no other connection to the syndicate.

Loansharking was another syndicate racket in the neighborhood. It was a service that was in considerable demand among lower class populations without favored access to legitimate credit institutions. The loanshark was sanctioned by the local syndicate to put money on the street at exorbitant rates of interest—funds available for lending could belong to the loanshark as well as to the syndicate. Although the risk was great, repayment was insured by Mafia intimidation and muscle. The loanshark's principal clientele was the street corner element weighted down by gambling debts and generally immersed in a free-spending economy. Like horse and numbers playing, this trade was buttressed by the presence of workers in local factories. On Friday afternoons, workers huddled with their loansharks in bars and on street corners. Loansharks also lent money to families to meet domestic exigencies; "family" loans were offered at fairer rates and on more friendly terms, perhaps because the risk was lower. Nevertheless, loansharks were held in low esteem. Their intimidating air was in clear contrast to the expansive personality of the bookie, and the service they performed was ruthlessly exploitative, although the services performed by the bookie and the loanshark were interrelated since loans were typically made to finance gambling debts.

Another syndicate activity was the sale of merchandise stolen from trucks and warehouses (*i.e.*, "swag") at prices that were often below wholesale. Although this was engaged in on a petty basis by truck drivers and warehousemen, any increase in scale warranted the protection and distribution networks maintained by the syndicate, largely because it was adverse to competition on its turf.

The syndicate made available regular supplies of goods to neighborhood Italians and to workers who patronized local bars and luncheonettes. Samples of stolen merchandise were cavalierly displayed on the street or inside a commercial establishment. Vendors hardly bothered to remove the items from their shipping cartons. Cigarettes, a popular bootleg item, were sold from the trunk of a parked automobile. Neighborhood shops, truck terminals and warehouses sold "hot" goods purchased in lots as a sideline. One candystore advertised appliances and men's sport shirts one week, boy's sneakers the next. Makeshift signs informed passersby of the current special, although the grapevine was a more effective manner of advertising.

Not surprisingly, the neighborhood supported this underground marketplace with enthusiasm. Highly regarded consumer goods, the conspicuous symbols of acculturation and upper class status, were made accessible to ethnic workers; there also seems to have been some satisfaction in the knowledge that upper class consumers paid more for the item and that a big company had been duped. Lamps, toasters, television sets and perfume (brands sold in uptown department stores) all made their way into the neighborhood as swag. Perhaps the only complication was when a scarce supply of stolen merchandise resulted in competition among neighbors, or when a neighbor endeavored to become a middleman and purchased caseloads to sell to friends and neighbors at a profit.

Since it generally regarded the Italian neighborhood as a field for its particular economic exploitation, the Mafia had myriad implications for legitimate business. It selectively invested in local ventures like trucking outfits and restaurant supply firms (perhaps an offshoot of liquor distribution during Prohibition). Some enterprises served primarily as "fronts" for illicit activities; in one case, a business was "set up" with the expectation that the proprietor would cooperate in the operation of syndicate rackets.

Legitimate neighborhood establishments were historically infringed upon by syndicate interests. Local businessmen were constrained to pay "protection" money as a tribute or tax to quasifeudal Mafiosi. Store owners were compelled to buy products or services marketed by syndicate affiliates. Thus, luncheonettes leased cigarette machines and juke boxes from a favored company and corner bars agreed to purchase liquor from a salesman with a relative in the rackets. Businesses that cooperated (i.e., accepted an offer they could not refuse) received special considerations, such as being able to rely on the syndicate to collect delinquent accounts and handle rowdy patrons, as well as not having their windows broken.

Enterprises that competed with syndicate interests were discouraged. For example, a luncheonette was not allowed to open because it was perceived as a threat to an establishment with syndicate ties; its windows were shattered on four different occasions until the owner withdrew. Legitimate businesses were also hurt by "swag" goods sold for less than their merchandise.

The Mafia performed the important function of providing employment for local men and even an occasional woman. It recruited young men with little formal education and whose background experience was a knowledge of the street. As a rule, the jobs that were made available offered greater financial remuneration, prestige and excitement than work that otherwise would have been their lot. For example, one man became a loanshark after working as an elevator operator. His new position gave him money in his pocket, the opportunity to wear expensive clothes and jewelry and respect since he now had "friends". Syndicate employment covered a wide range of jobs; there was a need for men to chauffeur cars, operate clubrooms and run errands, in addition to the more intimidating and illicit work. The Mafia was also able to find men employment through labor unions in which it exercised influence or control, and in companies which it owned.

Local Control

In addition to its economic implications for the neighborhood, the Mafia maintained an effective order in the South Village. An opportunity for such a role was created by the traditional remoteness of official agents of authority from the ethnic neighborhood. In light of an "absentee government" (Ianni, 1971:80- 83; Hobsbawm, 1959:32), the Mafia installed a network of control indigenous to the ethnic community. It was powerful enough to exploit this vacuum of authority for private material advantage.

A concern with order was a functional prerequisite. In general, the Mafia sought a local environment that would yield and ensure business profits. Above all, there was a need for a milieu that could shelter illicit syndicate operations and personnel. By taking responsibility for local control the Mafia could guarantee a "market peace" to its rackets. This reduced the scrutiny of authorities who had official jurisdiction in the neighborhood, thereby maintaining the secrecy of syndicate activities, although local police tended to integrate with syndicate clubs for a drink and a respite and were said to have been on the syndicate "pad".

Order was more than an organizational prerequisite. There was also an element of paternalistic responsibility for the Italian neighborhood as a Mafia fiefdom, plus the fact that Mafiosi had families in the South Village. In the neighborhood, this ideology of paternalism rationalized syndicate control. Elected officials were informed that "we take care of our own".

Mafia control had implications for a defended neighborhood. Strangers were closely watched. Unlike neighborhood Italians who understood the importance of keeping quiet (they saw everything but knew nothing), strangers could not be trusted. Of special concern was the possibility that strangers were law enforcement authorities. In one instance, an ordinary looking man who frequented a neighborhood bar for several months turned out to be a plainclothes detective and arrested a bookie for taking numbers. Therefore, caution was paramount since syndicate operations were in full view. It was facilitated by the extensive network of syndicate personnel on the street and in the club rooms throughout the neighborhood supervising gambling and other business operations. Moreover, the Mafia lent the neighborhood its reputation for total violence, serving to dissuade predators. Notwithstanding its exploitiveness in other areas (*e.g.,* loansharking), this protective function gave the Mafia legitimacy in the neighborhood.

Within the Italian community, there was recourse to the Mafia in the event of a problem or wrongdoing, especially if one had a "connection". The ability to recover stolen merchandise was at least partly due to the Mafia's fencing operations. Recourse to the Mafia reflected a popular belief that a more efficacious solution could be arrived at than if the local authorities were consulted. The Mafia knew the workings of the street and was not fettered by legal and bureaucratic restrictions.

The Mafia maintained a system of "courts" which meted out private settlements to concerned parties (Ianni, 1972:39). In one case, a businessman was ordered to compensate a former partner who claimed he had been cheated. The decision was reached in a "sit down", or hearing, where each partner was represented by syndicate connections. In another instance, a man caught burglarizing apartments was brought into a club where justice was dispensed with bats and fists (cornerboys were warned not to interfere when he tried to hail a taxi to take him to a hospital). In still another case, a man with syndicate ties was ordered to assume all medical expenses when an innocent bystander received a flesh wound from a gun fired by him. In all of these cases, there was the implicit assumption that recourse to legal machinery was precluded. This was one reason for the low crime rate in the South Village. Punishment frequently assumed a repressive character, since force was believed to be the most effective deterrent. It sometimes involved banishment from the neighborhood, a sentence that reflected the urgency of eliminating especially troublesome indivduals and suggests that there was a punitive aspect on being cut off from the neighborhood.

Mafia courts primarily settled internal syndicate matters. Cases often concerned the failure to repay a gambling debt or loan on schedule. A formal sit down would be arranged in one of the clubs when less intimidating methods proved unfruitful. A possible result was the refinancing of the original debt and cumulative interest charges, or the confiscation of real property. In one case, a debtor surrendered a small luncheonette when he defaulted on a loan, although he was retained on salary to manage the business. In another, indentured labor was prescribed, with the employer delivering the debtor's weekly wages to a syndicate representative. Debts were also discharged by engaging in risky undertakings; one debtor was pressured into hijacking a truck for its cargo. It was widely believed that individuals who "crossed" the Mafia were killed. To escape that fate, men fled to parts unknown, except perhaps to their families. Needless to say, it always helped to have someone with influence intercede. When the local syndicate tried to persuade a neighborhood merchant to give up his lease, the latter appealed to a contact in Brooklyn who negotiated a settlement that allowed him to keep the store.

68

The neighborhood was virtually a Mafia fiefdom. A Mafia leader, delegated authority by a more powerful figure in the "family", oversaw matters in the area with the assistance of "soldiers" and a retinue of other aides who were stationed at syndicate clubs throughout the neighborhood with the leader's own club serving as headquarters. In the neighborhood, the syndicate was entitled to prerogatives of an economic nature, including the collection of a tribute for "protection", and the deference befitting men of rank. In return, resident Italians were granted a neighborhood where their family and peer group life was secure.

In this scheme, the Mafia leader enacted a mediator role on behalf of local clients. A broker of major institutional resources, the Mafia leader rendered services in a manner comparable to the machine politician. People approached the Mafioso as they would the district leader; he likewise maintained a clubroom where favors were petitioned. The Mafioso obtained jobs within the syndicate as well as in companies and labor unions where ties were established. He could also intercede in legal matters since he knew politicians and judges.

The Mafia chief was often portrayed in local lore as showing a genuine concern for the Italian community. One priest who grew up in the neighborhood recalled one of the more ruthless "mobsters" in organized crime as "a lovely human being who was always helping people". It was widely maintained that Mafia chieftains kept narcotics out of the neighborhood while they were being introduced to other parts of the city. On this point, however, it appears that a concern for profits may have taken precedence over Mafia paternalism. Known narcotics distributors worked out of the neighborhood. In the fifties, there was a serious drug problem among Italian (and Irish) youth. To be sure, the distribution of narcotics would not have been possible in the neighborhood without at least tacit approval from the Mafia.

On the whole, beneficence would have been overshadowed by intimidation and exploitation. Even for those who minded their own business, the very presence of syndicate personnel was unsettling. Street cornerboys took care to laugh at their jokes, make way when they walked down the street and show concern for their well-being.

The Mafia
and Other Neighborhood Institutions

The Mafia was part of the fabric of the Italian community. It was entwined with neighborhood institutions and reflected a common normative order (*e.g.,* traditional notions of respect and personal loyalty).

69

The syndicate was closely integrated socially and economically with street corner life. Street gangs were the matrix and prototype for the new, second generation Italian American Mafia in contrast to the old ritual brotherhood (Ianni, 1971:88). Street corner life-styles generated a demand for syndicate services; playing the numbers was a facet of every day life. Street cornerboys articulated with Mafia clubs, or "horse rooms", which functioned as outposts for the administration of syndicate business and control. The clubs supported a convivial cornerboy atmostphere, along the lines of the other "members only" clubs in the neighborhood, by allowing men to hang out, play cards and watch television. The clubs served as centers for the consumption of syndicate services (*e.g.,* gambling) and the recruitment and socialization of syndicate personnel. From time to time, however, the club was cleared for high-level meetings among syndicate bosses (a reminder of their primary function).

The Mafia was also linked to district level politics and politicians. The trade in illegal liquor was secured by persuading the authorities, for a price, to "look the other way". Mafiosi altered voter registration lists and ballots, and pressured cornerboys to support a favored candidate. Mafiosi installed their own people in local district positions, a number of whom were reputed to have ties to "the underworld".

The Mafia had close ties with the neighborhood parish. On its side, the Mafia showed a concern for parish welfare. This seems to have involved a paternalistic regard for a symbolic neighborhood institution, a gesture that ennobled Mafiosi in the eyes of the community. It may also have been a matter of pleasing religiously inclined mothers and wives, or a desire for spiritual consolation in light of occupational demands (*i.e.,* a hedge against damnation).

This relationship proved salubrious for the church, especially given its persistent cash-flow problems. Mafia leaders reputedly made generous cash donations. A former pastor delegated the task of selling advertisements in parish yearbooks to Mafiosi. One Mafia leader recruited celebrities whom he supposedly helped "get started" to draw large crowds at parish affairs. Another used his influence to get Sunday services on the radio when there was a concern to stay in touch with former parishioners.

Rewards accruing to the syndicate were not entirely of a nonmaterial nature (*e.g.,* a good conscience). The annual parish feast, for example, was mined by syndicate interests for a profit. They purportedly had a say in the way concessions and sites were allocated, reserving the more promising ones for themselves. The syndicate allegedly realized a large share of the profits from the gambling concessions licensed by the city for the duration of the feast. It was suggested that one parish merely "fronted" for the syndicate.

The Mafia was rooted in the neighborhood family system. Racketeers had families living in the neighborhood who followed common traditions and "had it hard like everybody else". There was a dimension beyond the rackets that sustained a solidarity between them and the rest of the neighborhood. The families of Mafiosi were part of the network of respect surrounding wakes and funerals. Mafiosi were "good family men"; they "loved their home and macaroni on Sunday".

Conclusion

A Mafia syndicate, which was transformed from a ritual brotherhood into something resembling an urban gang in the second generation (Ianni, 1972), assumed an importance for the South Village Italian community on two levels. Since the Italian neighborhood was a home base for the exploitation of material advantages, the syndicate imposed on local business and introduced an underground economy that furnished locally valued goods and services. In addition, it constituted a system of local power relationships and control; it was an invisible governnment whose main objective was to guarantee a market place for illicit ventures. Coercion was at the bottom of both its economic activities and control function.

For the most part, the Italian community effected a *modus vivendi* with the syndicate. The general rule for coexistence was to "mind your own business" or "look the other way". This even went as far as a reluctance to mention the names of syndicate personnel and the habit of using more discreet terms of reference such as "the boys" or a knowing and accentuated "them" or "they". Still, the syndicate was accorded a measure of legitimation. There were tangible benefits in the Mafia contribution to a defended neighborhood and its ability to supply political leverage when other channels were closed. Moreover, as Ianni (1972) suggests, a common world view conditioned at least a philosophical acceptance of the Mafia in the neighborhood. Finally, although the Mafia was more ruthless, official authority was also exploitative. City police were referred to as "the Irish Mafia" because of the collection rackets they operated among neighborhood merchants. Precinct police and elected officials had ties to the Mafia, receiving payments in return for protection.

The South Village's status as a syndicate base tended to circumscribe communal expression. "The boys" had the capacity to usurp any facet of neighborhood life to secure private advantages. Neighborhood Italians found it difficult to argue.

The South Village in Transition

*i*n the period following World War I, the South Village
Italian community was significantly restructured. The
social frameworks and forms of solidarity that were
the basis of immigrant group life outside the family
eroded or were submerged. The community assumed a
shape that reflected the sociocultural position of the
second generation who had moved beyond immigrant
institutions but were still outside the mainstream. Their
communal adaptation combined specifically urban institutions like district politics with traditional ethnic
social and cultural forms such as Italian familism (although it was more properly an interaction between
the two). The sublimation of paesani distinctions meant
that communal solidarity was informed by a new and
expanded sense of ethnicity that itself was a product of
the second generation's acculturation and the social
structure of the city. Thus, rather than simply wither
away, the South Village Italian community absorbed
social and cultural changes beyond the immigrant
generation. The result was the emergence of a new
communal form *vis-à-vis* the immigrant colony, although
there were major social and cultural continuities. The
family group was still the centerpiece of local life.
However, with the eclipse of immigrant frameworks, it
articulated with a different set of communal institutions
(*e.g.,* the Italian neighborhood instead of the paesani
group, district political clubs instead of mutual benefit
societies).

A neighborhood-based community was the measure
of the second generation's adaptation to the city after
World War I. However, by the 1960s, ongoing population decline began to have a telling effect on communal
patterns. At the same time, the groups replacing the
Italians in the South Village began imposing their own
communal characteristics on the area and its institutions. The expansion of the SoHo artists' community in
the adjacent factory district after 1971 had far-

reaching implications (Simpson, 1981).

Dwindling Numbers

Although the Italian population in the Village began to decline after World War I, enough families remained to comprise the core of a restructured ethnic community. Grafted onto this element was the trickle of immigrants from the old towns (now that quotas and other factors had largely rerouted Italian immigration). By 1960, however, the cumulative impact of dwindling numbers was becoming evident. One of the local parishes expressed concern at the time that the loss of parishioners would undermine its viability.

Although the loss of population had been steady, there was an accelerated decline after 1950. Whereas the total population of the South Village remained virtually constant between 1940 and 1950, it declined 12.5 percent between 1950 and 1960. There was a further decline of 17 percent over the next 10 years, representing a loss of 3,510 persons. During the span, the population of the district that was Italian born or native born of Italian parentage declined by 3,239—a sharp drop from the 1950 total of 8,283.

The driving force behind this post-war demographic trend was the mobility aspirations of young Italian Americans. With family formation and mobility plans interrupted by World War II, they began opting, with determination, for more mainstream life-styles in the suburbs and outlying boroughs. Looking back on this time, a woman who moved to the suburbs in 1956 recalled that most young couples at least talked about moving away. Even Mafiosi were taking their families to pleasant residential sections in Brooklyn, Queens and the suburbs.

Actually the neighborhood experienced something of a renaissance immediately following the war. Returning G.I.s channeled their energies and capital into local business ventures. They breathed new life into the community when they married and started families. Parish records show a significant increase in marriages and baptisms from the end of the war through the middle fifties. Apartments were in demand, resulting in a local housing shortage. There was also a swelling of enrollments at the parish elementary schools. In the early fifties, one school stopped accepting students for the first grade class, while another had to combine grades to accommodate the influx of children.

The upswing, however, was rather short-lived. The young couples were not as much planting roots as getting their feet on the ground. Low rents made it possible to start a nest egg; in 1950, the median rent in two South Village census tracts were $23.83 and $23.00. Whereas their parents had been constrained by the Depression and the war, the post-war period held out the promise of significant socioeconomic advancement. With more education, second and third generation Italians were better prepared to benefit from the upturn

73

in the national economy; educational opportunities and job upgrading were available through the G.I. Bill, although the second generation remained largely blue-collar (Glazer and Moynihan, 1963:206). The federal government's housing policy made it quite easy for working class Italian Americans to own homes outside the central city. G.I. mortgages and FHA insurance made it possible to finance a house at four and a half percent interest over thirty years with a minimal down payment (often less than 10%). A three bedroom ranch house set in a neatly arranged tract development within twenty miles of the city could be bought for less than $13,000 in the mid-fifties. The time was ripe to abandon the three room flat on the airshaft with the bathtub in the kitchen, and many families did just that. The mailing list for a neighborhood reunion held in 1975 was full of former residents who live in post-war suburbs like Rochelle Park, New Jersey and Hicksville, Long Island.

The exodus of Italians to the suburbs was more than the result of favorable material conditions. There was an eagerness to leave the small world of the neighborhood and enter the mainstream of American life which they had been exposed to by the media, the school and the army. Social horizons were also broadened by occupational opportunities that were more varied than those faced by their parents. In the second generation, for example, women worked in offices and department stores instead of factories; in one census tract, 100 out of 353 women who worked in 1950 were salespersons. Italian Americans also faced less prejudice after the war; although one couple who moved to the suburbs in the fifties received a cold reception from Protestant neighbors, the majority of the famililies on the block were non-Protestants who had likewise left the city. Detaching oneself from the ethnic community was a precondition for acculturation and upward mobility, given the fact that the experience of Italians in the United States had been as a low status minority with a traditional peasant culture. Italians heartily embraced suburbia as the symbol of American life. A *New York Times* survey (November 14, 1978) found that Italians were the largest ethnic group in New York City suburbs, some 19 percent of those surveyed. More recently, Staten Island has been the promised land for Italian Americans who want to live in the suburbs.

In 1970, 4,160 people in the South Village claimed Italian ancestry and another 697 identified themselves as having Italian and some "other" ancestry (the 1980 census allowed respondents to identify with a particular ethnicity rather than make a determination of nationality background based on birth status). The 1970 census had counted 4,944 persons who were either Italian born or had Italian parents; since in all likelihood there was a greater decline in the Italian population over that 10 year span, it appears that the census affords a rather conservative demographic picture of the Italian South Village in 1970.

Since census data at the tract level are not given along ethnic lines, the characteristics of the Italian population must be roughly gauged. In two census tracts that were the "stronghold" of the Italian South Village, mean family income in 1980 was $21,345 and $24,900 respectively ($10,012 and $9,340 in 1970). Nineteen percent of persons 16 and over were employed in manufacturing, a decline from 31 percent in 1970. Twelve percent were employed in the retail trade where 20 percent worked in 1970. Thirty-one percent of the local labor force was employed in "professional and related services" in 1980. This group is probably almost entirely composed of non-Italian newcomers. Moreover, these occupations have a higher salary structure.

Notwithstanding its informality, a 1975 parish survey provides greater focus on the occupational characteristics of the Italian population. It showed that the men were most frequently employed in trucking, construction, factory work and maintenance. Women most often worked in a clerical capacity (*e.g.,* secretary, switchboard operator) or were in retail sales (the younger women preferred office work or department store sales postions).

South Village Italians sustained a modest working-class life-style. Most would describe themselves as "comfortable" or at least "not in want of anything" deemed a necessity. Low housing costs made a greater portion of their income available for discretionary purposes. In 1970 median rents in the census tracts considered earlier were $54.00 and $57.00 respectively; most rents ranged between $40.00 and $79.00. Even though median rents had risen to $215 and $277 respectively in 1980, Italians were paying about half as much in their rent controlled apartments. Therefore, Italians were able to afford the better cuts of meat at a private butcher, color televisions, air conditioners, vacations and automobiles. Of course, it must be remembered that tenement flats were without amenities that the majority of Americans consider standard (*e.g.,* full baths, privacy, spaciousness).

Some people could be described as "quite comfortable", although their life-styles were not qualitatively different from anyone else's; living in "the old neighborhood" tended to be a common denominator. Poverty was primarily a problem for the elderly; in 1970, 38.5 percent of family heads over 65, in one census tract, were living below the poverty level. This problem was compounded by poor health, so that some were shut- ins needing outside attention. However, inured to "doing without", the elderly knew how to survive with dignity with the help of social security and medicaid benefits. As younger people continued to move away, the elderly became a more conspicuous segment of the Italian community.

Newcomers
in the Neighborhood

Not all of the changes in the South Village were the direct result of Italian mobility. The arrival of new groups occupying places left by Italians also had implications for the Italian neighborhood.

In contrast to other ethnic areas, the South Village did not attract low status newcomers to the city. In 1950, for example, there were only 40 blacks out of 4,116 persons enumerated in three South Village census tracts; altogether, there were 68 nonwhite persons. In 1960 there were only 138 blacks living in this area. In two South Village census tracts the black population declined by 10 percent between 1970 and 1980 (from 122 to 110). The number of persons of Puerto Rican birth or parentage actually declined in two South Village census tracts between 1960 and 1980, from 327 to 114. A reason for this was the remoteness of the South Village from black or Hispanic settlements (even though blacks and Hispanics were employed locally). Moreover, Italians discouraged minorities from moving into the neighborhood. Perhaps more importantly, the core of the Village remained middle class all along ("the American Ward") and, after World War I, began to absorb contracting ethnic areas, the Irish section among the first to go. At the same time, the blocks to the west and south remained industrial.

Although the South Village was not threatened by waves of new immigrants, it was targeted by one or another plan to re-develop the district at the expense of its Italian population. One such plan was advanced in a WPA community study (1937). The researchers discovered "crowded slum-like conditions" in the Italian section of Greenwich Village that were "certain to be disturbing" and "a menace to health"; especially the 4 and 5 story walk-up tenements with "a shop, restaurant, or some other use" on the lower floor. The study also maintained that the adjacent factory district (now SoHo) was an "industrial slum" since much of the light industry, especially the garment shops, had moved out. It recommended that tenement and loft structures be leveled and "workers' housing" be constructed in their place. It avoided the issue of what was to become of the Italian population, nor did it show any appreciation for the cast-iron loft buildings that were designated historical landmarks by the city thirty-four years later.

The WPA plan did not materialize. A pattern continued whereby, as land values increased, houses and apartment buildings were renovated for middle class occupancy. The area below Washington Square Park, however, resisted easy rehabilitation for middle class use. In 1954, New York University, a major property owner in the Village area, turned its attention to the tenements and loft buildings below the Square. The university suggested that the South Village be subjected to government funded slum clearance, for which it was eligible in light of its sub standard housing.

The proposal for slum clearance was tendered as part of a study conducted by N.Y.U. School of Education (1954) to improve the quality of the schools in Greenwich Village. The study concluded that the latter was directly related to the district's ability to "hold a middle class population". This, in turn, depended on the availability of the requisite housing and other amenities. A plan was endorsed for three major development projects in the lower Village area which necessitated the removal of the Italian population. This was justified on the grounds that tenement life was insupportable, and that Italians were themselves discontented with the neighborhood. As evidence, it produced a survey which reported that "a larger percentage of the lower Village population expects to move than does that of the Upper Village". It did not address the status of Italians who did not have plans to leave. Nevertheless, the displacement of Italians was a precondition for the upgrading of Village schools.

One of these development projects was built in an industrial area southeast of Washington Square. By 1967, 1,826 dwelling units had been completed; altogether, there were four high-rise buildings on the site. A number of Italian families, some of whom were displaced by the construction, took apartments. For the most part, however, the new residents were middle class professionals—the leading edge of the gentrification in the South Village.

The other two renewal projects were to provide "slum- clearance housing in an area bounded by the Avenue of the Americas, Broome St., West Broadway and West Houston St., with the exception of designated buildings" (the latter were presumabably Federal Period landmark houses). This was the heart of the Italian South Village. However, these projects were not carried out. Notwithstanding the conclusions of the School of Education study, Italians were not prepared to cede the South Village which they never thought of as a "slum".

The South Village was also threatened by a plan to build a highway through downtown Manhattan at Canal Street (the Lower Manhattan Expressway) in the sixties. The highway called for the razing of buildings up to Broome Street; several buildings had actually been torn down on Hudson Street, near the Hudson River, in anticipation of the road. Italians living in the designated area were worried, and some were frightened into moving away. The plan, however, was scuttled by the end of the decade, partly due to local political action.

Although urban renewal and highway construction were held in abeyance, the South Village remained a "zone of transition".

Landlords were hesitant to make capital improvements. Rent levels stayed low, although this was partly due to the city's rent control law. As a result, students and other young, single persons found the neighborhood attractive. The area above Bleecker Street had been transformed into a bohemian quarter in the late fifties. The withering away of the hippie counter-culture left a seedy residue of bars, head shops, record stores and the infamous welfare hotels, including the imposing Greenwich Hotel on Bleecker and Thompson Streets. Many Italians in this section fled. The Italian neighborhood below Houston Street was largely untouched by these developments, although young people were filtering into the area in increasing numbers.

The transitional South Village also emerged as a settlement for Portuguese immigrants. Their numbers were insignificant in the mid-sixties, since they received no mention in the parish literature of the period. However, the 1980 Census counted 982 Portuguese in the area. Like the students and other young people, the Portuguese were attracted by low rent tenement flats.

A relatively small number of brick and brownstone houses attracted middle class professionals to the Village in these years. Many of these structures, built in Federal Period/Greek Revival style for upper middle class families before the Civil War, were refurbished when Italian families moved away. The purchases were often very reasonable; Italians were not sensitive to the area's real estate values. Besides being a good buy, there was the convenience of an intown location and the amenities associated with the residence in an urban village (*e.g.,* "community", good restaurants, safety).

A development in the early 1970s signaled the transformation of the South Village into something other than an Italian neighborhood, namely, the legalization of loft residence in the adjacent factory district and the crystallization of an "artists community". In contrast to renewal and the expressway, this was a development that would not be thwarted.

In the second half of the nineteenth century, the district which ran along lower Broadway was known as the "Venice of Industry". However, many of the small manufacturing concerns had vacated by World War II. As a 1966 parish yearbook noted, the "low ceilinged, narrow dark rooms with small windows only at the front and rear of the building" had been considered "impractical for conversion into residences". Into the sixties, however, these abandoned lofts were being occupied by painters, sculptors, musicians and film makers who demanded ample work space at low rents.

The artists entered a vacuum created by the uncertainty of development plans for lower Manhattan. Since the district was zoned for industry, they were forced to live in a clandestine manner.

They had to conceal their illegal occupancy from building inspectors by keeping their windows dark after work hours; household garbage could not be left at the curb. Artists also had to put up with the inconvenience of truck deliveries, noisy machinery and freight elevators. However, the "space" (a central concept in the *Weltanschauung* of loft residents) was unquestionably worth the sacrifice.

In 1971, the status of the squatter settlement was decisively altered. A community organization representing artists in the area pressed the city to legitimize their residence in the loft district. They were supported by prominent financial and cultural interests, including the Rockefeller family. With this backing, a municipal zoning amendment was passed in 1971 legalizing loft residence in a designated area for working artists who were officially certified by a committee newly established by the city (the area was bounded by Houston and Center Streets, and Lafayette Street and West Broadway which was its boundary with the Italian neighborhood). The city also instituted a program of tax abatements and exemptions for converted industrial property. The entire area was accorded the status of an historical landmark, which imposed restrictions on subsequent development, because of a preponderance of cast-iron facade buildings erected after the Civil War; landmark status gave the artists' community further distinction. Its official identity was established as "SoHo" a name which derived from its location South of Houston Street, and was not to be confused with "Soho" in London. The city was careful to emphasize that SoHo was not to jeopardize any further manufacturing jobs, which provided a livelihood for the city's minority groups (according to the local planning board, manufacturing jobs in the city declined by 3.4% between 1957 and 1955 while there was a 9.4% decline in Greenwich Village). However, city officials were able to justify SoHo on economic grounds since "art is industry". There were also possibilities that SoHo would help restore the middle class to lower Manhattan.

While art was secured against the building inspectors, legalization had turned the loft district into what a local TV news program referred to as "the hottest thing in New York real estate". The demand for lofts burgeoned among non-artists who craved space and a now fashionable address. In no time, "businessmen, doctors, lawyers, and retired persons...grabbed living lofts reserved for resident working artists" (*The Village Voice*, May 15, 1974). Developers bought commercial properties to be converted, with the aid of generous tax breaks, into loft apartments, or merely to hold for speculation; as a result, SoHo had become "a landlord's market rather than an artist's market" (*The Village Voice*, May 15, 1974). Wealthy artists profited too, becoming landlords and speculators. By 1977, 4,000 square feet of loft space that sold for between $3,000 and $7,000 in 1971 was selling between $50,000 and $100,000. Pioneer artists who had occupied illegal lofts before

1971 were forced into virgin industrial areas elsewhere in the city (NoHo, Tribeca, etc.).

Although the Italian neighborhood was not within the area designated by the City Planning Commission as SoHo, and had only a limited supply of commercial space, it nonetheless felt the full impact of the SoHo phenomenon. After 1971, there was a sudden surge of demand for apartments and storefronts in the South Village. Invariably, SoHo had an inflationary effect on local land values and the neighborhood rent structure, especially when the rent control law no longer extended to vacant apartments after 1972. To take full advantage of the prestige lent by SoHo, South Village landlords began listing apartments with a SoHo address and demanding SoHo rents. Italians watched all this behind the relative protection of the city's rent control law (allowing a maximum increase of 7½% a year).

Since loft space was minimal, the South Village held little interest for artists and others for whom space was an obsession and who spoke in terms of thousands of square feet instead of rooms. Nevertheless, it did attract a related and specialized group who came to the South Village to live in SoHo, but who either could not afford a loft or were not a vital part of the art scene. They tended to be in their twenties or early thirties, and at some stage preparatory to a professional career perhaps in a field related to the arts. They also tended to live alone or with a roommate.

Between 1970 and 1980, there was a marked increase in the number of persons aged 25-34 in the two South Village census tracts adjacent to SoHo. Whereas 22 percent of the total population was in this category in 1970, 31 percent were between the ages of 25 and 34 in 1980. This development was primarily responsible for reversing the population decline in the South Village. The census tracts mentioned above experienced a 28 percent increase in population between 1970 and 1980.

The young newcomers were drawn to the South Village for a number of reasons. In light of rents elsewhere in Manhattan, the apartments, which Italians had taken care of as their homes, were reasonable, although they were renting for two to three times what Italians were paying. Moreover, the neighborhood was interesting. A jazz musician felt "stimulated by the neighborhood". Similarly, an artist claimed to "feel the vitality" of the area, and valued the contacts it offered (via the bars, laundromats, etc.) for advancing his career. Many newcomers appreciated the South Village for its ethnic ambiance, although it was clearly fading. There was also the "reverse chic" of a tenement flat with a bathtub in the middle of the kitchen and a toilet in the hall. With Italian Americans making the "outward journey", the South Village had become an incubator of professional careers; as an ethnic enclave, it had been an incubator of mainstream Americans.

80

After 1971, apartments in the South Village were in great demand. Italians were stunned at the eagerness with which young newcomers paid as much as four to five times what Italians were paying for three small rooms and the inevitable toilet in the hallway (landlords discovered they did not have to renovate). To accommodate the demand, new housing was put on the market by ambitious developers. An old warehouse was completely dismantled, down to its steel frame, and reborn as a "luxury apartment house" with private terraces and a health spa on the ground floor; next to a chicken market and across the street from a candy store, it epitomized the "uneven development" that the middle class replacement or gentrification, was producing in the South Village. Two welfare hotels that were the scourge of the neighborhood were converted into middle income apartment buildings. The ground floor of one structure, which occupied an entire block and had a stately courtyard, was rented to a dry cleaning store and a donut franchise. In 1975, a one bedroom apartment rented for over $400 a month. In an interesting conversion, a corner luncheonette was renovated into four groundfloor duplex apartments, each renting for $440 a month in 1975.

Some tenement landlords sought to renovate and attract a middle income market for the upgraded units. In one building apartments were being renovated as Italians moved out. One landlord pressured Italians to leave by cutting back on building services. Another tenement was thoroughly renovated following a fire of suspicious origin. When it was ready for occupancy, neighborhood Italians, including former tenants, were unable to afford the new rent structure and the building was rented almost exclusively to young newcomers (median rents asked for vacant apartments in the census tract in 1980 was $325, six times the amount asked in 1970).

Private homes also warranted new attention. Two and three unit dwellings were refurbished for use by one family and, perhaps, an additional rental. One three-story house had a back porch overlooking a patio and flower garden; another was given a new look with freshly painted shutters and sycamores planted at the curb. A building that had been renovated into a townhouse possessed a private garage, fashioned out of an old storefront, with an electrically timed door that was the envy of everyone who jockeyed for scarce parking spaces on the street. In contrast to the renters, house owners belonged to a higher social stratum.

Apart from real estate, SoHo had other implications for the neighborhood economy. Traditionally, the heart of local economic life was the storefront shops selling groceries, meats, bakery products, fresh fruits and vegetables and other provisions to the ethnic population. There were also the bars and luncheonettes whose business was supplemented by the workers in nearby factories.

81

However, local commerce declined as population dwindled and light industry moved away. Many of the small food shops were affected by the supermarket chains; the urban renewal project added a supermarket to the area in the sixties. By the early seventies, there were only one or two grocery stores to a block where there were as many as five or six before World War II. There were only two Italian bakeries below Houston Street; packaged white bread could be seen peeking out of shopping bags. Candy stores, an important focus of street corner life, were becoming virtually extinct.

Before 1971, landlords had difficulty finding new commercial tenants. Some storefronts were left vacant and boarded up, giving the neighborhood a shabby look. In other cases, they were made available to neighborhood Italians for noncommercial use at low rents. In particular, they became club rooms for young people or were utilized as storage facilities for bicycles, baby carriages and other belongings that only cluttered up apartments.

SoHo reversed this economic decline, reclaiming the storefronts for entrepeneurial purposes. However, the renaissance was not oriented to Italians. The drab storefronts were metamorphosed into pretty shops selling antiques, silver jewelry and gourmet foods. Grocery stores and tailor shops gave way to boutiques featuring expensive European fashions. A butcher shop was transformed into a shop selling hand-crafted puppets and dolls. Another grocery store was rented to a potter; there were several craftspeople who lived and worked in storefront shops. One former "horse room" became an art supply store, while another became a cooperative sculpture gallery. A vacant metal shop became a quaint little restaurant specializing in Sunday brunch.

Some Italian-owned businesses closed because they were unable to absorb rent increases. One long-established candy store closed in 1982 when the landlord raised the monthly rent from $450 to $1200. Landlords reputedly offered both commercial and residential tenants payments if they agreed to break leases. The demand for commercial space also drove out the remaining social clubs.

Other Italian businesses, however, were rejuvenated by SoHo, although noteworthy changes were effected to accommodate a new clientele. A luncheonette that was about to close was reprieved since the young singles ate out often; this also helped the grocery stores and their sandwich trade. Another luncheonette that was resucitated by SoHo was renamed by its proprietor to identify with the art scene; walls and windows were decorated with posters announcing art shows and recitals. A bar owned by an Italian family in the neighborhood since the 1870s became a SoHo landmark. A hardware store, where everybody in the neighborhood had bought their venetian blinds, was similarly renovated when it catered to the renovation work going on in the area. SoHo gave new life to liquor stores, candy stores and many Italian food stores, which were transformed into specialty shops catering to the new middle class resident. The imported products carried by the shops were beyond the means of most Italians except on special occasions. Several shops changed their locale and modernized their facilities to better accommodate a middle class clientele.

Conclusion

A few years after legalization, the new SoHo community—a conception of city planners, real estate brokers and resident artists— virtually absorbed a distinctive Italian neighborhood in the South Village. Although Italians preferred not to recognize it, there was mounting evidence that this had, in fact, occurred. Thus, some of the new shops advertised themselves as SoHo establishments. The media played an instrumental role in effecting a change in identity. Articles in *The New York Times* referred to local restaurants as having a SoHo address. The centerfold pullout in *The SoHo Weekly News* was a guide to SoHo galleries that identified the South Village as part of the artists' community. On the other hand, the media, in particular the print media, fostered an impression of the decline of the Italian community. An article in *The SoHo Weekly News* juxtaposed photographs of rejuvenated SoHo storefronts and forlorn-looking elderly Italian women watching the neighborhood change; another photograph showed an elderly Italian woman passing in front of an art gallery. An article in *The New Yorker* (April, 26, 1976) magazine lamented the decline of "the South Village as a community". It portrayed the South Village as having "lost much of its old Italian flavor" and as "slowly disappearing as a neighborhood".

Subsequent chapters will focus on specific community institutions in light of the contraction of the Italian population and related changes in the neighborhood, in particular the expansion of SoHo. While these developments portend the eventual demise of a distinct Italian neighborhood,for the moment they have elicited new institutional responses and adjustments.

The Fragmented Family

*t*he South Village was a family neighborhood. The family group was a basic unit of membership and identification in a restructured ethnic community; neighborhood Italians defined themselves and were perceived by others primarily in terms of a family tie. The neighborhood was the locus of activities associated with family life, including childrearing and rites of passage like christenings and confirmation. Localized kinship mediated ties to persons outside the family, as evidenced by the "respect" paid at wakes and funerals. Ethnic family traditions comprised a cultural blueprint, informing a way of life that distinguished neighborhood Italians from other groups.

At the present time, the kinship substructure of neighborhood life is in eclipse. Families are not so much in evidence as are fragments of families. The kinship group has been dispersing and family life is not exclusively, even primarily, focused on the neighborhood. The transformation of local kinship has eroded interfamilial solidarity within the Italian community.

Neighborhood Households

In the present, families raising children comprise a minor segment of the Italian community. In two South Villages census tracts, the number of married couples with children under 18 declined from 608 in 1960 to 411 in 1970. In the latter year, this represented 28 percent of all families (in an adjoining tract largely inhabited by white-collar professionals, 33 percent of all families were of this type). The total number of children under 18 living with both parents declined from 1,079 in 1960 to 698 in 1970. The 1980 census shows only a slight decline from these figures. However, the ongoing decline in Italian families of this type is concealed by the prevalence of children among the Portuguese and, increasingly the SoHo newcomers. Since census data do not differentiate for ethnicity, parish records provide a closer look at this development. Whereas

777 Italian children were baptized at one of the Italian churches in 1916, only 35 received the sacrament in 1969 (16 others had one parent with an Italian surname). Less than half of the 270 students at the parish grammar school in 1976 had Italian surnames; before World War II, when the parish was predominantly Italian, enrollment was consistently over 1,000.

Relative to other households, the conjugal family has had a special incentive to leave the neighborhood. Besides the reasons associated with status improvement and securing better housing, these families saw in the suburbs and outlying boroughs a more propitious environment for raising children. More recently, parental concerns have focused on the erosion of social controls that were a positive feature of the urban village.

Recently married couples who have not yet had children are also scarce. These days, it is rare for couples even to start out in the neighborhood in order to save for a down payment on a house and stay close to the family. Instead, they have been taking apartments in one of the other boroughs or perhaps in one of the government subsidized buildings downtown (*e.g.,* Independence Plaza). With both spouses working, and armed with their wedding money (an advantage their parents did not have), they have been able to afford more modern and spacious apartments. Couples have often left the South Village because of the lack of housing commensurate with their standards (*e.g.,* space that can accommodate a five piece bedroom set). However, the issue has never simply been a question of housing stock, but of lifestyles that were not entirely compatible with the family-centered ethnic neighborhood.

The status of young families and married couples who have remained in the South Village is problematic; there is a tacit assumption that they should be living somewhere else. There are often complications which keep these households in the neighborhood. Money is a common problem, as are problems of an emotional sort such as when a woman is unable to move away from her mother, or a man cannot sever his ties to the street corner and the club.

Young families and couples just starting out, then, are an anomaly. As young Italians have made their way to the suburbs and boroughs, the majority of Italian households in the South Village have a quite different composition.

The elderly comprise an increasingly prominent segment of the Italian community. In 1980, 13 percent of the population of two South Village census tracts was 60 years of age and over, although their absolute number declined slightly between 1970 and 1980 (from 971 to 949). Of course, since newcomers to the South Village were relatively young (at least under 60), the proportion of Italians in this category was much greater.

85

The elderly are first and second generation Italians who have lived in the neighborhood for the greater part, if not all, of their lives. Although their incomes are low, they have retained survival skills acquired during earlier hardships (*i.e.,* low expectations, or "doing without"). Many talk about pride which keeps them from becoming a burden to their children. As long as they are able, they continue to shop for themselves and look after their flats; approximately half of all persons 65 and over lived alone in 1980. In agreeable weather, they congregate on park benches in their black cloth coats. However, children are usually not very far away, especially where poor health and advanced age are factors.

The status of quite a few neighborhood Italians is determined by a filial obligation to care for an aging parent. Looking after an elderly parent is often the source of considerable strain within the wider family, although the principal burden seems to fall on a son or daughter, married or otherwise, who was the last to leave the neighborhood. The "old-school" parents are said to demand or expect that their children look after them. One elderly shut-in adamantly refused the services of a visiting nurse, which would have been furnished through Medicare, because she "had a daughter" (settling into a sick role was a response to the disenfranchisement of household roles as well as a means of drawing the attention of distracted family members). Nursing homes are anathema to the elderly, who do not want to be entrusted to "strangers", and to children who could not live with their guilt.

Although many could be classified as elderly, persons who suffered the death of a spouse comprise a significant segment of the Italian population. In two South Village census tracts in 1970, there were 339 women and 128 men who were left widowed. In 1980, the figures were 322 and 91 respectively. The number of widows in 1970 represented 14 percent of all females over 18 (widows were 7% of females over 18 in the adjacent high-rise professional neighborhood). In one-third of these households there were children under 18. The majority, however, appear to be older persons whose children have grown and left. This group is probably reflected in the 175 women (out of 823) enumerated by a 1974 parish census as "living alone" (81 men lived alone). Their situation is typically characterized by loneliness, especially if children are not nearby and are preoccupied with their own lives. Widows are often found to exist on meager social security and, in some cases, pension benefits. Those who are young enough return to work to make ends meet and compensate for some of the loneliness.

In addition to the 14 percent of the women over 18 who were widows, 8 percent were divorced or separated (altogether, 18% of all families were female-headed). In 1980, 17 percent of all females 15 years and over were separated or divorced. This sharp increase may be largely attributed to the young newcomers. Within the Italian community, it appeared that the majority in this category were younger women, who are more immune to the stigma attached to marital dissolution. Several young women returned to the South Village following the dissolution of their marriages.

Another segment is comprised of older couples whose children have moved away (in 58% of all married couples in 1960, the husband was over 45). After all these years, they find it easy to "stay put". Empty-nesters tend to be in close touch with children in the suburbs.

In other households, grown children may still be at home. Those in their late teens and twenties may be enrolled in college or business school, a relatively recent phenomenon in the neighborhood. Others are working full-time. For these young people, it is taken for granted that one stays at home until marriage. This is less objectionable as living quarters have been made to provide reasonable privacy, in several cases combining two apartments.

Several of these households possessed somewhat pathological characteristics. In one case, family members spent a great deal of time together, mainly in the small flat, and there was considerable worry whenever one of them was out; the husband escorted his wife and their daughter when possible. Despite this clinging together, their home life was rather turbulent, no doubt a result of being in each other's company so continuously, although the husband's low occupational status and income was also a factor. As in other emotionally intense families the tie between mother and child was particularly intimate, perhaps as compensation for marital dissatisfaction.

Household arrangements that include older children become permanent as prospects for marriage are given up and parents become widowed. With the death of both parents, siblings often continue to live together. This was the case with a brother and sister in their fifties who only recently moved to Queens. Two unmarried sisters in their seventies are still in the house their family owned when they were children.

Some households in the South Village consist of reconstituted families in which individuals are reunited with parents and or siblings following the dissolution of a conjugal relationship. These households reflect the persisting importance of kinship ties, including the moral significance of familism. In particular, women are the mediators of this moral life by providing nurturance, performing domestic duties and promoting integration with the wider kinship structure. The man living alone is the object of pity, especially in the eyes of women whose role is defined *vis-a-vis* service to family and household, whereas men possess a trained incapacity in these matters, to which mothers and wives contribute. Single men are often "adopted" into the family circle of a friend, as are women whose families are not near at hand.

The Family Network

South Village Italians were part of a localized and closeknit kinship group. Grandparents, aunts, uncles and cousins, supplemented by compari and friends of the family, lived in the neighborhood and were the focal point of meaningful interaction even in the second and third generation. Over time, however, related households have left the neighborhood at varying speeds. This has been accompanied by a transformation in the character of kinship relations.

The dispersion of the kinship group may be illustrated by continuing with the example of Giuseppe and Carmela, bringing the family up to date. In the middle fifties, eight grandchildren—the third generation in the neighborhood—were married and living near their respective parents, Carmela and one another. Two grandchildren, Carmela's youngest daughter's children, were not yet married and were living at home (their father remarried after their mother died). Counting Carmela, who maintained her own apartment upstairs from one of her daughters, the wider family consisted of thirteen separate households living within a block or two of one another; there were also more distant kin and in-laws residing in the neighborhood. The kinship group was a close unit, although siblings and their families were closest with one another and their respective parents. The men socialized on the corner and the women wheeled baby carriages in Washington Square Park. The cousins were in each other's wedding parties and were godparents to each other's children. This solidarity was no doubt facilitated by residential popinquity; relatives were still neighbors. At the same time, living near one another reflected the solidarity of the kinship group.

In 1956, however, households started moving away. The process was initiated by Carmela's grandchildren, who wanted to be out of the city by the time their children were ready for school. The two youngest grandchildren left the neighborhood in 1958 and 1960, on the occasion of their respective marriages; neither spouse was Italian (one was Irish Catholic and the other was German Jewish). By 1970, only two of the grandchildren were left in the neighborhood—Carmela's oldest daughter's children. One was widowed in 1961, while the other preferred to remain near his job, although the fact that his wife had a mother and sister in the neighborhood seems to have also been a factor. Between them, they had three children living at home, although one was away at college during the school year. By 1980, only one child was still living in the South Village. The only other member of the family still in the neighborhood was the husband of Carmela's deceased daughter and his second wife. Although he thought about living near his daughters, his business kept him in the neighborhood.

The mobility of constituent households assumed a definite pattern that has been characteristic of other Italian American families (Femminella and Quadagno, 1976:77; Greeley, 1971:77). On the one hand, it was a two generational process. Siblings tended to move out together. Thus, Carmela's oldest daughter, who was now widowed, moved with her daughter and son-in-law to New Jersey. Within a year, a son and his family bought a house in the same suburban town; the two households were within a mile of one another. Carmela's second oldest daughter and her husband moved into an apartment in Brooklyn where a son had bought a home; she took a reluctant Carmela with her. Several years later, her other son moved to the same neighborhood. Carmela's other daughter and her husband moved simultaneously with their son's and daughter's families; the three households living in a family-owned building, which was sold at the time of the move. Each unit bought its own house in a pleasant section of Queens. Carmela's two youngest grandchildren were married and living near one another in Miami, Florida.

This dispersion process spanned fifteen years. Even before the process was complete, however, there were further meanderings so that the wider family is now even more dispersed. One of Carmela's grandaughters remarried and moved to Philadelphia where her new husband was employed, although her son remained in Queens with her mother and father. One of Carmela's daughters moved to the Miami area when her husband retired, followed by one of her sons and his family. Several years after this branch of the family had moved to Florida, Carmela's two youngest grandchildren moved from Miami to Buffalo; after one of the husbands was transferred, the other managed to find a job in the same area and the two sisters and their families were together again. Two of Carmela's great grandchildren recently married and now live in Minnesota and Maryland respectively; their parents were the only grandchildren of Carmela to remain in the neighborhood. As Italian Americans enter the middle class, this trend, largely dictated by the logic of the labor market, should continue.

At the present time, Italians living in the South Village find themselves members of a kinship group that is not localized. By itself, this has affected a change in kinship relations since kin are no longer neighbors. Relations between kin are also affected by significant differences in income, education and occupation, especially in the third generation. The kinship group, then, has become increasingly nonspatial and heterogeneous, having implications for the greater authority of the nuclear unit.

Interaction between kin varies with the specific kinship relation. The closest ties would seem to be between parents and adult children, especially mother and daughter, and between siblings. Even in the present, it is usual for at least one daughter to be living reasonably close to parents. This is especially true where parents are elderly, widowed or in poor health. As a rule, sons are not as available because of extrafamilial commitments, especially work, and because their wives are close to their own mothers. One elderly woman regretted the lack of a daughter in her old age, especially since she had become widowed and her health was poor. Although her sons wanted her to live with them in New Jersey, she was uncomfortable about living with her daughters-in-law.

Relations between parents in the neighborhood and married children who live elsewhere remain close, especially where daughters are concerned, and are evidenced by the frequent exchange of visits and phone calls. When visits are not that frequent, this seems to be primarily a function of unmanageable distances.

Although geographic distance poses a major and initial obstacle, the crystallization of new life-styles has also become taxing of kinship solidarity. Married children are immersed in jobs, homes, raising children and new-found friends.

Even where parents see children periodically, the arrangement is quite different from the relationship they had with their parents. This was noted by a woman with a married daughter in New Jersey, who lived on the same floor as her mother for the first twenty-seven years of her marriage, until her mother died. She saw her mother every day and, after her father died, would keep her company in the evening until she went to bed, occasionally staying over. In the neighborhood, kin were at hand and obliging.

Clearly, it is preferred that children be as physically close as possible, although there is some compensation in knowing that they have a good job, a nice house, etc. Widows and the elderly experience this as a special problem since there tend to be no satisfactory substitutes, although senior citizens programs at the church and settlement houses have attempted to fill the vacuum.

Geographical distance is a factor in relationships between siblings, as are disparities in income, education and occupation. Differential social mobility has implications for place of residence, involvement with kin and lifestyles in general. Status differences sometimes issue in jealousy and resentment.

A prominent source of strain in relations between siblings concerns the status of elderly parents who need looking after; it sometimes happens that one of the children "gets stuck" taking care of Ma or Pa. In some families, there have been animosities surrounding the disposition of a will. On the whole, however, siblings have maintained close ties. There is a readiness to provide assistance, both financial or emotional, in times of trouble.

The neighborhood used to be the physical setting for kinship life. Increasingly, however, interaction between kin has been shifted to places where mobile members reside. Thus, a middle-aged couple visits their daughter in Teaneck while a neighborhood woman visits a sister in Staten Island. One reason for this is that the suburbs, and the private house, can furnish a more satisfying environment for family gatherings; the meal can be served in the dining room, while the children can occupy themselves in the backyard or finished basement. Neighborhood Italians wax enthusiastic about these amenities. It also betrays the disinclination of many suburban relatives, especially the more status conscious, to return to the neighborhood. As a result, relatives make the trek out of town. Where transportation presents a problem someone may come in with a car. It is a common sight to see people on Sunday mornings waiting, with their boxes of pastry, to be picked up from the East Side.

Visiting relatives in the neighborhood has not been entirely eliminated. A common pattern is for a relative who works in the city to stop by for a brief visit while in transit. This is done, of course, without the rest of the family (*i.e.,* wife and children, who are firmly rooted in suburban routines).

The family circle that included a number of households interacting on a fairly intimate basis has been whittled down as nuclear families tend to go their own way and as subsequent generations have fewer children. Aunt, uncles and cousins, *compari* and friends of the family are not an integral part of everyday life. Disengaged from a neighborhood context, relatives become "distant" kin and interaction tends to become compartmentalized. In other words, kin become a more strictly ceremonial group who associate for the special event, the intermittent ritual gathering like the wake, the wedding and the confirmation party. They associate on neutral ground (*e.g.,* the funeral parlor, catering hall, etc.), rather than in one another's homes.

A central feature of this interaction is the exchange of gifts appropriate to the event. To a large extent solidarity with the wider kinship network has been collapsed within this mode of gift exchange; families keep a detailed account of gifts which is consulted when it is time to reciprocate. It is as if family get-togethers are impossible apart from incurring a significant expense; since wedding receptions are treated as symbols of having made it, occasionally becoming excessively opulent with their Las Vegas entertainment and conspicuous display of food, the size of an appropriate gift has reached alarming proportions. This has frequently generated negative feelings toward kin and matters familial. A rift is always possible where it is felt that a relative did not include enough in the envelope.

With the younger generation, the recognition of kin even for ceremonial or ritual purposes is not certain. This is especially true for those who grew up outside a localized kinship structure. Their reference group includes friends, schoolmates and colleagues. They are without an urgent and primordial sense of kin, genealogy and tradition. At wakes and weddings, they often have to be re-introduced to their parents' cousins. Obligations are not strongly felt and, consequently, are more onerous. In compiling a guest list for a wedding, priority is given to friends, neighbors and colleagues over more distant kin (a category that has enlarged as the family circle tightens).

Kin habitually lament that they see too little of one another. At wakes and funerals, one hears how it "takes something like this to get us together ". Upon leaving a wedding or a wake promises to renew a close association are tendered. However, despite good intentions, very little usually materializes; everyone seems to understand the context in which promises were made and, therefore, no offense need be taken. Kin simply wait for the next wedding or other special event.

Family and Community

In the past, the wider family articulated with the local Italian community. Relatives lived in the South Village. Kinship patterns were enacted within the neighborhood; neighbors participated in and scrutinized family life. The Italian community could be said to have consisted of family groups; family names and histories provided a handle on specific individuals.

Now, however, the South Village could hardly be considered "a family neighborhood", although Italian civic leaders still evoke this image for ideological purposes. Families have shrunk to but a few members, or have pulled up stakes for the suburbs. Most of the family businesses that dotted the neighborhood are gone.

Now that "all the old families are gone", the pattern of respect that constituted an underlying solidarity among families is in disrepair. Old-timers may persuade a son or daughter to drive them into the neighborhood to attend a wake. However, these obligations are not strongly felt by the younger generation. It is perhaps for these reasons that neighborhood wakes are not as crowded as they used to be.

Family groups have become disengaged from a communal base that nourished ethnic family patterns. Now that the family is more self-sustaining, ecclesiastical life-crisis rituals are less likely to be occasions for solidarity with other families. The traditional function of godparentage, for example, was to establish a fictive kinship tie with non-kin. However, greater affluence has diminished the instrumental reasons for expanding kinship networks. Moreover, the need to legitimate a relationship in this manner is superfluous since friendship has become a more personal matter, a relationship that is autonomous of the family. Individuals who stand up for one another at christenings, weddings and confirmations are frequently relatives (siblings, aunts, uncles, etc.). What this means is that a kinship relation is enhanced, not created out of non-kinship since godparents are already kin; it is difficult to tell whether this reflects the further privatization of the family or the need to shore up kinship ties. In any event, a traditional occasion for interfamilial solidarity is allowed to pass. Having left the ethnic neighborhood, the Italian American family is increasingly going it alone.

Familism defined a common moral life. However, many neighborhood Italians have had their moral system shaken by modern developments. The younger generation is not perceived to be as committed to family values. They have a range of interests taking them out of the family circle. Young couples have more going for them than having children, a trend that is reducing the size of the family group and undercutting a basis of family solidarity. Divorce is becoming more common. The wider family is becoming more spread out geographically and differentiated along social lines. It is held together by special events and the perfunctory exchange of Christmas cards. Older persons who were socialized into a world that revolved around the family are disconcerted by these developments. Many are unable to make a satisfactory adjustment.

Conclusion

Family groups have pulled up stakes, in some cases leaving behind vestiges of a kinship network that is no longer based in the Italian neighborhood. Moreover, new life-styles have diluted traditional forms of solidarity. For South Village Italians, these developments have upset a way of life that was centered on the family; neighborhood Italians are nostalgic for a past when "families were close" and "this was a family neighborhood". Nevertheless, South Village residents have made the most of what is still their "most accessible social capital" (Whitten and Szwed, 1970:47). Thus, married children serve as caretakers of elderly parents despite considerable personal sacrifice. Although conjugal families are rare, close kin compise household units. Links to mobile family members have been maintained. Mutual assistance is very much in evidence among close kin, although the wider family network largely functions as a ceremonial group. The enduring significance of kinship can be

93

attributed to its central role in Italian culture.Besides, most South Village Italians do not have access to alternate forms of social capital that would allow them to meaningfully refocus their lives.

A Neighborhood
of Strangers

*t*he neighborhood enclosed an ethnic group life outside the family. Localized interaction—in playgrounds,
on street corners, in settlement houses, etc.—focused
on informal peer groups supplemented by organizational memberships. Intensive use of the locality made
both the neighborhood and its inhabitants familiar
and trustworthy, although a sense of community was
predicated on a shared ethnicity and culture. This imparted to the neighborhood a strong measure of security, especially since the actions of "strangers" were
scrutinized by the residents themselves. The South
Village, then, was a "home territory" for Italians
within the city. In the present, however, this scenario
no longer holds.

Changes in Local Life

The social neighborhood has been noticably affected
by dwindling numbers. Street corner groups are relatively few and far between; cornerboys seem to have
regrouped on select sites to conserve their number.
There are only a few "members only" clubs remaining
and these are syndicate "horse rooms". The only authentic social/athletic club in the neighborhood was on
borrowed time; a handful of members approaching
retirement age used the club a few nights during the
week for card games. As the Italian population shrank,
bars, luncheonettes and candy stores closed down,
taking away sites where people socialized. In 1976,
there were only two "neighborhood" bars and an equal
number of candy stores below Houston Street where
cornerboys could hang out. There were three luncheonettes in which neighborhood women could have
coffee and exchange news. In the evening, there were
only a few locations where men and women gathered to
wait for the *Daily News* truck; no one group consisted of
more than a dozen regulars. For a "family neighbor-

hood", there were few youngsters in the streets. The playground never seemed filled to capacity, except when black and Hispanic students from a nearby commercial school came over on their lunch hour. No one could remember when the last stickball game was played in the neighborhood.

The social neighborhood has also been affected by lifestyle changes. As households have become smaller and living conditions have improved, people spend more time in their flats. In the summer, it is more comfortable to stay inside with the air conditioner on than to sit out on a bench in the company of others. People watch television instead of the neighborhood; the vicissitudes of characters in situation dramas are more absorbing than the events that make up local life. The telephone has obviated the need to stop by for a chat and has virtually put an end to the practice of yelling from the street or the bottom of the stairwell. The social aspects of shopping are lost where supermarkets, pizza parlors and liquor stores make deliveries. Where people cannot provide for their own needs, government welfare sustains relationships of dependency; the elderly, then, are able to arrange for visiting nurses and homemakers through Medicare. The combined effect of these developments has been to make neighborhood life much less public, although in some cases they may be a response to the withering away of group life.

For many Italians, social life has shifted beyond the neighborhood. Relatives tend to be the focus of this supralocal life. Thus, Sunday afternoon is set aside for visits to a daughter in Long Island or a brother in New Jersey. In the process, relatives have opened up a wider suburban connection. Journeys are taken to shopping centers in New Jersey, a restaurant in Westchester County, and a golf course in Staten Island. Several neighborhood couples have had their wedding receptions in suburban catering halls (this tends to enhance their prestige, as does the suburban connection in general). Those with the means talk about consummating their tie to the suburbs, moving "by my daughter in Teaneck".

Greater affluence has furnished access to a still wider world. In a local beauty parlor, neighborhood women talked about their trips to Las Vegas and which hotel offered a "better deal". One couple visited Fisherman's Wharf in San Francisco, while another had recently taken a cruise to Bermuda.

Those who are locality-bound can be defined in terms of some constraint (Pahl, 1970). Older cornerboys, following peer group patterns initiated in their youth, are often unemployed for medical or other reasons. Hanging out picks up the slack of no longer working; betting on a horse and going for coffee are among the things done to "kill some time". Many of the younger men and teenagers are either unemployed or have quit school. Hanging out together is a "social compensating device" (Parsons, 1954:94), and

96

is spiced with drugs and alcohol; their alienation and hostility are occasionally vented on unsuspecting "strangers". Probably the most locality- bound are the elderly whose infirmities have made them shut- ins.

Formal organizations have been variously affected by changes in the neighborhood. The Knights of Columbus, for example, has been contracting due to an inability to recruit new members. The remaining members maintain a club room for playing cards and for parties with the wives on Saturday nights. Both of the business and professional men's clubs continue to thrive, but only as they become more detached from the local Italian community. Their memberships, which partly overlap, reside mainly outside the South Village. The more prestigious club is a meeting place for the city's Italian American elite (*e.g.,* second generation politicians, judges, lawyers, building contractors, etc.). One of its principal contributions to the Italian American community of the city is a scholarship program for the study of Italian language and culture at Columbia University. The club once hosted a formal dinner in its exquisite dining hall to raise some money for Italian philanthropies; the Italian ambassador was in attendance. At the same time, the club's remoteness from the neighborhood is conspicuous. Although the club was menaced by the welfare hotels on Bleecker Street like the rest of the South Village, it waged a separate protest by lobbying with politicians and writing letters to local newspapers.

Social settlements that serviced the neighborhood have also been transformed. Those that have survived are no longer geared to slum youngsters, although neighborhood teenagers may continue to use facilities like the gymnasium; the mothers' clubs have disappeared. One of the first settlements initiating a "work" among South Village Italians is now a community center for middle class Villagers. Where it once provided a health clinic and day nursery for Italian children, it is now known for sponsoring radical political forums, experimental theater, avant garde film and dance presentations and homosexual consciousness raising sessions (Kempton, 1966). Another landmark Village settlement now specializes in adult education courses, with offerings that range from conversational French to arts and crafts. However, it did inaugurate a senior citizens' program in 1971 that was principally aimed at Italian elderly left behind by mobile family members. The director of the program was the wife of a prominent Italian civic leader. She considered the program as the settlement's major link to the Italian community; seventy percent of the individuals in the program in 1974 were Italian.

The Embattled Neighborhood

The erosion of a local community had direct implications for a defended neighborhood. Although the means for defending against predators were not exhausted, dwindling numbers and altered lifestyles undermined the basis of local control. An unprecedented number of apartment break-ins in 1974 signaled the neighborhood's vulnerability. Since that time, the fear of crime has been a major motif in local life, although the South Village still has a low crime rate compared to other parts of the city.

Safety has been a function of lifestyles that were locality-based. There were always knots of men on the corner, so that even a person venturing home late at night was reassured. Women sat at their kitchen windows and surveyed the goings-on in the street; little passed unnoticed. Strangers were closely monitored, especially after dark, since their intentions could not be guaranteed; where primary group life was so accessible, the people who inhabited one's world had to be trustworthy. It was possible to at least "know of" most of the people who lived in the immediate area. Outsiders found acceptance difficult in this in-grown community. Bars, candy stores and playgrounds were the private preserves of neighborhood groups. Apartments were handed down to relatives and friends before they actually became vacant.

The crime wave, which included some purse snatchings and muggings, hold- ups of neighborhood merchants and the rape of a young artist, was directly related to the ungluing of this provincial system. There were simply fewer cornerboys of all ages on the street to keep a watchful eye out for "troublemakers". Looking out the window has become passé. One comfortable October evening, burglars carried a large heist out the front door of a building. Perhaps the streets were desolate and the burglary was not detected by spying neighbors because Frank Sinatra was on television that night. Italians were quick to point out that such incidents were rare in the past.

The breakdown of the defended neighborhood was also related to the withdrawal of syndicate commitment to the neighborhood. With gambling and other operations to protect the syndicate had a vested interest in keeping order. Now, however, there are a few "horse rooms" left open and a reduced contingent of syndicate employees on the street. Even though the syndicate has taken a new interest in the South Village, these operations do not demand similar kinds of control; in fact, the new syndicate ventures are geared to strangers. Finally, liability is limited where the families of syndicate leaders live elsewhere.

The defended neighborhood was decisively undermined when strangers came to live right in the neighborhood; hitherto, stranger and neighborhood were mutually exclusive categories. In the first place, neighbors were now "not like us". The newcomers were not Italian; with the exception of the Portuguese, they were not "good family people", but were immersed in careers and lifestyles that Italians found inscrutable. Perhaps most important, the newcomers were unknown. They came into the neighborhood without an introduction; when they took an apartment, it was the result of responding to a newspaper ad or a transaction with a rental agent and not the mediation of someone who lived in the building. For many Italians, anonymity was unsettling at such close quarters.

The newcomers transformed the defended neighborhood into a "community of limited liability" (Janowitz, 1967). Artists and middle class residents did not hang out on a street corner or take over a candy store. Their neighborhood was not a social medium Apartment windows were for leafy house plants, not for an unobstructed view of the street (this was a rough gauge of who lived in the building). Indeed, these newcomers spent comparatively little time at home—perhaps the majority would regard their stay in the South Village as only temporary. Careers and other interests frequently took them away. Apartments were sometimes sublet to friends or persons answering advertisements. Their life-habits, in other words, were not conducive to "defense". Many Italians believed that the newcomers, not being street-wise, attracted "creeps" and other predators sensing an "easy mark". It was pointed out that one newcomer who left his window open so his cats could wander out on the fire escape was especially naive. The neighborhood was now a world of strangers that could not be effectively controlled. The proliferation of galleries and bars exacerbated the problem.

The crime wave made Italians anxious. People were reluctant to go out at night; the women hurried home from bingo in groups. Apartments were fortified with window gates and police locks; hardware stores had a brisk business in these items, standard in other parts or the city. Unfamiliar faces encountered in the hallway elicited suspicion. The elderly were instructed not to open the door for anyone. The tenants of one building arranged to have the outer door locked so that not even the vestibule was accessible from the street. The only possibility of reaching people inside was by telephoning in advance. For the initiated, a key was kept in the "members only" club next door. Those who were admitted for the first time had to submit to an interview conducted by a wary cornerboy.

When local Italian leaders decided to address the crime problem, they tendered assurances that they had matters in hand; cornerboys had their bats poised. However, enlisting the services of additional foot patrolmen was a tacit admission that informal mechanisms of control were inadequate; conveniently, this was not announced at community meetings because policemen were being laid off at the time throughout the city for budgetary reasons and the assignment of additional patrolmen to a neighborhood that had a low crime rate would be hard to justify. The inadequacy of neighborhood defenses was also evident when a new community organization emerged around the crime issue; it initiated a campaign for buzzer and intercom systems, and worked with the local precinct on a civilian patrol force. Cornerboys and civic leaders were well aware that their defenses were down, they just were not letting on. Perhaps there was the hope of living a while longer on their reputation; they may also have been protecting their self-image. One Italian leader was irked at a local newspaper story publicizing the increase in crime in the South Village. He felt that this would be an invitation for predators to test neighborhood defenses. The urgency of keeping this secret was evidenced by a jittery cornerboy who asked, making sure that no one was looking over his shoulder, "Do you know how vulnerable the neighborhood is?"

The crime problem was interpreted in community meetings as the work of outsiders, in particular, blacks and Hispanics. Much of the blame had focused on the clients of two drug treatment centers in the area. While outsiders may have been responsible for the bulk of the incidents, a share of the crimes was committed by young Italian men and teenagers who took advantage of lapsed neighborhood controls. They were intimate with the routine the residents kept and knew the network of alleyways running between tenement buildings. Some "bad apples" had actually been apprehended by cornerboys and reckoned with in syndicate clubs. It appeared that Italians were somewhat relieved that insiders were involved, perhaps fearing unknown predators more. However, Italian leaders did not acknowledge this in public. It apparently could not be divulged that Italians were not taking care of their own house. Leaders also wanted to spare the Italian community, and themselves, additional criticism from Villagers, particularly as the latter became concerned about "gang" activities.

Relationships
with Newcomers

The South Village was an Italian neighborhood—any Italian living there would attest to that. The term "neighborhood" was synonymous with the Italian community. Neighbors shared a common ethnicity and culture, and interacted within a common institutional framework; resident non-Italians were exceptions to the rule, a fact that was sometimes noted in nicknames. There were ecological boundaries that set the Italian community off from other ethnic neighborhoods and the middle class Village. However, the recent influx of Portuguese immigrants and the expansion of the SoHo artistic community have introduced new divisions at the local level. The neighborhood and its social fabric are no longer exclusively, even primarily, Italian. These changes have rendered the concept of an Italian neighborhood untenable, although Italians act as if this were not the case.

The Portuguese

By the early seventies, a Portuguese community had coalesced in the South Village. Their numbers were apparently insignificant as late as the mid-sixties since they received no mention in the parish literature of the period. The South Village was by no means a major Portuguese settlement; the 1980 Census enumerated 982, although half this number was concentrated in one census tract. Nevertheless, there were enough immigrants to constitute a distinctive communal system alongside the Italian community. A Portuguese friar was secured who led a contingent of nationals within the erstwhile Italian parish. This Portuguese wing attended Portuguese language masses and celebrated the feast days of national saints. A self-contained Portuguese community also included a Portuguese social club, a travel agency that performed various services for an immigrant clientele and a youth center. These settings embraced the greater part of Portuguese social life; only school children had informal social contact outside the community, although their parents kept them closely tied to Portuguese culture through language instruction at the club after school and trips to Portugal in summer. After a while, there were Portuguese-owned grocery stores where the immigrants concentrated their shopping.

Initially, cultural differences and a separate institutional life minimized contact with Italians. There was never any great rush of immigrants which would have disrupted the population balance; their relatively small numbers were easily accommodated. There was no competition for housing, as the Portuguese took apartments that Italians were abandoning. Portuguese men became janitors, a job that Italians were no longer willing to perform. The Portuguese were not seriously impinging on communal resources; the men even hung out on corners that Italians were not using. In contrast to the middle class, they were indifferent to local politics, although the revolution in Portugal commanded their interest. In general, the Portuguese adopted a low profile in which, as recent arrivals, they deferred to Italians, a fact that the latter noted with approval.

However, as the Portuguese further acclimated themselves to the neighborhood, minor tensions became evident. Their expanded role

101

in the parish provoked disagreements with Italians. When a fourth Portuguese-owned grocery store opened there were rumblings that "the Portuguese are taking over everything". There was disapproval of Portuguese clannishness. A young Italian electrician complained that a Portuguese grocer would not hire him to rewire his store because he preferred a fellow countryman. Another Italian accused several Portuguese of monopolizing parking spots on his block by coordinating the movement of automobiles so that spaces remained occupied. There were also complaints when one of the grocery stores flew a Portuguese flag on Independence Day, yet an Italian flag was flying across the street.

In general, disapproval of the Portuguese stemmed from the fact that they were newcomers and that the neighborhood was changing. However, there was also resentment of their apparent material success. This was evident in the criticism of a Portuguese immigrant who worked as a janitor in several buildings in addition to his regular warehouse job. Despite his lowly occupational status and recent arrival in this country, accounting for his broken English, both he and his son drove brand new automobiles; his son had just bought a house in New Jersey and he was planning to do the same. It was especially galling to Italian tenants when he showed up on Saturday evenings, before going over to the Portuguese Club dance, to take out the garbage in his pin-stripe suit and diamond stick-pin, exercising care so the garbage cans would not scratch the metallic finish on his late-model Oldsmobile parked at the curb. Italians simply shook their heads and wondered "How do they do it?", criticizing "this country" for allowing "foreigners" to fare as well as they have.

In the main, however, intergroup antagonisms are minor. Teenagers have not formed rival gangs; ethnic tension is not reflected in any of the graffiti on buildings. On the whole, Italians have grown to like the Portuguese. They remind them of their own immigrants and, perhaps above all, they are "good family people". They are distinctly preferable to other low status minority groups. Moreover, they are ideal neighbors since "they mind their own business". Although the second generation is still young, there is some evidence of intermarriage which should increase now that half the student body at one of the parish schools is Portuguese.

SoHo

The artists and other middle class newcomers constituted a more imposing communal development. They were more numerous than the Portuguese and decidedly less insular; they also represented a

102

greater capital investment in the area. They were making the South Village theirs in ways that the Portuguese were not. As a result, they had greater implications for the structure and tenor of Italian community.

Before the City Planning Commission officially recognized an artists' community adjoining the South Village at West Broadway in 1971, the artists and students living in the vicinity were essentially an appendage of the Italian community. They patronized Italian shops and luncheonettes. A day care center for artists' children was housed in parish facilities. For all intents and purposes, the artists were guests of the Italian population. Their low profile was virtually guaranteed by illegal occupancy since the loft buildings were zoned for industry.

In 1970, artists who were living illegally in the adjacent factory district formed a civic organization that sought to establish solidarity with the Italian community; its principal sponsor was a famous American sculptor who was one of the first artists to move into the area. The organization focused on issues of practical concern to squatter artists, like sanitation pick-ups and police patrols. Significantly, there was no attempt to distinguish an "artists' community". Rather, loft dwellers and local Italians were portrayed as members of the "Downtown Manhattan Community". This communal breakthrough was the goal of a newspaper that the organization published on a weekly basis. It recruited Italian businessmen and civic leaders to attend its meetings in renovated lofts. Influential Italians helped their cause with the city; a friendly sanitation inspector who hung out in a local candy store overlooked household garbage left at the curb. The organization's newspaper was distributed free of charge from neighborhood shops. In a symbolic gesture, an early issue reproduced a photograph, submitted by an Italian woman who was a neighbor of one of the publishers, showing local Italian women protesting the closing of a neighborhood school in 1930.

A breakthrough never materialized and the organization collapsed within a year; there were few Italians who could identify with a "Downtown Manhattan Community". More importantly, by 1971, an artists' community had taken shape as "SoHo". It had official boundaries, recognized by the City Planning Commission, and an emergent communal infrastructure. From this point on, artists living in the area were no longer an appendage, or guests, of the Italian community. A new civic organization representing local artists had crystallized in the legalization struggle and confidently referred to SoHo as "a viable, self-contained community". The same message was proclaimed by a new SoHo newspaper that aspired to be "bigger than *The Village Voice*"; the paper publicized the artists' community and aggressively asserted its viewpoint. Both the civic organization and the newspaper took up positions against the interests of the Italian community immediately after legalization.

Not only did SoHo become a distinct communal entity, it wasted no time encroaching on the Italian neighborhood and its resources. This took the form of a residential influx, consisting primarily of young people in the arts and the professions. This precipitated a rise in real estate and rents; apartments that rented for $75 a month brought $300 a month when they were decontrolled. There was a proliferation of boutiques, bars and restaurants which soon became more numerous than the galleries. These establishments lured a young and affluent clientele who found the area to be "an attractive experience and a chic one" (*The New York Daily News*, 1/28/79). Within five years of legalization, the Italian neighborhood had been effectively absorbed, as evidenced by the increasing use of the name "SoHo" when referring to South Village blocks. A "SoHo Fair" was held on Prince Street between Sixth Avenue and West Broadway, until recently the heart of Italian territory; an article in a fashion magazine made reference to local "Italians, whose neighborhood SoHo encompasses". Slowly but surely, Italians were no longer living in an Italian neighborhood.

SoHo descended on most Italians from out of the blue; there was little general understanding as to what was happening in their midst. For a while, Italians were unable to comprehend exactly who the newcomers were. In particular, it escaped them that the people moving into their neighborhood and the adjacent loft district were artists, students and professionals. Even after legalization, the newcomers were referred to as "beatniks" and "hippies", largely on their physical appearance. This negative, but not intolerable, status was reinforced by the pattern of loft residence around which SoHo developed. The industrial wasteland beyond West Broadway was a no-man's land of dreary lofts where many Italians had worked that only "hippies" would consider for living purposes. However, this image was seriously challenged by extensive media coverage that depicted the actual dimensions of the conversion phenomenon. Italians began to notice that the young people moving into their tenements were quite educated and with career ambitions that did not square with the bohemian stereotypes. They also discovered that the art work in local galleries was high-priced, even though they did not think much of it. Perhaps Italians had every reason to be confused by these developments. For years, Italians had left the ethnic slum to "better themselves" and enter the cultural mainstream. Now, they were witnessing the middle class literally scramble for available lofts, store fronts and tenement flats with bath tubs in the kitchen. Even more ironic was the appreciation that the newcomers showed for the sediment of ethnic culture left in the move to the suburbs.

104

Although Italians hated to see the neighborhood change, and had an ingrained suspicion of "strangers", the new influx did not elicit the concern comparable to the encroachment of Chinese immigrants on the East Side (Little Italy). The artists and students seemed to be "nice kids" who were, after all, effecting improvements in the neighborhood's physical character. Civic leaders pointed out their concern with issues like police protection and property ownership, and that some artists were married and had children. Newcomers added color to the neighborhood; a sculptor who wore a bandanna and claimed he was a gypsy was a particular favorite. At bottom, however, the artists and students were preferred because, in the words of one Italian, "When you attract poor people, you sometimes attract crime and violence".

On their side, the newcomers found the ethnic neighborhood to have numerous benefits. A lawyer liked the fact that "the people here use the street a lot; they sit outside talking, or sit on the stoops, and the kids play everywhere". He felt that this gave the neighborhood a certain "kinetic feeling". On a more practical level, the newcomers were of the opinion that Italians ran a safe neighborhood; Italians were aware of this and seemed to want to live up to expectations.

Nevertheless, Italians regarded the newcomers as strangers. They were fundamentally marginal to the Italian community; in particular, they were not connected to its network of kinship and peer groups. They did not share a way of life or a common ethnicity. A *modus vivendi* emerged where each group went about its own business; a resident artist called it "a comfortable symbiosis". On the one hand, there were the family, the street corner group, parish bingo games; on the other, there were art, careers and new urban life-styles. Italians wondered where the newcomers' families were. The latters' afamilial life-style removed an important common ground that did furnish a moral consensus between Italians and Portuguese despite ethnic differences. Italians walked past galleries shaking their heads at the paintings and sculptures. Artists and other newcomers considered Italians provincial, in particular, "uptight" about strangers. One artist commented that "Italians are so insular they won't even step across the street to visit a gallery", although he figures that this was probably a good thing since their moral sensibilities would be offended.

However, the *modus vivendi* showed signs of strain. There was an underlying ill-feeling that typically develops when another group is perceived as "taking over"; although Italians would have been more hostile toward what was happening were it not for the city's rent control law which limited rent increases to 7½ percent a year. Newcomers were restive about the reluctance of Italians to accept them in the neighborhood. Noting that conversations seemed to stop abruptly when he entered a grocery store or the hallway of his building, one newcomer complained that "the term 'neighborhood' applies only to Italians who've lived here all their lives".

Much of the conflict between SoHo and the Italian community was manifest in the political arena (See, Chapter 12). However, there were other areas of disagreement as well. A cooperative day nursery maintained by SoHo residents was the focus of one such incident. The "play center", which charged a fee of thirty dollars a month per child, had been allowed to use the parish basement rent-free. This elicited criticism from the Italian community, which was also upset with the "progressive" methods employed at the center (See, Chapter 11). In an article in the SoHo newspaper, the director of the play center stressed the need for conciliation. He believed that the nursery was capable of "increasing the understanding between the two divergent cultures of SoHo and the 'old neighborhood' ". He emphasized that, as far as attendance at the center was concerned, there was "an open door policy for the entire neighborhood, not just SoHo". To further understanding, he proposed a kind of cultural exchange program involving a round of "loft tours" for children and adults. The proposal, however, never materialized. The nursery remained an exclusively SoHo institution. When it moved over to the parish school, it was distinctly isolated from the mainstream of school activity.

Perhaps the greatest amount of friction between the two divergent cultures involved Italian teenagers and young men. The latter resented SoHo for usurping their turf. The artists and middle class "moved right in" and imparted their character to the South Village, transforming it into SoHo. According to one cornerboy, the newcomers "act like it's their neighborhood", flagrantly disregarding the Italians' historical claim. One group of young cornerboys, then, were irked by the posters on buildings and lamp posts advertising events like gallery openings and recitals. Although their objection was that they made the neighborhood "look sloppy", they were essentially reacting to turf markings which signified that a successful invasion had taken place.

Young Italians manifested their displeasure with this turn of events at various levels. There was the bellicose stare that strangers encountered when they ventured past cornerboy haunts. This sometimes escalated into antagonistic remarks. One artist claimed that young Italians passed "wisecracks" when he was out jogging or with a woman friend. Further up in the Village, local youth had a reputation for harassing homosexuals. In the playground, there was an unwritten rule that neighborhood boys had a priority on handball and basketball courts; when strangers were included in the game, it was not appreciated if they prevailed over locals. There were more serious incidents. It was believed that young Italians slashed the tires on eight automobiles as revenge for the newcomers exacerbating the parking problem (none of the cars belonged to neighborhood Italians). At the HEW housing complex for artists in the West Village, Italian teenagers were singled out for harassing artists' children. An actor who lived in the neighborhood died as a result of an altercation with Italian teenagers when he opposed their designs on a delivery truck.

The more violent incidents elicited forceful denunciations in the local press and the community planning board. The whole matter assumed the dimensions of a gang problem in which "young marauders" (according to a report by the local planning board's public safety committee) attacked two auxiliary policemen. The situation further deteriorated when neighborhood youth clubbed "anyone with dark skin" with bats during a rampage in Washington Square Park. A city social worker who lived in the urban renewal housing off Houston Street diagnosed the problem as one where

> *Italian American youth are currently expressing overt, hostile behavior in the community. They are in need of programs where they can change negative behavior patterns through constructive use of their free time.*

In a less professional and sympathetic tone, she suggested that the young men were "probably auditioning to become Mafia hit men", adding that "the Mafia is always looking for hit men". In the local planning board, the problem was given considerable discussion. A South Village community organization with a certain rapport with cornerboys (the Problem Center) was delegated the responsibility of "cooling things out"; local merchants were supposed to make jobs available through their storefront. However, official solutions did not amount to much; few jobs actually opened up and the storefront organization could not secure funding. Although matters quieted down after the park incident, it seemed largely the result of police surveillance. Moreover, the Mafia supposedly put the word out that anyone evidencing "negative behavior patterns" was looking for trouble (although the syndicate reputedly assisted some of the neighborhood boys involved in these incidents).

Cornerboys regarded SoHo as an infringement on their traditional role, that is, to "keep order in the neighborhood", largely by waylaying troublemakers. Turf defense has been a means of channeling the aggressive behavior of young males on behalf of the defended neighborhood, although in the past they were also kept in line by adult cornerboys and the Mafia. However, middle class newcomers were not supportive of this arrangement, especially when they themselves felt intimidated. Therefore, according to one young man, although the newcomers appreciated a safe neighborhood, they were "the first to squawk when someone gets hurt".

Young cornerboys had a different interpretation of the "gang problem". As far as they were concerned, the artists and middle class did not "belong in the neighborhood". In the words of one young man, "the newcomers never lived like us". He added that "all we care about is surviving", whereas the newcomers "don't know what the world is like out there". He summed up the difference between the two groups by portraying Italians as "streetwise" and newcomers as "bookwise". However, this distinction betrayed a sense of relative deprivation and shame. Artists and middle class were resented, not just because they were taking over the neighborhood, but because they accentuated the lack of symbols of success to the cornerboys (*e.g.,* good jobs, education, articulate speech, attractive housing, money). The newcomers were not bohemians who repudiated mainstream status symbols and could be looked down upon. Moreover, Italians felt excluded from the world represented by SoHo. They were out of place in SoHo bars. They could not afford the boutiques or understand the art. The young men "got nowhere" with SoHo women; often, the latter's neighborliness was misinterpreted as a "come on". Perhaps to signify that he had made it, a cornerboy in his twenties used "fifty dollar words" at planning board meetings, unaware that his malapropisms were amusing middle class Villagers. In encounters like these, most Italians privately sensed they were out of their league. Invariably, SoHo introduced invidious status distinctions into the neighborhood. Historically, it could be assumed that "no one was better than anyone else", largely because ethnicity established a common ground and the upwardly mobile were channeled out of the neighborhood. Newcomers did not belong in the South Village, then, because they made Italians uncomfortably aware of their own social status.

Whereas cornerboys had a gripe with SoHo, some members of the Italian community were enthusiastic about some of the changes being effected (even cornerboys heartily approved of the young women who lived alone or with roommates). Obviously, property owners were happy with the rise in real estate values, although most of the buildings were in the hands of non-Italians. Businessmen were receptive to the purchasing power of the new middle class residents. There was also approbation for SoHo from a social standpoint. One neighborhood woman, who lived in the South Village all her life and walked to a part-time job in a candy factory, humorously observed that she "had to wait all these years" to encounter different life-styles first-hand. She was fascinated with the likes of a young writer whose husband lived in California for most of the year, trying to find work as an actor; she swapped stories with a friend who knew a musician up the block whose South American raccoon lived on a perch over his bed. The proprietress of a vegetable store found her new customers willing and able to discuss classical music. The housewife who could not go to college in the thirties because Italian women "didn't do that then" now has "intellegent conversations" with a music critic and the author of a book on rooftop gardens. In a sense, SoHo has enhanced the social status of Italians who have stayed in the neighborhood by providing them with middle class neighbors and a fashionable address. Perhaps this is part of the reason that mobile Italians, who relate to the neighborhood as a measure of how far they have come, have trouble understanding the changes that SoHo has wrought in the South Village.

Five years after SoHo was officially acknowledged, it had substantially transformed the character of the South Village which had almost ceased to exist as an Italian neighborhood. The old buildings have an entirely different atmosphere. Except for the stereo music or perhaps a muscian practicing on an instrument, they are more quiet and subdued. The aroma of garlic and oil no longer dominates the hallways; there is now competition from incense and patchouli and the distinctive Portuguese preparations for codfish and lamb. The newcomers have not bothered to hang clotheslines and are generally indifferent to the airshaft; roofs are more likely to have gardens than pigeon coops which once sent birds swirling above the neighborhood. The names on the mailboxes are not Italian, familiar or even stationary for any length of time. The young newcomers come and go and operate on different schedules. New neighbors are mistaken for visitors and even burglars. Now that "the old families are gone", an elderly woman lamented that

> you never know your neighbors anymore. You meet people in the hallway and you nod your head. That's all.

The rhythms of the street have also changed. The storefront shops are no longer geared to Italians. Even at night, most of the people on the street are strangers. In particular, SoHo has put cornerboys out of joint. They noticeably clash with the new activity in the neighborhood. Many of the locales for hanging out have been surrendered to SoHo establishments. The new SoHo shops are not conducive to street corner life; no rapport emerged with the new "paper store" that sold Le Monde, The New Left Review but not the Daily News. Nevertheless, SoHo did supply an interest and involvement with the street; hands clasped behind their backs, cornerboys have taken to surveying the spectacle generated by the restaurants, galleries and boutiques. They are also the cordial attendants of visitors who stop to ask directions to SoHo, and the conoisseurs of SoHo women.

The restaurants, boutiques and galleries have incorporated the South Village into the city as SoHo. Previously, the neighborhood was an enclave for ethnic group life. It was even more insulated than the East Side, which had a plethora of Italian restaurants and specialty shops, and has since become the city's "Little Italy". However, following legalization and media exposure, the neighborhood was inundated with tourists. Busloads began arriving for gallery tours. Taxi cabs discharged well-dressed shoppers and patrons of the arts.

On Saturday and Sunday, tourists wandered about with cameras and guide maps.

Once in SoHo, tourists discovered the vestiges of an ethnic community that was not indicated on their maps. Down for the super-realism or the brunch at the charcuterie, they came upon some charming storefronts and real flesh and blood ethnics. They stopped and studied the storefronts, their cameras poised. On one occasion, two sightseers experiencing a neighborhood candy store were disappointed that the overhead fans had been replaced with air conditioners although they did enjoy their egg creams and a convivial exchange with cornerboys. An old family bakery was a special find for tourists. In addition to the loaves of bread picturesquely arrayed in the storefront window, they were taken with the elderly proprietress in her black dress and chignon, and the framed portrait of the Sacred Heart over the cash register. After scrutinizing the store from the street, they often came inside to buy some biscuits which looked interesting and whose name they struggled to pronounce. To enhance the cultural experience, customers frequently requested that the large loaves of bread not be halved and wrapped in paper so they could be carried under the arm or left to protrude from shopping baskets.

Sensing commercial benefits, some merchants have cultivated an Italian atmosphere. In this spirit, both a neighborhood bar and an Italian bakery have gone *al fresco*. An unassuming luncheonette refurbished its interior in a Mediterranean motif and added a red, white and green awning. Its name was changed from "Tony's Coffee Shop" to "Tony's Casa di Cafe".

On the whole, Italians are not pleased that their residential neighborhood has been turned into a tourist attraction. Besides the implications for social control, it has created a nuisance. The neighborhood has become infested with pedestrians and automobiles; bars and restaurants keep the neighborhood hopping into the early morning. Tourists invade residents' privacy.

Conclusion

In the present, the parameters of a social neighborhood are defined by the attrition of communal membership and the expansion of SoHo. The former has attenuated expressions of sociability that distinguished a local community, like street corner groups, although life-style changes are also a factor. At the same time, SoHo has imparted a different character to both the physical neighborhood (galleries, boutiques, etc.) and its social fabric. Within this framework, Italians have clung to familiar communal patterns and, despite their physical proximity, Italians and newcomers move within their respective social orbits. Local Italians have used ties to mobile relatives to expand their social networks beyond the neighborhood, so that the latter is no longer congruent with Italian group life. Notwithstanding this adjustment, the erosion of a neighborhood community is experienced as a loss, especially by those who are more embedded in the locality such as the elderly. The lapsing of provincial defenses has exposed the neighborhood to predatory elements, and bureaucratic substitutes have proved ineffective. Fear of crime has precipitated a further retreat from involvement with the neighborhood. The blurring of boundaries between the neighborhood and the city, the emergence of strangers as neighbors and the metamorphosis of the tenement neighborhood into SoHo have further disrupted the life-world of erstwhile urban Villagers.

The Italian Parish
in a Changing Neighborhood

*t*he loss of parishioners has been a fact of life for both Italian churches in the South Village. As a result, their status in recent years has been determined by various strategies for survival. One strategy has been to retain loyalty of parishioners who moved away. There has also been an attempt to reach out to new groups in the South Village, although Italians have been reluctant to acknowledge the claims of "outsiders" to their parish. Finally, the parish has aspired to become something of a sight for tourists and a welfare center for disadvantaged segments of the Italian community.

The decline in parish membership has been persistent, becoming especially sharp in the last fifteen years. Membership at the older parish dropped from 1,500 families in 1964 to 400 families in 1976. The decline has had an effect on every facet of parish life. There are fewer masses performed, and they are less crowded. In the 1960s, the beautiful basement church was converted to an auditorium since there was no longer a need to accommodate an overflow from the main church; an auditorium was more practical now that the parish had to hold affairs to raise money (*e.g.,* bingo). Since there were fewer parishioners to administer to, the number of priests stationed at the rectory also declined. Recently, the rectory was taken over by the order house and parish priests moved to smaller quarters. Membership in parish organizations has withered; the Fathers' Club at one parish had fewer than fifteen men. Moreover, belonging to a parish society no longer had the prestige it was said to convey in the past (*i.e.,* a reputation for probity). Some parish organizations expired. The Dramatic Society has not staged a production in years; the big parish socials and picnics belonged to another era. One of the more conspicuous changes in parish life is the infrequent occurence of marriage and christening ceremonies. In 1974, there were only 91 christenings, a far cry from the 896 children baptized at the church in 1912. Moreover, in only about half of the christenings were the parents Italian. This was another sign of the times. Finally, the parish school has been left tottering. Between 1964 and 1976, enrollment at one school went from 982 to 240; the number of pupils at the other school declined from 1,430 in its heyday (the 1930s) to 270 in 1976, surviving thanks to an infusion of non-Italian students. Each year, registration for the kindergarten is faced with much anxiety.

At least one of the Italian parishes—the old parish founded in 1866—sensed something in the wind a while ago. Its 1966 anniversary publication attributed parish decline to the fact that "many of the young Italian Americans returned from the battles (World War II) to a waiting G.I. Bill which enabled them to buy homes and educate themselves beyond the traditional reaches of the laboring class". As the parish saw it, the upwardly mobile were being drained away, leaving the relatively less advantaged. In light of these developments, successive pastors were preoccupied with "promoting the parish welfare during the lean years". However, their efforts could not prevent it from becoming "an urban parish in the stagnated core city". While the West Village (formerly an Irish neighborhood) had become a fashionable place to live, the South Village did not have the supply of housing that might accommodate new and more affluent residents. Ironically, the parish saw what is now SoHo as an additional obstacle since there were "too many commercial lofts and small factories that are impractical for conversion to residences". As a result, the parish saw urban renewal as the only solution. In lieu of slum clearance, the South Village could "never be turned into an enclave for the well-off".

The parish enjoined Italians to be realistic. Urban renewal seemed inevitable since developers could not "ignore the choice real estate adjacent to the fashionable Village". It expressed the hope that "much of the neighborhood's Italian character" would be "preserved by giving local residents, especially those displaced by renewal, first crack at any new apartment units". It was noted that "rare indeed is the parish...that can claim to have gone through 100 years— even 50 years—without any disruptive social change". It added, however, that it was "no cause for Christian concern" if the Italian character of the parish would some day entirely disappear, leaving only a rich heritage.

The parish did not get slum clearance, although it later got its new and more affluent residents. Still, in its lean years it was forced to find other formulas for survival. One of these was the feast of the parish patron. Introduced in the early fifties, "badly-needed revenue was thus brought into the parish's hungry coffers".

The feast had been a symbol of peasant religious expression and, consequently, was vigorously opposed by the Church hierarchy and more progressive elements within the Italian community. As the number of parishioners dwindled, however, it became a critical device for keeping the parish solvent. Previous objections were now suspended with the tempering of its folk-religious aspects. Appropriated by the parish, the religious ceremonies and the procession of devotees were no longer sacrilegious; parish priests escorted the statue of the saint past parishioners who occasionally left their place on the sidewalk to affix dollar bills to the image for a special intention (in the 1960s, the procession of parishioners went as far as Washington Square Park). Actually, religion was a small part of the celebration; the feast was music, games and sausage sandwiches. As time went on, the feast became even more secular and commercialized.

The feast easily became the major event on the parish calendar and in the neighborhood as well. It consisted of concessions selling Italian food and trinkets like the kind sold at amusement parks. Some of the stands were run for the parish by parishioners who donated their services; this was exclusively true of the gambling booths. Others were operated by parishioners for personal profit, although a fixed amount went to the parish sponsor. All of this caused great excitement in the neighborhood, especially among the youngsters who saved their coins to go on the rides and local merchants who worked overtime to supply the concessionaires. Former parishioners came back to attend and renew old ties, and perhaps showcase their prosperity.

The feast achieved unanticipated success, attracting outsiders in increasing numbers. As this happened, its scope and import widened. Its duration was extended from seven days to two weeks (allowing more time for rainouts). As the number of concessions increased, competition for a stand and a good location was intensified. There was grumbling that the parish was favoring certain individuals over others; syndicate interests were rumored to receive the more desirable concessions and locations. By the mid-sixties, the feast had become a supra-neighborhood affair. The Lindsay administration designated the feast part of the New York City Summer Festival Program along with other events like band concerts and theater in Central Park. The parish estimated that half a million people attended the 1976 feast; patrons included the urban middle class out for an ethnic experience and mobile Italian Americans renewing a contact with "the old neighborhood". In recent years, the feast has become even less Italian insofar as Greek, Mideastern, Mexican, Korean, Thai, Vietnamese and Japanese foods can be sampled along with the scungili and calzoni. It was a sign of the changes taking place in the neighborhood when a SoHo restaurant opened a stand selling a French sausage, although vendors of Italian sausage made them call it something else. Adding to the international flavor of the feast, devotional masses were said in Spanish, French and Portuguese, as well as Italian; perhaps it was a typographical error that referred to the feast in an advertisement as the annual *Fiesta*.

The event's financial success has warranted more sophisticated packaging. Preparation is said to begin six months in advance. The feast is advertised in the city's major newspapers and on radio. Each year there is television news coverage invariably showing a patron trying to manage an abundant calzone and workers in undershirts frying peppers and onions. The parish's public relations were especially elaborate for the Bicentennial. It prepared a nine page brochure complete with photographs of previous feasts and an interpretive text. The latter characterized the parish as "steeped in tradition", having "begun as a natural expression of the energy and pageantry typical of the Italian life-style". The brochure noted that the parish itself "evokes a feeling for another time and place, when the church in the piazza was the center of the Italian village". Reading the promotion, it was almost possible to forget the earlier ban on Italian *feste* and the hope that urban renewal would bring new and more affluent residents. In deference to the Bicentennial, the brochure noted that the land on which the church was built between 1882 and 1888 "was a storied plot, as Aaron Burr, Vice President to Thomas Jefferson, had originally surveyed the site". Even the parish was steeped in America's traditions in 1976.

By the late seventies, the feast had ceased to be a neighborhood function. It was primarily geared to strangers—Italians sardonically point out that only a stranger would pay $2.50 for a sausage sandwich. Many of the concessions were run by strangers. Several neighborhood Italians claim to stay away and resent the noise, garbage and crowding which accompany the festivities. Still, the popularity of the feast has generated a sense of pride in both the neighborhood and the Italian heritage. It has easily become the principal source of revenue for the parish; this was probably the reason the other Italian parish initiated one of its own in the early seventies.

There have been other measures calculated to sustain the older parish. As a shrine church, it was hoped that the relic and special devotions to the parish saint would attract a loyal following beyond the parish (in the past, devotion to the saint was the main reason people attended the feast). In addition, the parish erects a manger scene on a busy thoroughfare alongside the church each Christmas. The parish yearbook noted that "local newspapers and national magazines have spread the fame of the crêche with their full color representations"; like the feast, the display reflects "the Italian community's love of pageantry, the flair for the picturesque, its consummate artistry". Into the sixties, the enterprising pastor who introduced the feast enlivened the manger scene with parochial school children and their mothers singing Christmas carols in the December night.

The parish actually saw itself as competing with the Greenwich

Village bohemian quarter for tourists. The 1966 anniversary book criticized "the hoopla of the nightly side-show that brings tourists and would-be beatniks storming into the Village". "On the edge of Bohemia", however, it felt that it could still hold its own as a tourist attraction with the likes of the Christmas display, "an immutable reminder of the Christian structure as opposed to the fads of secularism". It confidently asserted that the feast and the manger scene combined to "usurp the Village's neon brilliance twice yearly". As "a paragon of Old World tradition existing cheek by jowl with the avant garde culture of bohemia", the church did wonder, in a moment of reflection, whether "the flamboyance of the Village has rubbed off on the parish".

The parish has also tried to retain the loyalty of former parishioners. In the fifties, it began the practice of broadcasting the Tuesday evening novenas in honor of the parish saint over a local radio station (Schiavo, 1958:332). The church also sponsored annual parish reunions in an uptown hall. Parish newsletters kept them abreast of events. Of course, the feast is seen as a magnet for former parishioners.

Ties to former parishioners were especially emphasized by the other parish, which seemed more intent on preserving the Italian character of the parish and was disinclined to adopt the commercialism engaged in by its neighbor (although it introduced a street feast in 1970 that was much more low-keyed and distinctly less successful). Perhaps the reasons for this inhere in the traditions of the Italian missionary order that has operated the parish since 1892 (one of the priests criticized the other parish for compromising Italian ways). The pastor recently expressed his hope to "keep the Italo-Americans here" and retain "the nice little community we have". He noted, however, that the parish would have to supplement this base. He proposed to "draw back the people who at one time or another passed through the doors of the church", and to interest the children and grandchildren of former parishioners as well (perhaps banking on the social trend of resurgent ethnicity). This would be accomplished by holding special events like street feasts and processions. There was also a plan to rejuvenate the various shrines at the church since, he believed, Italians were partial to religious devotions. This would restore an active parish and solve pressing financial problems.

It remains to be seen whether ethnic nostalgia can generate support for the ethnic parish. There are signs, however, that former parishioners have not entirely abandoned the church. On the first day of each calendar year, they trek in from the suburbs to secure preferred dates for special masses; they also come in (or send in) for mass cards. When a *New York Times* article pointed out that one of the parishes was in debt for $160,000 because of water leaks

116

that destroyed art work and the church basement, a chord was struck with mobile parishioners. Money came in from places like Teaneck, New Jersey and Elmhurst, New York. Two men who lived in the neighborhood more than twenty-five years ago contributed $2,000 and $1,000 apiece for the repairs. The pastor was overwhelmed and encouraged for the future. However, the loyalty of children and grandchildren is rather dubious.

In still another development, both churches have come to emphasize, community service, in particular, vis-a-vis disadvantaged segments of the parish. One area of concern is the elderly, many of whom have little family left in the neighborhood and are functionally disinherited (e.g., no one for whom to cook and clean). Each parish instituted senior citizens programs which received no mention in parish literature as late as 1966. At one parish, 150 senior citizens met in the church basement twice a week for arts and crafts, bingo, movies, birthday parties and coffee and cake. The priest responsible for the program has become a geriatric specialist. His parish duties are focused on the needs of this substantial contingent. In 1976, the parish was looking to expand this facet of its operations; the priest who directed the program hoped to be able to visit more of the elderly at home and to hold more regular meetings.

Besides a senior citizens' program, each parish has shown a heightened concern for youth problems. The latter has been thrown into relief by incidents involving middle class residents, who made an issue of "aggressive" Italian street youth in local newspapers and in the planning board. Various civic groups and the planning board have looked to the Italian churches as perhaps the only legitimate neighborhood institution that can deflect youthful beligerence (these organizations were not prepared to work through the Mafia). For their part, the churches have sought to bolster social and recreational programs aimed at teenagers. One had over one hundred youngsters participating in activities in the settlement hall and gymnasium on a regular basis.

The concern of the parish for the problems of the young and the old perhaps reflects the availability of government money in these areas. As a welfare agency dispensing community services for which funding is available, the parish could possibly remain solvent and viable. A move in this direction was evident when an Italian civic leader used his influence with a Democratic party "boss" to get $33,000 for a summer youth program at one of the churches. Still, it is doubtful whether the provision of welfare services is a preferred alternative to the performance of traditional parish services.

The prospect of the declining South Village parishes were buoyed by the influx of Portuguese immigrants in the late sixties. Even the old German church, now holding on by a thread, took heart. The Portuguese represented the possibility of restoring a thriving parish,

117

not just a shrine or a tourist attraction. They were reassuringly similar in their earnest peasant backgrounds to the earlier Italian immigrants.

As it turned out, the prospects of a general revival from this source was limited; there simply were not enough Portuguese to go around and South Village churches found themselves in competition for parishioners. However, it was never really a contest. The older Italian parish held a peculiar advantage. By a twist of fate, the patron saint of the parish was actually Portuguese, having migrated to Italy later on in his religious career and making a name for himself as an Italian saint. While this probably had nothing to do with the settlement of Portuguese in the area, it seems to have been a factor in their preference for this church over the others. What really decided the issue was the church's good fortune in obtaining a Portuguese priest to minister to the immigrant community. The old German church had similarly petitioned the order for a native friar but was unsuccessful. The pastor there lamented that this probably sealed its demise. Although no attempt was made to secure a Portuguese priest at the other Italian parish, one of the priests there conceded that the immigrants would certainly have brightened its prospects.

The Portuguese definitely invigorated the old Italian parish. They buttressed sagging church attendance and were reputed as generous financial contributors. In 1975, approximately 40 percent of the student body at the parish grammar school was Portuguese, equalling the size of the Italian contingent (the rest of the students were from Central and South America and Puerto Rico). In the lower grades, however, there was an even greater proportion of Portuguese students. In addition, the Portuguese were increasingly the focus of ceremonies held at the church. In 1976, the parish estimated that there were 2,000 Portuguese parishioners at the church, although only 982 Portuguese were enumerated by the 1980 Census in four South Village census tracts. The Portuguese community comprised a parish within a parish. They did not join the Fathers' Club or The Holy Name Society, nor did they patronize the Las Vegas Nights and bingo games. Their religious expression was enclosed within immigrant communal frameworks headed by the Portuguese friar. The immigrants related to the parish through him. They attended his Portuguese language mass. He baptized their childrn and listened to their problems; he taught Portuguese to immigrant children after school; he organized the devotion and procession of our Lady of Fatima, whose statue the immigrants had donated to the church.

The parish school was the only setting in which the immigrants had been integrated and, even here, only the children took part; parents did not belong to the P.T.A. and rarely went to the school. For the youngsters who spoke English and were exposed to media

118

culture (*e.g.,* "Donny and Marie" posters, "Star Wars" T-shirts), ethnic differences were less of an obstacle. Portuguese children jumped rope and played stoop ball along with their classmates. Still, Portuguese students were highly conscious of their ethnicity and constituted a distinct group within the school. In one fifth grade class, a geography lesson dissolved into a battle over whether Italy or Portugal was "better"; since their connections were fresher, the Portuguese children were better informed than the second and third generation Italian youngsters. Fluency in Portuguese marked them off from other classmates; the more recent Portuguese students spoke little or no English, necessitating a bilingual pupil to serve as mediator in the classroom. After school, most Portuguese children attended classes on Portuguese language and culture; for a while, these classes were taught by the friar at a local settlement. The children also attended affairs at the Portuguese Club.

The *modus vivendi* of a parish within a parish eventually showed signs of strain, although nothing approaching a "Portuguese problem". Neighborhood Italians became restive over the role of immigrants within "their" church. At a P.T.A. meeting, several mothers agreed that the Portuguese were "taking over". There was resentment of their financial support, which perhaps reminded Italians that they could not carry the church by themselves. The church was criticized for catering to the immigrants. The pastor, in particular, was faulted for taking the trouble to read a speech in Portuguese at a procession for Our Lady of Fatima. An elderly woman, who donated considerable sums of money and time to the parish, thereby claiming for herself a voice in parish affairs, also felt that the Portuguese were receiving special treatment. She was perturbed when the statues of Our Lady of Mount Carmel and Saint Maria Goretti—the latter donated in her parent's name—were sent to the warehouse to make room for Our Lady of Fatima.

Relations between Portuguese and Italians were complicated by the peculiar historical irony that the popular parish patron saint was really Portuguese and not Italian, as had been believed. Some of the Portuguese delighted in pointing this out to Italians, which insulted their ethnic pride. This revelation virtually precipitated a crisis of belief in the neighborhood, and many Italians refused to accept it. Some appeared betrayed by both the saint and the priests. For a while, the whole issue was hotly debated in bars and on the corner. Italians were not prepared to let the Portuguese take away their patron saint too.

Despite their smooth relationship, differences soon emerged between the parish and the Portuguese community. The problem started when a new pastor was appointed. One of his initial projects concerned the status of the Portuguese friar, who was now the associate pastor. Seeking to unify the parish, and perhaps gain more direct control over the Portuguese, the new pastor suggested that the native friar give up his exclusive commitment to the immigrant community and be assigned for general parish duty. The Portuguese were displeased, and threatened to quit the church and remove their children from the parish school. To make their point, they staged a protest demonstration outside the church during Sunday mass. However, the confrontation was abruptly terminated when the order transferred the friar elsewhere. While the Portuguese did not agitate further, they were disconcerted and their ties to the church seemed to have weakened. The language class taught by the priest, for example, was taken over by a young Portuguese woman and held in the Portuguese Club. It was surprising that the parish should take steps to alienate the Portuguese, unless it felt that they were safely ensconced within the parish frameworks.

Nevertheless, the Portuguese made their mark. Recent parish literature gives the impression that the parish has ceased to be exclusively, Italian. With specific reference to the Portuguese, it was now the "melting pot" for all nationalities". This new image has even led to a revision of parish history. The parish had previously portrayed its past as bound up with the local Italian community; it even minimized the role of the Irish in early parish development. However, a recent booklet noted that the parish "has historically served the needs of a community as diverse as America itself".

The artists and other young middle class newcomers have presented both Italian churches with another kind of challenge. The younger parish has largely remained aloof; its identification as the "Immigrants' Church"—the theme emphasized in *The New York Times* article—has led it to concentrate on former parishioners and the vestiges of Italian community. It may also have trouble seeing the new residents as material for a Catholic parish, although in what may be construed as a concession to the changes in the neighborhood, the pastor proposed that the parish grammar school be made nondenominational to keep it going. The other parish, however, actively embraced "the transformation of the surrounding community", recommending "an ecumenical outlook" *vis-a-vis* artists and other newcomers. Nonetheless, integrating the latter would probably pose a greater problem than that represented by the Portuguese.

The pastor at this forward looking parish was actually quite enthusiastic about the effects that SoHo was having on the neighborhood. He even welcomed the changes and the newcomers from the pulpit one Sunday. Parish literature referred to the loft conversions in "the new artists' community" as a "renaissance". SoHo was evidently not the bohemian "hoopla" of the sixties. Perhaps these finally were the "new and affluent residents" that urban renewal was supposed to bring. With any luck, there would be practicing Catholics among those moving into the renovated lofts and tenement buildings.

The pastor was eager to accommodate the newcomers. He allowed a day care center in the church basement for artists' children and later allowed them to use an empty classroom in the grammar school without charging the center any rent, and was happy that the space could be put to good use. Parish facilities had already been made available to other middle class groups. Tenants of the urban renewal housing on LaGuardia Place were meeting in the church basement. It was announced that "a group of professional people use the parish hall for their 'Country Dances' ". The hall was also the site for a classical radio concert that likewise was a middle class function.

The pastor had apparently hoped that accommodation would result in much-needed parishioners. However, this did not materialize. The newcomers either are not Catholic, only nominally Catholic, or prefer the nearby New York University chapel which is more attuned to their educational and social status. They have not sent their children to the parish school. A fifth grader whose parents are artists was perhaps the only exception and, according to a teacher at the school, "stuck out like a sore thumb".

Thus, while some newcomers used parish facilities, they nevertheless remained essentially marginal to parish frameworks. The SoHo day nursery was physically and socially isolated from the parish grammar school; even when the former was moved to the school building, it followed a different schedule so that there was little or no interaction between the two. Moreover, the nursery has been the object of neighborhood criticism. Neighborhood women were upset at the report that toddlers romped around the church basement without clothing. Teachers at the parish school were critical of open-classroom methods. There was also a complaint that the nursery paid no rent, even though it was a profit-making enterprise. In all of this, there was an undercurrent of resentment toward strangers who were "taking over".

If SoHo was not supplying the parish with new members, there was at least the benefit derived from the "gentrification" of the neighborhood. Even so, the parish discovered that this was not without its problems. In 1976, new middle class residents became quite vocal in their opposition to the feast. Articles and letters published in local newspapers denounced the event as a bane to the residential character of the neighborhood (*e.g.,* traffic congestion, noise, garbage). There was similar protest expressed in planning board sessions. It was also anonymously charged that the Mafia ran the feast, giving only a percentage of the proceeds to the church. A proposal was tendered in the planning board to ban events like the feast in the future.

The parish was appropriately concerned since the feast was its principal source of revenue. A week before the feast began, it distributed a brochure which, besides promoting the event, addressed itself to the criticism levied by the newcomers. Its tone was conciliatory and apologetic; it assured its critics that special interests were not the main beneficiaries, that the feast was run by and for the parish and its proceeds allowed the church to provide "social, cultural, and religious programs" for "the whole community, not solely for the stalwart Italian members". The parish maintained that it was sorry that the feast was such a nuisance. If it did not need the revenues there would not be a feast, and residents would not be burdened with "the noise, the smell, the unsanitary conditions, etc.". It promised to "supervise more closely the causes of such inconvenience experienced in the past".

There was no comparable protest the following year, only the standard mumbling from Italians who would never dream of having the feast canceled. However, one thing was clear, the parish and the neighborhood were no longer one and the same; from here on, the parish could not take "community sentiment" for granted. The middle class regarded the church as just another property owner and civic organization. As such, it was expected to submit to wider community norms fixed and enforced by the local planning board which was dominated by the middle class.

Conclusion

The Italian churches have been exploring ways of remaining viable as Italians have moved away. The younger parish may be less flexible than the other because of its historical commitment to an Italian national parish (*i.e.*, the "Immigrant Church"), although it may be rejuvenated by the "rediscovery of ethnicity". It has also recently allocated space in the parish school to a school for Italian businessmen and diplomats featuring instruction in Italian. The other, as a territorial as well as an ethnic parish, is not similarly constrained. although it is difficult to envision just how artists and the other newcomers will comprise a base of support. It is possible that as population continues to shift, both will wither away. Each initially inhabited buildings that once housed Protestant churches whose congregations left the area.

The New Political Scene

*a*t present, neighborhood politics are defined by the erosion of former capabilities. Very broadly, this predicament is related to the "gentrification" of the lower Village; the middle class has become dominant in precincts that were previously Italian. South Village Italians have tried to hold their ground in the face of the advancement of "reform" interests. There was also an attempt to forge a coalition that would mine bureaucratic centers of power and resource distribution.

Politics in the Wake of Reform

Throughout the 1950s, the middle class was becoming numerically dominant in the 64th (formerly the 2nd) Assembly District. Significant challenges were mounted against the regular club, dominated by Italians and their Irish allies, in the name of political reform. The structure of formal political power was about to be fundamentally altered.

The event that signalled this power shift was the defeat of Carmine DeSapio as district leader. The leadership had been contested in the late fifties by a reform club, which had a sizeable Jewish and professional contingent and included the present Mayor of New York Edward Koch, representing the view of middle class Villagers. In contrast to the groups traditionally served by machine governments, their interests "lay more in the realm of ideas and policies than bread and butter" (Connable and Silberfarb, 1967:297). The publication of *The Village Voice* gave expression to their political interests.

The quintessential boss survived initial challenges. However, he was defeated by a small margin in 1961. DeSapio himself attributed the loss to the fact that, with the middle class, local politics had become "ideological" (Connable and Silberfarb, 1967:313). A neighborhood civic leader put the blame on the failure of Italians to vote for DeSapio. Another civic leader contended that DeSapio had "betrayed" a loyal Italian constituency for grander political fortunes. He "forgot the neighborhood" and "stopped doing the little things like helping a civil servant get a promotion"; with his picture on the cover of *Time* magazine, he had gotten "too big for his boots". As a result, Italians wouldn't vote for him.

With the ascendance of the middle class Italians became increasingly marginal to district politics. The neighborhood did not identify with the reform club and its leadership, and the latter did not have to serve the neighborhood. Since Italians had a poor voting record, the new district leadership could pay them little attention.

Ironically, DeSapio's defeat was coincident with the reelection of his godson to the assembly seat from the district (he was first elected in 1954). The latter's father, an immigrant from Italy who became wealthy as a manufacturer of paper stock, had organized a reform club opposing Dan Finn and subsequently backed DeSapio. His own position was apparently liberal enough to exempt him from the tag of "bossism". Moreover, he was a lawyer and spoke without a trace of neighborhood argot. Italian and middle class, he was an attractive "fusion candidate". As a result, he was endorsed by the new reform club and other liberals in the Democratic Party.

His regular reelection since 1961 reflects the extent to which he has embraced reform and the middle class constituencies in his district, including large professional and homosexual communities. In contrast to neighborhood Italians, these constituencies join civic organizations, attend community meetings, submit letters to local newspapers and monitor their representative's legislative performances. Recent campaign literature listed sundry accomplishments that would satisfy their interests—addressing his constituents' concern with ecological issues, his biography mentioned that his father's papermill supply company would today have been referred to as "a paper recycling plant". On the other hand, there was nothing that would specifically interest Italians.

Although he commands respect as an attorney and state assemblyman, Italians have felt betrayed by his middle class orientation and liberal views. He was criticized in the Knights of Columbus for voting in favor of abortion in the state assembly. A young Italian activist, who contemplated running against him as a Republican, pointed out that he voted for legislation restricting social clubs, a measure strongly favored by middle class Villagers intimidated by street youth. At one of his community meetings, several Italians derided the agenda, in particular a discussion initiated by a Villager regarding a children's arts and crafts center, as superfluous. They were there to talk about the presence of black "hustlers" in local playgrounds (seating arrangements reflected the polarization between Villagers and Italians).

The assemblyman tries not to alienate Italians. At the above mentioned meeting, he sought to reassure Italians of his concern with their problems. He established a common identification with a nostalgic foray into the old days. Lapsing into the neighborhood idiom, he recalled that some of the men in the audience were "two and three sewer boys", referring to prodigious distances for a stickball batsman. He also mused about the time when "our mothers had nothing better to do than lean out the window sills".

Despite his public profile, Italians have continued to support him because he is Italian and from the neighborhood, and perhaps out of respect for an Italian who has made it in higher circles. Moreover, he still aligns himself with the Italian community in the form of favors to old friends. His overall strategy in handling Villagers and Italians seems to work because they occupy different worlds; Villagers are largely unaware of his informal ties to the Italian community, while Italians are marginal to local political discourse and are disinterested in matters affecting the rest of the Village. In the final analysis, however, it is the middle class, and not the Italian neighborhood, that keeps him in the assembly.

Politics were considerably different in the 62nd (formerly the 1st) Assembly District which included the lower portion of the South Village, the loft district (SoHo) and the East Side Italian community (Little Italy). In this district, control had not been relinquished by the regular clubs.

The stability of the regular organization can be attributed to the more recent penetration of the middle class. Italians on the West and East sides had been able to provide comfortable electoral margins for district elections. The status quo was helped along in 1971 by a redistricting plan that transferred South Village blocks that had become middle class to the 64th Assembly District. According to a liberal political analyst for a local newspaper, the result was to render the 62nd Assembly District "something of a wasteland for reformers".

Recent developments have produced changes in the district, however. One was the legalization of artists' residences in the factory lofts abandoned by industry between West Broadway and Lafayette Street. The expansion of SoHo, wedged between the South Village and Little Italy, constituted an incipient challenge to the wasteland theory. Shortly after legalization in 1971, a reform club was spawned and approached several Italians believed to have liberal sympathies. The club endorsed an Italian who managed to defeat the incumbent district leader, although the latter retained his assembly post. However, the new leader proved to be on intimate terms with the regular organization as well as the local Conservative congressman, and in the next election the betrayed reformers were referring to him as a "Democratic Boss". Still, the reform club had become a factor.

The other development was the proposal of a restoration plan for Little Italy, the Italian neighborhood bounded by Canal and Houston Streets, Lafayette Street and The Bowery. In 1973, the city backed such a plan with the promise of substantial funding and other assistance. The "Little Italy Restoration Association" (LIRA), which was to be the development agency for the plan, became the center-piece of political power in the district. It was dominated by Little Italy businessmen and was closely aligned with the new district leader. LIRA consolidated Italian political power on the East side against an expanding Chinatown and halted, at least temporarily, designs by a new SoHo reform club. With the events in Little Italy, the South Village took a back seat in district politics.

Neighborhood Italians continued to support the incumbent as-semblyman until he retired in 1978 to accept a lucrative appointment with a state regulatory commission. They seemed to vote out of habit, even though he did not always serve their best interests. In 1974, for example, he voted against rent control. Approaching retirement, he was not visible in the district and barely even bothered to campaign. His successor was a young, educated Italian American who was affiliated with the regular Democratic club on the East side and was barely known in the South Village.

The Republican Club in this Democratic district is still in the hands of a family that had gained control of it during Prohibition. However, neither the club nor the leader has much weight these days—the family never managed to convert its political position into upward mobility. It has been a number of years since the club has run candidates for political office except to make the election "look good" and afford club members a lark. In 1974, it was behind a cornerboy with no political ambitions, but who "got a kick" out of having his name on the ballot. The club has little patronage at its disposal; the leader is able to manage only a few lower level government jobs.

The clubhouse itself has been reduced to a hangout for elderly men who play cards and discuss a few political issues. The clubroom's paneled walls are covered with photographs of club socials, party luminaries and old campaign posters of Nelson Rockefeller; window sills and shelves are decorated with trophies won by social/athletic club teams of yesteryear. The leader still has an office, but the door that separates it from the main clubroom seldom needs closing any more. It is a club whose heyday is gone.

Probably the most important political figure from the standpoint of service to the Italian community is a second generation Italian in his late fifties (hereafter known as "the community broker" to

126

protect his anonymity). He has never held, nor run for, elected public office. Instead, he has built a record in local civic organizations. His most important institutional affiliation has been the community planning board of Greenwich Village; since the mid-fifties, he has been elected to eight nonconsecutive terms as chairman. However, a foundation for his political career was laid as a member of Carmine DeSapio's club which perhaps explains why he still harbors a wariness for "liberals".

The community broker combines accessibility with political know-how. A local merchant, he is in close touch with the neighborhood. He is the one to whom people complain about potholes in front of their buildings or a boiler that a landlord is slow to repair. With his many contacts in government, he can still "get things done", although he is more of an ombudsman than a traditional leader trading material "inducements" (*e.g.,* jobs). He is also capable of navigating among middle class Villagers who regard him as being more open-minded than the average "neighborhood" leader, and respect him as a political veteran. In the fifties he aided Jane Jacobs' block association in its protest against the widening of Hudson Street, although he thoroughly enjoys shedding a different light on the incident. Jacobs explained the eventual defeat of the proposed street widening as an example of what could be accomplished by community organizations and assertion; she described residents signing petitions and writing letters to city officials and local newspapers (Jacobs, 1961). The community broker contends that it was not solved through community activism as Jacobs believed but in behind-the-scene negotiations. He and a number of political allies applied pressure "in the right places", ultimately enabling him to get through to the borough president. Jacobs and the block association were unaware of these developments. The community broker added that, although the matter had already been decided in private, a public hearing was staged "to make the borough president look good".

Wider civic involvement has offered the community broker an opportunity for the validation of his "civic self" lacking within the Italian community. He is still sleighted by the neighborhood's failure to appreciate his efforts in securing a playground in the early fifties, the only one below Houston Street, and has been embarassed by the irresponsibility of Italian appointees on the planning board. However, there is a social gulf that separates him from middle class Villagers. He is rather self-conscious about his background, frequently calling attention to the fact that he has "only" a high school education and is not a polished public speaker. For these reasons, he gives himself credit for succeeding in a middle class world.

His marginality has made him especially sensitive to communal differences and tensions, contending that Villagers have long been

127

antipathetic toward Italians. As evidence he cites a "permissive attitude" toward transients and the lack of support for Italians in their fight against the welfare hotels foisted on the South Village by the city. When Italians moved against these intruders on their own, Village liberals castigated them as "racists". In the political arena, Villagers have labeled Italians as "bosses" while claiming political virtue for themselves. Finally, he notes the recent criticism of the parish feast. He was particularly offended by the casual comment of a planning board member that if the parish really needed money, "Why don't you rent a boat and sail around Manhattan with an Italian band?".

The community broker likes to point out a certain hypocrisy in these charges. He argues that while Italians have been called racists, it was all right for Villagers to propose tight security for Washington Square Park, including a chain-link fence and guards, and a cleanup of vagrant types attracted by fast food restaurants. He notes that the welfare hotels were not closed when Italians complained, but when they were to be redeveloped for "middle income housing". He also finds it ironic that although Italians "have the name", the reform club operates in much the same manner as the old clubs, especially when it comes to handing over appointments to club members. Finally, he observes that while the feast was considered a residential nuisance, the same did not apply to the annual Village art show.

Although he rises above neighborhood provincialism now and again, the community broker is unequivocally a neighborhood figure. He is more at home with behind-the-scenes maneuvers than public debates; he subscribes to the philosophy "it's who you know". He can also be chauvinistically loyal to the neighborhood. He was once approached by a spokesperson for an insurgent club to run for district leader against the Italian incumbent, but could not countenance an affiliation against the neighborhood and a lack of respect for the old leader. He particularly resented the instigation of a split within the Italian community—another example of how treacherous liberals can be. He also believed that the club was merely using him to undermine Italian political dominance in the district and then withdraw its support, replacing him with a non-Italian (a belief that probably reflects his social insecurity *vis-a-vis* the middle class).

The community broker is the last of a breed in terms of the service he performs for the South Village; in fact, he sees himself as the heir of Carmine DeSapio. The bakery that he owns with his elderly mother becomes an office and clubroom when the morning deliveries are completed. Neighborhood people drop by to air complaints and solicit advice; folding chairs are on hand should the discussion become too lengthy. Conversation, as well as commercial transactions, are interrupted by incessant telephone calls from board members and representatives of citizens groups. These sometimes require that he consult committee reports filed on the shelf next to imported pasta and decorated tins of olive oil. His mother is annoyed by these claims on her son's attentions since he works so hard at the business. However, she is somewhat appeased by the gilt-edged photograph of herself with the community broker, his wife and the mayor taken at an award dinner that hangs over the cash register near the icon of the Sacred Heart.

Although the community broker still knows his way around city officials—recently, he was instrumental in obtaining funds for a senior citizens' program at a local parish—his political capital has diminished as a new generation of politicans have replaced old contacts. His influence on the planning board has waned with the appointment of professional administrators as full time salaried "managers" (the first elected board member was from outside the community)and by the ascendance of new constituencies within the district.

Taking On SoHo

In the mid-seventies politics was flavored by several issues focusing on the differences between Italians and the emerging SoHo community. Meanwhile, sensing an opening, a new organization was spawned that claimed to represent still another position; it created additional problems for the established structure of power represented by the likes of the community broker.

In 1973, a proposal for consideration by the local planning board signaled the arrival of the SoHo artists' community as a political force in the area. A private developer requested a variance for the construction of a sports center, or gymnasium, across the street from the old German church on West Broadway, near Canal Street, the main thoroughfare of the new SoHo neighborhood.

The proposal was heartily endorsed by Italian civic leaders, including the community broker. Besides the prestige the sports center would lend the area; Italians were assured by the builder that neighborhood children would be allowed to use the gym at slack hours, although it was admitted that it was primarily geared to office workers in the nearby financial district. There would be employment for some eighty persons and Italians were to have first crack at the support jobs. The center would also benefit the local economy (*e.g.,* luncheonettes and candy stores) depressed from the departure of Italians and the loss of factory jobs.

No one counted on opposition from SoHo. Until this time, the artists occupying the abandoned lofts had kept a low profile, mainly because the area was zoned for commercial use and their occupancy was illegal. Moreover, artists were on amicable terms with Italians. They jointly opposed the construction of the Lower Manhattan Expressway, which would have gouged out portions of the South Village and SoHo for roadways and exit ramps.

The legalization of loft residence for working artists in 1971 threw the inchoate artists' community into relief as "SoHo". Reinforcing this special identity, the City Planning Commission declared the SoHo area an historical landmark because of the cast-iron facades distinguishing the 19th century industrial buildings. Now that the expressway was no longer a threat, there was new capital investment although the original idea of providing cheap space for artists was undermined as loft conversions became fashionable for well-to-do non-artists.

Legalization gave the artists sanction to articulate their collective interests. The SoHo Artists Association (SAA), organized during the legalization struggle, became a capable interest group. It self-assuredly declared the concept of a sports center incompatible with an artists' community and historical landmark. A boundary dispute was imminent.

The SAA informed the planning board that the sports center would destroy the fragile new artists' community. It contended that it would attract an insupportable number of people and automobiles (the latter exacerbating the air pollution). It also argued that the complex would open the area to commercial exploitation, having deleterious consequences for artists seeking affordable space.

The SAA was persuasive. The planning board adopted its position and advised against the complex. Italians were quite angry and taken off guard by the artists' assertiveness in the matter. The community broker felt that the sports center was "none of their business". He also felt betrayed. He insisted that "if it wasn't for the Italians, there wouldn't be a SoHo".

Not to be outdone in their own neighborhood, the Italian community responded with a written appeal to the planning board, composed by the community broker, although it was anonymously authored to preserve his official neutrality as planning board chairman. The appeal began by saying that "We in the Italian community do not raise our voices too often, however, we cannot remain silent any longer". There were the familiar signatures of neighborhood leaders: the parish pastors, presidents of parish societies, the Republican district leader, the president of the local Little League, officers of the Knights of Columbus and American Legion chapters, the president of a businessmen's club, the director of the Italian American Civil Rights League chapter and the president of a "members only" club. The community broker signed as a member of a Greenwich Village civic association.

130

The appeal astutely countered the charges made by the SAA. It pointed out that the galleries and bars had already precipitated the untoward effects expected from the sports center. Parking was particularly nettlesome on weekends; tour buses worsened the pollution created by automobiles, including taxi cabs which, heretofore, were rarely encountered in the neighborhood. Especially incisive was the observation that the rent structure had already been disrupted, in the South Village as well as in SoHo. It was noted that commercial tenants were being driven out, despite the fact that the Planning Commission supported SoHo with the proviso that there would be no further loss of jobs. Finally, it was observed that marginal artists were likewise leaving for less expensive space in other loft areas.

Committed to SoHo culturally and economically, the planning board turned down the appeal. Confronted with a protracted and expensive litigation, the builder quietly withdrew. However, in the neighborhood, Italians were bitter. The community broker was seething and intent on settling the score. Italians seemed more deeply alienated from the planning board; although a believer himself, even the community broker was disillusioned. There was a sense that, after all these years, Italians were being brushed aside for latecomers.

In the ensuing years, there was increasing antagonism toward SoHo, in the abstract if not in the concrete. It was manifest in criticism of the artists' physical appearances and life-styles, as well as a derogation of the art work on display in local galleries insofar as it was visible from the street. It was informed by a fundamental difference in class and ethnic backgrounds, although it was essentially a question of "strangers" who were perceived as "taking over" the neighborhood.

Two years after the sports center embroglio, simmering tensions with SoHo culminated in another confrontation. The occasion was a hearing held by the local planning board's traffic committee for the purpose of determining whether the residents of the district bounded by Broadway and Hudson Street and Houston and Canal Streets, would favor the erection of bus stop shelters in their area (the shelters had just been introduced in uptown shopping and office areas). While the whole matter seemed rather innocuous at first, it again raised the volatile question of communal boundaries, identity and control.

The glass bus stop shelters (one panel was actually a billboard generating revenues for the city) were proposed by a new South Village community organization, the Problem Center, which aspired to become the neighborhood's answer to the SoHo artists' Association. The shelters were a good promotion. The community broker

131

remained indifferent to the proposal and cool to the Problem Center although he sensed a rival.

The traffic committee narrowly approved the measure, although actual sites were not specified. However, a strident minority report contended that the structures were an "abomination" to the "historic SoHo and Charlton-Vandam districts". It maintained that the shelters were being foisted on the area by representatives of the Italian community, and that this did not repreent "community" opinion since Italians were a numerical minority *vis-a-vis* the inhabitants of SoHo and Charlton- Vandam and the planning board district generally. In fact, an Italian "neighborhood" was granted only "a couple of blocks", and even these, the report added, were not predominantly Italian. Therefore, it was recommended that a public hearing be held to give residents of SoHo and Charlton-Vandam the opportunity to repudiate the odious plan once and for all. In concluding, the report censured the directors of the Problem Center, two Italian men in their twenties, for their "rude" behavior before the traffic committee.

Still smarting from the sports center defeat, the community broker, who was chairman of the planning board at this time, was unnerved by the minority report. He had been suspicious of the shelters. which he regarded as a ploy by ambitious upstarts. Like the report, he had been critical of the Problem Center's directors, although he did not make this public, because their abrasiveness was an embarrassment to the entire Italian community. However, he was piqued by what he considered as the emasculation of the Italian community before the planning board. In particular, he was angry that the minority report reduced the Italian neighborhood to "just a few blocks", and that it regarded SoHo as the focal point of the South Village area. He also felt that upbraiding the spokesmen for the Problem Center was out of hand since it was a matter internal to the Italian community.

The bus stop shelter proposal had escalated into another confrontation between Italians and newcomers. The community broker looked toward the upcoming hearing, which was to have demonstrated the opposition of SoHo/Charlton-Vandam, as an opportunity to restore the sullied dignity of the Italian community. On a more personal level, it was also a chance to reassert his own political capabilities *vis-a-vis* SoHo and the Problem Center as well. In the intervening weeks, he contacted Italian organizations and civic leaders to muster support for the reckoning with SoHo and other detractors of the neighborhood. Most Italians seemed to need little prompting to be convinced that they were being "walked on again".

The hearing was scheduled to take place in a parish hall; this was a coup for the community broker since the familiar surroundings would probably buoy the confidence of Italians. However, at the urging of the community broker, the hearing was postponed for two weeks in deference to the parish feast. This was a symbolic victory, especially since criticism of the feast from the SoHo/Village community made it an issue in its own right which only added fuel to the fire (*See,* Chap. 11).

To be sure the feast was not especially popular in the neighborhood. For two weeks, the influx of "strangers" caused considerable havoc. The noise and the bright lights interfered with sleep; the garbage generated by the festivities left a stench that hung over the entire neighborhood for a week after the feast had run its course. Many Italians avoided the feast altogether. Nevertheless, it was a neighborhood institution and it did afford something of a contrast to the usual routine, despite the unpleasantness. Moreover, it provided needed revenues for the parish. The community broker especially objected to the charge that the Mafia was running the feast, although every Italian knew it had "a share of the action". Again, Italians bridled at the outside interference. The assault on their communal institutions and prerogative was becoming too much to bear. There was an air of agitation in the bars and club rooms.

In the two weeks before the hearing, Italian forces were rallying on two fronts. On its side, the Problem Center obtained letters of support from local civic organizations and politicians. Its strategy consisted of the submission of these letters in open session backed up by a contingent of vocal young cornerboys.

Meanwhile, the community broker was busy addressing himself to the purely political issue of whether anyone was going to tell Italians what to do in their own neighborhood. He planned to settle accounts with SoHo and other enemies. In the bargain, he was going to upstage and neutralize the Problem Center. Whereas the center obtained letters of support, he got politicians and civic leaders to attend the hearing. He also mobilized the obstreperous and occasionally intimidating middle-aged cornerboys attached to the Community Control Center, a members only club with civic pretensions.

There was excitement in the neighborhood on the evening of the hearing. A half hour before it was scheduled to start, the community broker could be seen circulating through the church hall, providing "his" speakers with pertinent information and coordinating his attack. When the person chairing the meeting noticed this, he half-seriously remarked, "You're supposed to be objective", in reference to the community broker's status on the planning board. In the same tone, the latter quickly rejoined, "Don't try to make a neutral out of me".

The traffic committee faced the hearing with understandable trepidation. Several times in the past, similar occasions were disrupted by angry Italians protesting an infringement on their communal sovereignty. Italians did not otherwise make their presence felt at public meetings. Even the community broker denounced this behavior. However, rowdiness may have been the only way to counter "the verbal skills and experience in handling meetings" available to middle class people (Feagin, 1974:58; Pahl, 1970:91).

Something similar could have developed this time. The hearing had been billed in the neighborhood as an opportunity to "get SoHo". As they walked over the the church hall, people invited others to come along for this explicit purpose. However, SoHo never really showed up. There were only two speakers opposed to the bus stop shelters; both were members of the traffic committee reponsible for the minority report. One was a SoHo artist, while the other was a media professional who lived in the North Village. In the audience, there were only Italians.

The opposition speakers presented their arguments first. They basically reiterated the points made in the inflammatory report. In the first place, the shelters were "simply lighted signs" bound to "pollute an historic district". The other reservation, perhaps too confidently articulated by the second speaker, maintained that the Italian neighborhood had been superseded by SoHo and Charlton-Vandam. The latter had a larger population and determined the character of the area. It was a mistake to assume that an organization representing the Italian community reflected the opinion of all the people in the district.

The first speaker departed immediately after his speech, taunted by Italians on both sides of the aisle that led to the exit. The other deliberately stood his ground as it was the Italians' turn to approach the microphone. The cultural argument was disposed of straight away by a young man from the Problem Center. Apologizing for not having the time to change out of his work clothes, he insisted that the shelters were not an "abomination", but were actually quite handsome. Moreover, it was not essentially a matter of aesthetics or history (*i.e.,* landmarks), but of practical service. He suggested that the shelters would obviate the need of having to wait in a doorway when it rained, which made one prey to muggers. The aesthetic argument was later given a real jolt when a Republican district leader considered it "amusing that these shelters can be found in Paris and Amsterdam, but they are too ugly for Wooster Street".

Except for blind endorsements by the two Italian assemblymen who had come out for the community broker, subsequent speakers became increasingly vituperative; the meeting degenerated into a personal battle between Italians and SoHo. A civic leader from the Mafia-linked storefront denegrated the artists' lofts as "filthy and dirty", he made a similar reference to their physical appearance employing categories left over from the hippie period. In contrast,

134

he called attention to the "spotless" homes in which Italians lived, a point that elicited wild support from the audience. The director of the Problem Center, going with the flow, criticized the art displayed in local galleries as "immoral". He noted that there was an irony in the charge that the shelters would desecrate an historic district; he contended that the neighborhood had been given a shabby look by the myriad posters advertising gallery openings, films, poetry readings and the like.

The fray stirred up communal passions. Through all of this, the opposition speaker who stayed in the hall remained riveted to his chair and said nothing for the rest of the night. A district leader evoked a pleasant and safe neighborhood "before SoHo". Respect was paid to their Italian heritage; the well-dressed salesman from the company that manufactured the shelters received an ovation when he cleverly admitted that he was "a paisan". A cornerboy solemnly acknowledged "this neighborhood which the Italians created".

It was generally agreed by Italians that SoHo was "too big for its boots". The excitable young director of the Problem Center was most militant about this. He bellowed that "SoHo is against everything we're for". He also warned the audience that "it's time we woke up and took the neighborhood back before it's too late". As the street corner came out in him, the traffic committee blanched.

The community broker was more tactful. He pointed out that he was not adverse to SoHo, but simply wanted to preserve the integrity of the Italian community. He was particularly upset that the minority report had reduced the neighborhood to "just a few blocks". He reminded those in the hall that the Italian community was still viable, politically and otherwise. In conclusion, he expressed his disappointment with the "ingratitude" of the SoHo community. Becoming a trifle dramatic, he asserted that "if we didn't support them, they wouldn't be a fact" (afterward, he specifically called attention to his support on the planning board for loft residence).

The hearing did not appear to have resolved the larger issue of relations with SoHo, despite the fact that the planning board approved the bus shelters. The victory was a hollow one. The bottom line was the disappearance of the Italian neighborhood. Although there were concrete differences with SoHo, the latter was being blamed for the fact that the South Village was becoming something other than an Italian neighborhood. At the hearing, then, it did not matter that the main opponent of the shelters neither lived in SoHo nor was an artist, nor that the SoHo Artists' Association had sent a qualified letter of support which was read at the hearing by the director of the Problem Center.

The hearing highlighted an emerging split within the Italian

135

community. As the principal sponsor of the bus stop shelters, the Problem Center purported to represent the South Village and had been recognized by the planning board and the SoHo Artists' Association. It had acquired a storefront and official letterhead, as well as a growing staff of energetic young people, many of whom were non-Italian newcomers. However, it did not have popular support in the Italian neighborhood and the community broker (and others) was going to make sure that it would not. After the blow dealt to SoHo, he turned his attention to the renegade director of the Center.

The upcoming Bicentennial celebration furnished an opportunity for the further crystallization of these currents. Into the month of June (1976), the Bicentennial had not been publicly acknowledged in the neighborhood. However, coincident with the bus stop shelter dispute, and while the parish feast was in progress, the Problem Center strung flags and banners from fire escapes in honor of the national event. It was a promotion device, intended to call attention to the Center and attract supporters. The Center also sponsored a fireworks display, a favorite with cornerboys at this time of the year (the sale of illegal fireworks was traditionally a source of income for cornerboy entrepreneurs). If the promotion was unsuccessful, the Center, hurting for funds, would at least go down in a great gesture; this reflected the cornerboy influence in the organization which ultimately alienated middle class staff members.

The Problem Center had decorated only two adjacent blocks with banners and flags, either because it ran out of money or because the rest of the neighborhood was not cooperative. However, two weeks later (one week after the bus stop hearing), almost the entire South Village was festooned with Bicentennial banners. On the surface, they appeared to be an extension of the earlier project initiated by the Center. Instead, they turned out to be the work of the community broker. These new banners had a twofold purpose. First, they symbolically restaked the Italian community's historical claim to the South Village. Second, they were intended to upstage the Problem Center's display.

The project orchestrated by the community broker was a neighborhood enterprise that was deliberately intended to stimulate communal solidarity. He solicited the participation of cornerboys and organizations. The Mafia also backed the effort. The latter donated money and strung banners from horse rooms.

Each block was mainly responsible for hanging, as well as financing, its own flags. When one block was unable to generate enough money, costs were subsidized from the general collection. Although there were reservations about sharing with another block, the community broker pointed out the importance of the entire neighborhood "making good". He was genuinely pleased with the degree of cooperation in the project, since it was unusual. He also felt that it redounded to his credit, which it did.

The flags were not the same as those hung by the Problem Center. The tiny vinyl flags put up by the latter were red, white and blue. The ones procured by the community broker were red, white and green—the colors of the Italian flag. In each case, strings of smaller flags were dominated by a large banner as the centerpiece of each display. The Center's banner carried a message proclaiming "Greenwich Village...A Cradle of Democracy". The community broker's banner read 'Happy Birthday America From the South Village Italian Community and Its Friends". Moreover, the community broker decorated blocks that were no longer predominantly Italian. Besides the area south of Houston Street, banners appeared as far as West Third Street. It did the community broker's heart good to see the old neighborhood take shape again under the flags and banners; he was especially delighted to see a banner suspended over a Bleecker Street cafe which Italians tried to close in the early sixties.

The young director of the Problem Center was duly impressed with the community broker's organizational acumen. As a cornerboy, his personal inclination was to be chauvinistic about the neighborhood. He had been given a lesson by a veteran. However, both men looked bad when the banners were left hanging through the winter, giving the neighborhood a seedy character, which many artists and other newcomers, who considered the whole project tacky from the very beginning, did not fail to notice.

The Problem Center

The Problem Center was founded in 1974 by a young Italian man and some neighborhood friends. As an "activist neighborhood association", it proposed to serve residents of the area bounded by Houston and Canal Streets, Sixth Avenue and West Broadway. In contrast to the old practice of ceding initiative to local leaders, it sought to engender civic participation on a broad scale and bring the South Village within the mainstream of urban resource distribution (Cloward and Piven, 1975:316).

The beginning of the Problem Center came with an unprecedented rash of apartment burglaries and, to a lesser extent, muggings and hold-ups. People were agitated; there was a pervasive sense of physical insecurity, compounded by the realization that communal institutions were eroding. There was no organized response until a meeting was anonymously called to discuss remedies for the crime problem. The meeting had been arranged by the young man who was

137

to become the director of the Problem Center. It was held in the hall of the old German parish on West Broadway; as with other community meetings, this gave the gathering legitimacy, as did the presence of the parish pastor who began the meeting with a benediction and introduced the soon-to-be director. The two hundred or so people in the hall were predominantly Italian, and they seemed to know, or know of, the young man who organized the meeting; in a short biography, he noted that he lived in the neighborhood all his life. He spoke informally and acknowledged a great many people in the audience. He proceeded to detail the events that comprised the local crime wave, and turned the meeting over to a liason from the police precinct who recommended methods of securing apartments against burglars. The pastor closed the meeting with a prayer; people seemed relieved by merely coming together.

Two weeks later, another meeting was called to assess interim developments. Already, the number of break- ins and other crimes reported to the local precinct had substantially declined. Probably as a result, fewer people attended than at the previous meeting. Nevertheless, they were informed by the young man who seemed to be running things that a community-wide organization representing the South Village had coalesced. Its agenda, moreover, would be much broader than mere block-watching.

The organization was to be premised on a "militant attitude" toward rights that South Village residents were entitled to, but were not receiving, largely because of their leaders' complacency and their own apathy. The organization would "go after" money and services that federal, state and municipal governments were diverting to more outspoken groups. It would activate the neighborhood's electoral potential, sponsoring voter registration drives and endorsing candidates for local office. Its storefront operation would mediate between landlords and tenants, with a view toward remedying housing abuses and would institute job programs for young people and provide free legal advice for persons with an income of less than $7,000. The director asserted that the Center would try to obtain subsidized housing for the South Village, similar to the units proposed for Little Italy. The Italian audience cheered the organization's ambitious agenda, but the feeling was one of "wait and see".

The director adumbrated a redefinition of community along locality lines; the Problem Center would be responsive to all groups in the South Village, not just Italians. Its posters were printed in Portuguese, Italian and English; the director noted that he was "in touch" with the Portuguese community, although the Portuguese were conspicuously absent at both meetings. In particular, the Center appeared to be a vehicle for the integration of young newcomers; heretofore, there was little or no common ground with "clannish"

138

Italians. Their presence at the meetings was conspicuous. They participated in the discussion and volunteered for important staff positions. It appeared that they would be the backbone of the "activist community organization"; a law student, a tax lawyer and a social worker were among the early disciples. In addition to the director and several lieutenants, the major input from the Italian community were young cornerboys who formed a civilian patrol, a rationalization for and a legitimation of "busting heads".

Despite the purported inclusiveness of the organization, the director began acting as if the Center was an Italian organization. He seemed to be singling out the Italian community for support and legitimation. He assured the audience, "We're common people; we all know each other". He called attention to the fact that his family "has always lived in the neighborhood", and introduced his mother, who was sitting in the audience with a broad smile, as if to verify his claim. He spoke of his youth when "this neighborhood used to be great" and insisted that "we can make it great again". He paid his respects to the Italian leadership, that is, the community broker, the local assemblymen, church pastors and, in a roundabout way, the Mafia.

In the promise of the moment, the fact that the neighborhood power structure had not been heard from was suddenly apparent; the director felt obliged to announce that the community broker had to attend another meeting. In fact, there were very few men present; cornerboys and club members with other allegiances had stayed away.

Non-Italians, including those who had volunteered for staff positions and were now sitting at the front of the hall with the director, were becoming visibly uncomfortable. They downright bristled when the director, getting carried away, proposed that the organization be named *Avanti,* (meaning forward) and began referring to the South Village as "Little Italy West". Several non-Italians immediately objected that this excluded anyone who was not of Italian descent. One man stated that he felt "misled" by the organization's original posture. Interestingly, Italians supported their contention that "We're Americans, not Italians", an observation with which everyone heartily concurred. The director conceded to the ethnically neutral title, although this was clearly a portent for non-Italians.

Despite earlier claims and the fact that the sinews of an activist community association were the educated, middle class newcomers, it was apparent that the Problem Center was primarily addressed to the Italian community. This intent was spelled out in a series of articles that appeared in a new SoHo weekly whose publication also coincided with the crime problem (the column was designed to further understanding between artists and Italians). They were

139

written by two young, college educated, non-Italian women (apparently with the collaboration of the director of the Center) who had recently moved to the South Village.The imagery conveyed by the newletters naively romanticized the beleagured Italian community:

> *We relaxed our vigilence. For many years, our neigh-*
> *borhood was the safest in New York City. People sat*
> *outdoors while children played, we had large community*
> *gatherings, excursions for young people, jubilant feast*
> *days. We didn't have to lock our doors, and we were safe in*
> *the street after dark.*

However, crime and the general drift of American culture undermined the ethnic *gemeinschaft.* One of the newsletters observed:

> *Now, as we know too well, times have changed and modern*
> *American culture is quickly moving farther from the*
> *traditions we grew up in. The Italian American community*
> *has traditionally been family oriented, unified and alert to*
> *community problems. In the past few years, as New York*
> *fell apart and started to rot, and the whole country seemed*
> *to abandon moral standards, we in the neighborhood*
> *have allowed ourselves to be part of the decay.*

Just when they thought they had found an explanation for the anomie and atomism of modern society, these young women from middle class backgrounds discovered that the Italian neighborhood had its problems too.

Despite this note of crisis, there was a possibility of moral regeneration "if we wrest our community from those destroying it and make it our own once more". An example of the destructive forces that had to be extirpated were "the numerous methadone clinics shoved on us by the North Village and the planning boards". It discerned in the reaction to the crime problem and the number of people who attended the first meeting "a sudden community coalescence, a sharp awareness of the urgent need for unified action". The new Problem Center would be a vehicle for the restoration of the old neighborhood.

Putting ideology aside, the Center took on the crime wave in deliberate fashion. It articulated a number of grievances, and organized community energies to exert pressure on the appropriate authorities. It petitioned the local precinct for better police protection and formed civilian block-watcher cadres. The director informed residents about buzzer and intercom systems, noting that landlords had to comply with these safety measures under the law. The Center also took on a methadone clinic and a seedy topless bar which were isolated as trouble spots. When it learned that none of the addicts treated at the clinic were from the immediate area, it pressured the city to reduce its treatment load and subsequently relocate the clinic. The Center notified the State Liquor Authority of violations which caused the bar to close for a period of time. Its efforts paralleled those of the SoHo Artists Association and there was even a measure of cooperation between the two. The new SoHo weekly sensed that the crime problem "dissolved the dense cultural barrier between SoHo and its neighbor to the west". "Ironically, but predictably", according to its editorial, crime had become "an effective unifying force between the artists and Italian Americans who principally comprise the community". A manifestation of this unity was the regular column for the Problem Center's newsletter.

While the Problem Center was busy following this strategy, another effort to solve the crime problem was underway. It was organized by the community broker along the usual "neighborhood" lines.

Shortly after the first meeting held by the Center, the community broker arranged his own meeting in the basement of the old Italian church. The audience was composed entirely of Italians; the meeting was chaired by a spokesperson for one of the members only clubs. There were several notables from the Italian community present, including the community broker; the director of the Problem Center was in attendance, although no one paid him any heed.

The tenor of the meeting was in marked contrast to the sessions held by both the Problem Center and the SAA. This was a conclave of cornerboys. The audience was agitated and the proceedings were chaotic. Someone blurted out that "some of the boys" would be on the lookout with baseball bats, the traditional symbol of neighborhood order. The consensus was that the men on the street would not hesitate to take matters into their own hands if the situation called for it, and they seemed hopeful that it would. Several persons put the crime problem in a racial perspective.

The ambiance was captured by the editors of the new SoHo weekly who covered the meeting. They were highly critical of the conclave; in particular, they were aghast at "the cries to restore the death penalty, to lock up 'these animals' and to restore police foot patrols". They noted the contrast with the more sensible meetings held by the SAA and the Problem Center. Their editorial concluded that "crime will be prevented by the cooperation of residents in a reasonable, nonviolent manner".

Typically, the meeting was just "window dressing" and a chance for the neighborhood to discharge some of its anxiety. The community broker and representatives from the clubs had actually orchestrated a solution to the crime problem prior to the meeting in the church basement. That afternoon, they met with the precinct captain

141

who pledged twenty-five additional foot patrolmen, the majority of whom would be plainsclothesmen. They informed the captain that heightened vigilance on the part of the cornerboys would be forthcoming.

The agreement could not be divulged, presumably because it was difficult to justify an increase in police manpower in a relatively low crime area when the city was in the middle of a fiscal crisis (1975). The precinct captain, who spoke informally with the community broker and cornerboys, tried to reassure the audience that something was being worked out in conjunction with community leaders. Taking his leave, the captain requested that Italians leave enforcement matters to the police.

When the number of break-ins and muggings declined, and a few perpetrators had been apprehended by the police, the community broker regarded the whole business as a feather in his cap. He scoffed at the efforts of the Problem Center (and the SAA)—times like this demanded someone who "knows where to go to get something done". The directors of the Problem Center suggested at a subsequent Center meeting that efforts initiated by his organization were responsible for the abatement of crime. This became a problem for the director when it got back to the community broker and the clubs.

As the crime wave receded, the Problem Center struggled to maintain a constituency. Whereas over two hundred families paid membership dues of two dollars the first year, subscriptions were practically halved the following year. The storefront operation was received with little enthusiasm in the neighborhood. Highly motivated staff workers waited around with nothing substantial to do. Only a handful of people attended community meetings, which were eventually terminated.

There were several reasons for the organization's decline. One factor, acknowledged by the director himself, was a disinclination to accept assistance outside the circle of primary relationships. This was especially true of the elderly. Some of them spoke of their monthly social security pittance as if it was not deserved. Many were reluctant to subscribe to Medicare and only began to utilize the program when they heard others were doing so. The storefront experienced difficulty signing people up for food stamps and dispensing mass transit discount cards for senior citizens. Since the storefront was right in the neighborhood, people who would otherwise seek assistance were afraid that "everybody would know their business".

It was questionable whether there was a great demand for the Center's services in the first place. Perhaps most people had sufficient private resources, or thought they did, or else were receiving an adequate measure of assistance from government transfers. The churches and settlement houses sponsored various institutional services for the elderly. Neighbors still comprised informal networks of support; a woman whose apartment was damaged in a fire received over $1,000 from people in the neighborhood.

There were already problem-solving mechanisms at the communal level for matters of concern like crime. Moreover, Italians had little trust in the activist politics advocated by the Problem Center. In temperament, they were in accord with the style of the traditional "leader" who had connections and discretely negotiated results. This betrayed a reluctance to "rock the boat"; while people may have telephoned the storefront about a lack of heat, they would not divulge their identity or file a complaint. They were afraid that their rents might go up, or that they might be evicted, despite assurances that they had certain rights as tenants. When a young Italian American who was active in civic affairs organized a rent strike in his building with a Legal Aid lawyer he was called a communist and asked whether he was "sending the rent money", being held in escrow, "to Moscow".

These attitudes completely baffled and frustrated non-Italian staff workers. One complained that Italians had a "lack of convictions" to effect the changes envisaged by the Center. A young woman who lived in the South Village for just a few months resented "working long hours without cooperation".

The Problem Center might have been accepted by the neighborhood over the long run. However, it was never able to overcome the fundamental tension that inhered in its hybrid nature. It never clearly defined its constituency, at bottom, the director desired an Italian community organization that would somehow restore the "old neighborhood", while middle class staff members had a broader concept in mind (*i.e.,* a community that included themselves). It confounded community activism with cornerboy expressiveness (the contradiction was embodied in the director himself). The decisive moment came when the director ran afoul of the neighborhood power structure, including the community broker and the head of a storefront with syndicate ties. When the director of the Problem Center took credit for solving the crime problem and, in general was making "too much noise", he was paid a visit by some of the "fellows from the club" who ostensibly "straightened things out". From then on the director was hardly enthusiastic about the role the Problem Center was to play in the South Village. The neighborhood power structure had checked the director's personal ambitions as well as the activist orientation of the organization, which was bypassing existing communal controls and gave a significant role to "strangers".

143

The alienation of educated newcomers was a decisive blow to the Problem Center since they possessed the technical know- how to broker the service bureaucracies. However, they became disgruntled by the director's political maneuverings and the organization's essentially "neighborhood" orientation. The last newcomer to defect was a young black artist who saw the Center as an opportunity to ingratiate himself with Italians, since he had been living in the neighborhood "very precariously". He finally withdrew after the display of "tribalism and clannishness" at the bus stop shelter hearing; although he presented a feasibility study for the shelters, the hearing convinced him that the term "neighborhood" did not include "anybody who wasn't Italian and lived here for more than thirty years".

The Problem Center, then, was unable to resolve its fundamental contradictions, and lost its initial promise. It did not serve as a vehicle for the fraternization of Italian and middle class newcomers, or Portuguese immigrants for that matter. In fact, it seemed to have aggravated class-cultural differences. A disappointed staff member concluded that her experience with the Center confirmed a negative stereotype of Italians in the culture. As staff members fell away, the Center became a vehicle for cornerboy self-expression, although it always had this significance for the director and other young men from the neighborhood. The ramshackle storefront became a place of exile for the director and a hangout for street kids.

The Center would have closed but for a timely youth gang problem in the Village. For a number of years, Italian teenagers allegedly harassed homosexuals and passersby in the West Village and, more recently, artists in the Westbeth housing complex. When an actor who lived in the Village was killed in an altercation with neighborhood teenagers, the local planning board suggested that the Problem Center play a role in the solution of the juvenile problem. With the summer imminent, the Center was to function as an employment exchange for local youth, with jobs furnished by local businessmen. The Center was also holding out for a grant from the New York City Youth Board for a facility and a director's salary amounting to $8,000. A real estate management company that operated the Westbeth complex donated $3,000 to keep the storefront open, although $1,000 of this was spent on the Bicentennial display and fireworks to the displeasure of middle class staff members.

It was at this time that the Center became the focus of an article on the South Village by a freelance writer for *The New Yorker* magazine (Harris, 1977). The article went on about the essential value of a neighborhood community like the South Village, and the need to preserve such a communal form in the face of large-scale urbanism. It followed the Problem Center's attempt to initiate a program of community self-help, which was depicted as a preferential method for dealing with local problems, especially since government was

144

indifferent or incompetent. The author was apparently unaware of issues relating to the Center's legitimacy or the fact that it was itself a symptom of the eclipse of a more traditional form of community.

Although the publicity was welcome, outside support was not forthcoming. The New York City Youth Board grant did not materialize. Perhaps the denouement was when a summer job program was given to a local parish and a rival "civic organization", with syndicate ties, largely through the efforts of the community broker. That summer, the director settled for running a federal CETA sponsored youth program at the old German parish.

In the late fall, the storefront had its gas and electric, as well as its telephone service, shut off because it had stopped paying the bills. With the rent three months overdue, the landlord had the Center evicted. There seem to have been bad feelings because the storefront's windows were smashed (in cornerboy fashion) on two separate occasions following the eviction. By the summer, the storefront had given way to a boutique, the kind that the director charged "made the area expensive and drove out the little family shopkeepers". The boutique was paying four times the rent paid by the Problem Center.

When the storefront closed, the director warned that he was "not out of the picture". With some supporters from the Italian community he established a "political organization" that was to be an alternative to the middle class reform clubs in the Village and SoHo. Their flyer announced, with clumsy phrases and misspellings, that they were going to "run somebody for office", presumably the director. However, it did not have one noteworthy endorsement.

The organization was not heard from after this time. The Problem Center had signified a new political development for the South Village by aspiring to become a pressure group that could extract benefits from public bureaucracies and politicians. This was important given the "decline of the machine" and the accession of new groups to power in the district. However, community action never really materialized because the organization was mired in neighborhood provincialism (*e.g.,* streetcorner expressiveness, a disdain for the politics of group advocacy, factionalism). The neighborhood's political structure remained essentially unchanged, although the ability of leaders to perform special services for constituents is increasingly limited *vis-a-vis* "a complex and bureaucratic government" (Cloward and Piven, 1975:80), and a power shift related to the influx of middle class residents. As their power wanes, some neighborhood leaders have shown a preoccupation with the symbolic aspects of their position, perhaps to console themselves for their loss of power, although they are unmistakably fading from the scene. Others, most notably the state assemblyman from the 64th

A.D., have successfully adapted by becoming aligned with new constituencies.

The Mafia:
Adjusting to a New Setting

*L*ike other neighborhood institutions, the Mafia has been affected by social change. The importance of neighborhood racketeering has progressively diminished with the cultivation of more profitable, and often legal, ventures in the larger society. There has been an erosion of demand for ilicit syndicate services in the neighborhood with the ongoing replacement of the lower class population. Nevertheless, the Mafia has found ways to adjust and even solidify its presence in the South Village.

Economic Operations

Prohibition was perhaps the signal event for the entrance on any large scale of Italian crime families into areas of profit outside the ethnic economy. This trend has intensified since World War II. Major areas of involvement have been land development, counterfeiting and theft of stocks and bonds, labor racketeering, pornography, arson and drug distribution. Within this broader trend has been the penetration of legitimate businesses where profits from illegal activities are laundered. This has brought the Mafia into enterprises ranging from construction and trucking companies to real estate firms and hotels. As the interests of syndicate organizations have become increasingly diversified, they have also spread out over a wider geographical area. Like corporate executives, personnel are transferred to other parts of the country where the syndicate conducts business.

These developments rendered the neighborhood a backwater of syndicate operations. A neighborhood like the South Village held diminished interest in light of opportunities elsewhere. Revenues yielded by traditional rackets such as gambling and loansharking eroded with the contraction of a lower class clientele (not only neighborhood Italians but workers in local factories). There was no demand for these services among the new middle class residents. Also, legalized gambling and the institution of the state lottery siphoned business away from the bookies. An offtrack betting parlor, taking bets on harness racing and the flats, is a leisurely five minute stroll from one of the syndicate club rooms. As a result, the number of bookies working the neighborhood has been considerably reduced, although they still have a monopoly on numbers and professional and college sports. Similarly, there is also a smaller market for stolen goods although neighborhood Italians still favor these purchases when available. Moreover, this operation has been given a legitimate aspect in the form of a retail outlet which is reputed to make stolen merchandise available to the general public.

Accompanying the shift of syndicate interests from the Italian neighborhood has been the flight of syndicate personnel to better residential areas; after all, organized crime has been a "ladder of mobility" (Bell, 1961). They have moved to bedroom suburbs in New Jersey and Long Island where their children attend the local high schools and their wives keep lovely homes. To their new neighbors, they are known as businessmen who commute to jobs in the city. There are only occasional problems, as when a local Mafioso tried to bribe the police captain in his affluent suburban town. Other Mafiosi have moved to middle class sections of Brooklyn and Staten Island that are predominantly inhabited by Italian Americans. In some of these second settlements, local networks of control and profit-making have been recreated; in a neighborhood of one and two family homes in Brooklyn, the Mafia is said to screen home buyers via influence in the local real estate industry.

Some syndicate personnel have stayed in the area. One Mafia chieftain lives in a modern apartment building and another in a townhouse. Lower level personnel have remained, perhaps because they tend to be immersed in a free-spending economy and many are unmarried. Moreover, in the neighborhood, hanging around the horse room, they are "somebody". One loanshark, who was divorced from his wife and had moved back with his mother, still is able to swagger and intimidate the men on the corner. Like other neighborhood Italians, these syndicate workers are simply too embedded in neighborhood life to live elsewhere.

Despite the decline of former rackets, the neighborhood still serves as syndicate headquarters; their new suburban neighborhoods are inappropriate for gatherings of Mafiosi. As a result, members only clubs are maintained as board rooms for syndicate "big shots". One Mafioso commutes to his "office" from the suburbs. From time to time, meetings are convened; shiny new automobiles with New Jersey license plates are parked out front, although one club maintains parking spaces in a vacant lot for visiting dignitaries. On

148

these occasions, the neighborhood buzzes with interest and speculation. Of course, the neighborhood continues to afford syndicate
conclaves the requisite anonymity.

After 1971, Mafia interest in the South Village from an economic
standpoint was resuscitated. However, the impetus had nothing to
do with the Italian community, but with SoHo. When loft residence
was legalized in 1971, real estate conversion and new business
activity had turned around the local economy. The beneficial effects
had spilled over to the South Village. To be sure, traditional syndicate
services were of little value to the artists' community. However, the
precipitous rise in real estate values created new opportunities for
wealth. Once syndicate interest perceived the implications of SoHo
for local real estate, they began acquiring property in the neighborhood (as with other Italians, comprehending the SoHo phenomenon
seems to have taken some time). The Mafia was accruing a stake in
the disappearance of the Italian neighborhood.

Within a short time, a general offer to buy any residential and commercial property was circulated and syndicate agents armed with
ample cash told landlords to contact interested parties when they
decided to sell. In three years, seven or eight properties were purchased in the South Village. Commercial properties were bought
and converted into modern rental units. Tenements were also submitted to renovation. Renovated apartments reflected the new rent
structure effected by SoHo. The new tenants in syndicate buildings
or renovated apartments were middle class newcomers.

The Mafia did not coerce landlords to sell, nor did it intimidate
Italians into giving up rent controlled apartments which could be
renovated into more expensive units. Intimidation of this sort was
practiced by one landlord who owned a string of buildings in the
neighborhood with several other investors, precipitating a rent
strike in one of the buildings. Instead, new syndicate owners waited
for Italian tenants to vacate.

Mafia interests have been decidedly more ruthless with commercial properties. The owners of a neighborhood candystore were
notified that their lease would not be renewed after being there 30
years. A local bar was forced to move to another site when its rent
was quadrupled. The owner of a butcher shop was sent to a pre-
mature retirement when his rent was raised to a prohibitive level. In
these cases, the new occupants were businesses catering to the
SoHo community. When a building housing a groundfloor jewelry
shop was purchased by syndicate interests, the proprietor was
harassed in order to persuade him to give up his lease that had eight
years to run; the windows of the store were broken and when a
metal gate was erected as protection, glue was inserted into the
lock fastening the gate closed. Italians were upset about these
tactics, especially since the closing of establishments like a candy-

store meant that another piece of community had been broken off. However, complaints were predictably muffled.

SoHo opened up economic opportunities for the Mafia in other areas as well. Several of the ground floor stores were retained by syndicate interests themselves for business purposes now that the neighborhood was bustling once again. Two Italian cafes were opened intended largely for the tourist clientele drawn to local galleries and boutiques. The prices of the black coffee and the pastry did not have neighborhood Italians in mind, who still preferred luncheonettes and taverns. Syndicate interests also opened a bar which tried to replicate the atmosphere of a SoHo establishment with its hanging plants, wood floors and exposed brick, and sandwiches on pita bread. A kind of general store was opened, selling everything from shampoo to children's toys, merchandise that may have been stolen.

In a more familiar vein, it is possible that the syndicate has enacted various considerations from SoHo businesses. In particular, it may be demanding protection money, at least from the restaurants and boutiques if not from the galleries. Restaurants and other establishments may also have been imposed upon to deal with syndicate concerns. One fashionable SoHo restaurant was reputed to have been involved in this manner. If broken storefront windows were any indication, this was a more general phenomenon.

Local Control

The Mafia seems to be less of a force in formal Village politics. Syndicate influence has receded *vis-a-vis* middle class civic activity based on the airing of myriad local interests within the community planning board (traditionally, "mafia" was premised on a political vacuum). This has not necessarily been a setback, since the declining significance of local rackets removed a pressing need for political protection at the district level. Still, in the district extending over to the east side, there has been little organizational change through the years, although SoHo now portends a threat of reform.

Regardless of its role in district level politics, the Mafia retains significant influence within the Italian neighborhood, which has traditionally comprised a separate jurisdiction as far as most Italians and Villagers are concerned. This is reflected in the fact that syndicate associates are still garrisoned locally, although their ranks have been depleted. This includes several who are alleged to be highly placed in the syndicate hierarchy. Only one of them is especially visible since he personally supervises a horse room and other interests in the neighborhood. From time to time, conclaves attract

150

other "big shots" to local club rooms. As in the past, these notables make their presence felt; their comings and goings are events to the men on the corner and the women in grocery stores.

The Mafia's influence in the neighborhood continues to hinge on its business operations. It exercises control out of a vested interest in market peace. Although the volume from rackets like gambling and loansharking diminished and only a few horse rooms remain open, there are still operations to protect. SoHo afforded new opportunities for profit and the basis for a new interest in neighborhood affairs.

Mafia rule in the neighborhood continues to take traditional forms. Individuals are called down to syndicate courts for gambling debts and other transgressions. Justice is still meted out to those who cross the organization as when one man who supposedly owed the syndicate money "fell" from a tenement roof. Syndicate personnel throw their weight around on the corner. In general, the atmosphere of intimidation remains; cornerboys have to avoid displeasing syndicate personnel. There is still a desire to deflect attention from syndicate operations, as well as the broader responsibility of policing the neighborhood. It was in this spirit that warnings, "not to act up", were issued to a clique of young Italian men who were notorious troublemakers. The "members only" club/horse rooms remain command posts that keep an eye out for troublemakers, a fact that still elicits the approval of Italians.

In recent years, there have been uncharacteristic manifestations of Mafia influence and control in the South Village. In 1969, a chapter of the Italian American Civil Rights League was established in the neighborhood. The principal aim of the League was the removal of prejudice and discrimination against Italians, particularly the stereotypes propagated by the media. It sought to raise ethnic consciousness, drawing on the ideology of the nascent white ethnic movement, as the basis of political solidarity. The League's slogan became "We are #1"; its green, white and red decals appeared on apartment windows, storefronts and automobile bumpers. In an impassioned speech, the president of the League warned that "it's time that the Italian Americans woke up and demanded what's rightfully theirs" (Weed, 1973:50). The organization's ethnic assertiveness and manipulation of the media was resonant of the Black Power Movement, despite the fact that ethnics often found themselves in conflict with the claims of racial minorities.

Although not publicly acknowledged, the League was a syndicate project; its founder and president was the head of a Brooklyn crime family. It was no coincidence, then, that so much ire was directed at the gangster image; League officers constantly complained of unwarranted F.B.I. harassment. Pressure by the League eventually resulted in a decision by the Nixon administration to expunge the word "Mafia" from official federal pronouncements; the implication was that there was no such organization.

The League was supported by other New York crime families who mandated chapters in their respective territories. The Greenwich Village chapter was estimated to have had some 500 dues paying members. The substantial membership was reputedly the result of syndicate pressure on cornerboys; neighborhood Italians were less than enthusiastic about the League in light of its affiliations, although there was popular support for Italian solidarity in principle. The crowning moment for the South Village chapter, and the League, was its participation in the 1970 "Unity Day" rally at Columbus Circle. It sent a large delegation in rented buses; neighborhood people were encouraged to attend and merchants were pressured to display Unity Day placards and close their shops on the afternoon of the rally. However, Unity Day saw the League dissolve in ignominy when an assasination attempt was made on its president and founder. Ironically, it was attributed to a dispute between rival crime families.

The defunct League chapter gave rise to a storefront community organization headed by the former chapter president who was reputed to have syndicate ties. The storefront purported to represent the Italian community in Village and city politics. Its director and several aides attended civic meetings, usually to take umbrage at developments believed to be harmful to neighborhood welfare (*e.g.,* the transient hotels). In reality, the storefront was a members only club with a bar and tables for card games and a place where cornerboys could bet on numbers. The director, who ran the club, had a reputation for having "friends" and being a "tough guy". His inflamed speeches at planning board meetings were an embarrassment to other Italian leaders. Nevertheless, the organization was taken seriously outside the Italian community. For several years, it distributed jobs and free lunches as part of a government sponsored Summer Youth Corps program although people in the neighborhood accused the director of giving jobs to his friends' children, as well as falsifying the need for free lunches.

Another local horse room assumed an enlightened civic role. It referred to itself as the Neighborhood Control Center, even though "Members Only" was stencilled on its storefront window, which was coated with thick black paint reinforcing the impression that the premises were off limits. Occasionally, a contingent left the club to attend community meetings and forcefully articulate a provincial point of view. A delegation from the center, accompanied by a top syndicate leader, once disrupted a City Council hearing for a proposed construction of a women's detention complex in the South Village. Members spoke out of turn and stomped folding chairs; when the councilwoman chairing the hearing noted that residents of the city had to assume responsibility for the rehabilitation of deviants, they sent back the stock reply "we take care of our own". Their unruly behavior brought about the postponement of the hearing and eventually the complex was not built in the South Village.

The center took an active part in dealing with the recent crime wave. A meeting held in the church basement was chaired by the president of the center, flanked by members in good standing. After reassuring the people in attendance that his cornerboys would be more vigilant, he introduced the precinct captain, who referred to the president by his first name. The Neighborhood Control Center became involved in other issues as well. For example, it endorsed the Sports Center, along with the Knights of Columbus, the two parish churches and a local assemblyman. The center was also a major supporter of the community broker. Notwithstanding its civic pretensions, however, Italians perceived the center as "the horse room".

Mafia influence could be seen in another direction. It applied pressure to stifle the Problem Center, the activist community organization that sought to integrate the South Village with an array of bureaucratic institutions offering various "program benefits". Interests in the syndicate were opposed to such politics, apparently because it undermined the neighborhood's low profile. Moreover, the Problem Center had made a power play by criticizing South Village leaders who "let the community down". The horse room that ran the Summer Youth Program was especially threatened since the new organization aspired to become a clearinghouse for all types of services. Established neighborhood leadership may also have been anxious over the role that middle class newcomers were playing through the Problem Center. It was not long, then, before the director of the Problem Center was informed that he was out of line. Its wings clipped, the Problem Center further alienated the middle class newcomers who were the backbone of community activism. With its founders isolated, both from the neighborhood leadership and middle class newcomers, the community organization atrophied.

The Mafia and the Middle Class

The Mafia was culturally compatible with the Italian community; it was comprehensible as a pattern of social relationships and as a state of mind (Ianni, 1972:46-47). Although it imposed a tyranny, the Mafia did provide an order within the Italian neighborhood and satisfied a demand for goods and services that were not otherwise

153

obtainable. However, the middle class and artists who were replacing the Italians in the South Village did not appear to have the need for social mediation (Ianni, 1972:47). Moreover, their cultural backgrounds and political socializations were not compatible with the idea or concept of "mafia" and its role as an invisible government. Newcomers privately criticized the Mafia on moral grounds. This surfaced when the parish feast was attacked in a community newspaper and in planning board circles as a Mafia racket.

For the most part, however, the Mafia and the middle class have effected a comfortable symbiosis. There are no tensions apart from the feast issue, which never really amounted to much. Most newcomers are not directly or fully apprised of Mafia activities in the neighborhood. With their middle class backgrounds, they are not cognizant of members only clubs or syndicate headquarters. They are unable to recognize a bookie or a loanshark; many newcomers find it perplexing that certain men are on the street all the time. they are not tuned in to the grapevine which carries news about local syndicate developments. It is possible that, given the Mafia's reputation, they prefer remaining ignorant and occupied with other matters. As long as they mind their own business, the Mafia will not complain. Neighborhood Italians mind their own business, but they know.

Even though newcomers have no use for loansharks and bookies, they have figured in syndicate business interests. They are the unwitting patrons of syndicate-owned cafes and restaurants. They are also the reason syndicate interest bought apartment buildings in the neighborhood; newcomers did not question the high rents in renovated units. Middle class newcomers have made local Mafiosi businessmen and landlords. The syndicate, then, had no reason to oppose the changes in the neighborhood.

Only vaguely aware, newcomers are able to derive certain benefits from the Mafia presence in the neighborhood. Above all, there is the feeling that "the Mafia keeps the neighborhood safe". This assumption has been a motive for their settling in the Italian neighborhood in the first place; newcomers refuse to believe that the Mafia would allow the recent spate of apartment burglaries. Moreover, rumors generated about the Mafia add color to the neighborhood.

Conclusion

Like other community institutions, the local Mafia syndicate has not been immune to change. The movement to the suburbs, the decline of industry and the expansion of SoHo resulted in a lower demand for traditional syndicate services like gambling and loan-sharking. At the same time, however, the syndicate has been cultivating involvements outside the ethnic neighborhood; thus, the scale and significance of local operations diminished, although the old neighborhood apparently continues to serve as a base for the administration of wider syndicate operations.

SoHo has altered this scenario. It afforded investment opportunities in legitimate enterprises.More than any other communal institutions, the Mafia has a vested interest in SoHo. Its role is more inconspicuous than it has been in the Italian community, where it is a more integral part of the underlying cultural fabric. Even in SoHo, however, the Mafia syndicate is capable of traditional methods of exploitation *vis-a-vis* the local economy. It is difficult to determine how far this has gone. Nevertheless, it would appear that SoHo will have to come to terms with syndicate practices.

Another Look
at the Italian Neighborhood

*a*s far as the South Village is concerned, the categories employed for an understanding of the ethnic neighborhood are inappropriate. The South Village cannot be reduced to a "staging ground" or "decompression chamber" for the processing of immigrants into the larger society. These metaphors reflect an assimilationist bias in American social science (Greely, 1972:2; Blauner, 1972:6; Lyman, 1974:186-191). They do not allow for the presistence and restructuring of the South Village Italian community in the period following World War I. The South Village did not become "disorganized" as a result of "Americanizing pressures" (Ware, 1965), nor has it persisted as a residue of the original immigrant settlement—as a haven for ethnics who failed to make it (Lopreato, 1970:46; Nelli, 1970:44-45) or an Old World enclave (Wallace, 1977:129-138; Queen and Carpenter, 1972:145). Social and cultural changes issued in a new ethnic communal form *vis-a-vis* the immigrant colony with its paesani frameworks (itself a communal adaptation to the city). Traditional institutions and values remained substantially intact and articulated with urban institutions (*e.g.,* the intervention of the family via mothers' clubs in settlement house programs). Slum social structures crystallized in place of immigrant frameworks; a new communal organization included streetcorner groups, machine politics, the urban gang and the defended neighborhood, although each had a precedent in Italian peasant culture (*dolce far niente, clientelismo,* Mafia, *companilismo*).

A restructured community reflected the interests and needs of second generation Italians who remained in the original settlement, as well as the institutional means available to them at a particular historical juncture (Kramer and Leventman, 1969:21-34). Its basic component was the family group. The family probably had greater institutional significance for the ethnic com-

munity following World War I since the early settlement contained a disproportionate number of male sojourners whose experience was organized around the padrone, the lodging house and the aid societies, and whose primary goal was to earn money and return to the paese. Notwithstanding "Americanizing pressures", traditional family patterns were very much in evidence after World War I. The family continued to determine the individuals principal status. Localized kin comprised a closeknit network which articulated with the Italian neighborhood on a number of levels. Neighbors were critics of deviation from the code governing family life, and demonstrated a mutual "respect" for the sanctity of families and for familism in the abstract. Neighborhood families evidenced common traditions which distinguished them from "the Americans" and countered the acculturative "pressures" of the larger society. To this extent, neighborhood replaced the paesani group as the moral context for ethnic family traditions. The rhythms of family life were a defining characteristic of Italian community ("a family neighborhood").

Family ties and familism were supplemented by peer group relationships which became more available and autonomous in an urban setting. Italian American males, in particular, adopted a classic street corner pattern, reminiscent of the gatherings of peasant men in the piazza and the cafe. This included the formation of social/athletic clubs, a phenomenon that Ware noted for the Irish in Greenwich Village (1965:355). Male street corner groups were settings for sociability, but also exercised informal control within the Italian community (e.g., keeping an eye on "strangers", making sure that adolescents behaved themselves). Neighborhood women also evolved a peer group pattern around mothers' clubs, bingo and other parish activities, the supervision of children and the daily shopping; it was built on a traditional domestic role and included female kin (in particular, there was a need to accommodate "Mama"). Neighborhood youth achieved considerable autonomy in the schoolyard and playground and in settlement houses and parish activities which gave organizational expression to their peer group life.

The South Village Italian American community possessed an institutional superstructure formed by the parish, the local district clubs and the Mafia syndicate—it was not just a neighborhood of family-centered peer groups. Membership in these voluntary organizations had a formal and instrumental character and mediated ties to the larger society. Parish priests, club politicians and Mafiosi had leadership roles although the latter two primarily pursued narrow, special interests. The urban parish and machine politics were handed down by the Irish; despite animosity and conflict, the Irish served as models for the adjustment of South Village Italians to American urban institutions. Still the parish and the political club had somewhat different roles in the Italian Village owing to historical circumstances (e.g., New Deal reforms which undermined district organizations) and the logic of ethnic succession (the Irish retained power at the diocesan level and in the county Democratic organization), as well as a cultural background which assigned a more central importance to kinship and was outright wary of political and religious institutions. Mafia traditions imparted a distinctive character to crime syndicates operating out of the Italian neighborhood. The American Mafia combined elements of the urban gang found among other low status ethnic groups with traditional patterns of social organizations and an "Old World" moral code (*e.g.,* the web of kinship, *omerta*). The role of the Mafia perhaps did not have a parallel in other ethnic neighborhoods with its implications for social control and the ethnic economy, and its articulation with underlying cultural mores.

Whereas the immigrant community was an extension of the paese, in the second generation group life was embedded in the Italian neighborhood. The neighborhood enclosed the bulk of meaningful social interactions. This was true because kinship and peer group relations were localized. In contrast to the alien and threatening city, the neighborhood was a safe moral world. A greater degree of trust obtained within the neighborhood because one was widely known and knew, or knew of, a ramifying network of individuals and families (where social life was localized and families remained over the years). There was also a sense of security in a shared ethnicity and common culture. Perhaps most importantly, informal controls were in place. The neighborhood acquired the properties of a protective enclosure where residents encumbered the movements of strangers, usurping official authority. Carving out a "social turf" (Greeley, 1971:95-102) and a "defended neighborhood" (Suttles, 1972:21-43) is common to working populations in the city. It may be argued that the bounded ethnic neighborhood was indispensable for coming to terms with the strangeness and dangers of the city, especially in light of a peasant background which regarded the unknown with fear and craved familiar patterns of behavior and response.

A change in the ethnic identification accompanied the transformation of ethnic community. In the second generation, paesani identification was subliminated within an expanded concept of ethnicity; the second generation was Italian (American) and the South Village was an Italian neighborhood. This development reflected common acculturation experiences; second generation Italians drew invidious distinctions between themselves and immigrant paesani who were "just off the boat". Ethnicity set the South Village and its residents apart in a city where the principal social divisions are the ethnic ones.

These communal changes presupposed certain ecological and structural conditions. There were no serious invasions of unacceptable groups or industry which impart a classic instability to ethnic slums and other zones of transition (Ward, 1971). At the same time, there was ample employment for working class Italian Americans in the vicinity as well as access to transportation routes (Yancey *et al.,* 1976). This made it possible to exercise the cultural preference to remain within the ethnic community, especially in light of ethnic prejudice before World War II. Although the tenement neighborhood precluded a middle class existence, particularly home ownership, it was able to accommodate substantial improvements in the living standards of working class families.

The South Village Italian neighborhood, then, was able to absorb social and economic changes in the second generation, becoming a viable communal alternative to both immigrant frameworks and mainstream social settings. However, families that stayed into the second or third generation have left in the third or fourth. Somewhere along the line, ethnic localism is experienced as too provincial and there is a desire for "something better" than the tenement neighborhood. The South Village Italian population continues to contract and, in recent years, a distinctive Italian neighborhood has become more absorbed by the SoHo artists' community. In light of these and other developments, a number of observations may be tendered concerning the nature of neighborhood life in the present:

1) Institutions that structured a neighborhood community for the second generation are either withering away (political clubs, street corner groups and social/athletic clubs, the protective enclosure, the localized kinship groups and interfamilial solidarity) or becoming disengaged from the neighborhood (the mobile family, the prestigious businessmen's clubs, the Mafia syndicate, the parish), or else oriented in the direction of new groups in the South Village (the Mafia syndicate, the neighborhood economy, the parish social settlements). With the influx of so many non-Italians, the historical identity of the South Village as an "Italian neighborhood" has been rendered untenable. At the same time, acculturation has further diluted distinctively Italian customs and tastes (*e.g.,* the use of dialect, amulets and charms protecting against the evil eye, familism itself); because of their peasant origins, they have often been incompatible with a rise in social status (*e.g.,* meals reflecting a subsistence economy such as escarole and beans).

2) Several trends portended another restructuring of local life. Neighborhood Italians have been increasingly integrated within social welfare programs directly or indirectly funded by government. A large segment of the community receives Social Security income, participates in the Medicare and food stamp programs, or is on welfare. In recent years, local parishes and settlements have initiated senior citizens' programs with

159

the help of state and federal grants. A Greenwich Village hospital has enrolled elderly Italians in a federally financed program that provides hot meals at home. Teenagers are another problem constituency, especially in light of gang activities that have threatened the middle class. In recent years, settlement houses, civic organizations and local parishes have vied for government funded youth programs. Perhaps the most significant development along these lines was the ill- fated Problem Center which aspired to procure bureaucratic resources for the local population (*e.g.,* senior citizens rent exemptions, half-fare transit passes). It also adumbrated a new definition of community which included young newcomers and the Portuguese. However, its hybrid character contained too many contradictions. Intergroup differences could not be reconciled although it was the old-guard neighborhood power structure, responding to what seemed like a usurpation of their influence, that delivered the decisive blow. Local Italians had been reluctant to give the Center their mandate and approach it with their problems, preferring not to advertise their personal business or lodge complaints that might "cause trouble". Where possible, Italians continued to rely primarily on customary solutions. Thus, the elderly were looked after by their children and local leaders, still thirsting for recognition, performed small favors. Increasingly, however, traditional resources were becoming strained.

3) Some civic leaders and other residents envisioned a reorganization of community along the lines of the restoration, or *risorgimento,* proposed for the East side by local Italians and the City Planning Commission. The East side was designated a "special district" by the city with a view toward preserving its Italian character, which was threatened by the mobility of Italian residents and the expansion of Chinatown (and, to a lesser extent, the Hispanic community beginning at The Bowery). A restoration plan was to include the upgrading of existing buildings, the construction of moderate-income housing, expanded community services, street improvement and an Italian American cultural center (New York City Department of City Planning, 1974). This was intended to keep upwardly mobile Italians in the neighborhood and even lure them back from the suburbs. The plan was heralded by the mayor, Italian American politicians and organizations and urban planners and received considerable coverage in the city's newspapers. Inevitably, Italians in the South Village, which historically has had close ties with the East side and was part of the same assembly district, hoped for a risorgimento in their neighborhood. There was talk that if adequate housing was available young couples would stay in

160

the neighborhood. A South Village civic leader proclaimed in a LIRA phamphlet that "a new feeling of togetherness" was evident that "we must take advantage of in order to reaffirm in our minds and in the minds of others our unique identity as Italian Americans". At one point the director of the Problem Center intended his organization to be a mirror image of LIRA, referring to the South Village as "Little Italy West". (However, this concept generated little interest.)

To begin with, South Village Italians were not threatened by an influx of low status groups as were East Side Italians, and so were not defensive and mobilized for direct ethnic confrontation.[1] Perhaps most important, South Village business interests, the Mafia included, were revitalized by SoHo. On the other hand, the ethnic economy of the East Side, which always had a great supply of Italian restaurants and specialty shops, was endangered by the new immigrants. It was no coincidence the local Italian businessmen and real estate interests were the backbone of LIRA and that the main thrust of the Little Italy plan was a *risorgimento* for the ethnic economy (none of the rendered objectives materialized). SoHo afforded favorable investment opportunities for the South Village as well as the factory district; in particular, it precipitated a sharp rise in land values and new profits for neighborhood shops. Moreover, the city was not about to designate another Italian "special district".

4) Although the South Village was not destined to become the city's Italian quarter, its Italian heritage has undergone a degree of elaboration and commercialization as a result of events in Little Italy and the recent interest in ethnicity. As it withers away as an Italian neighborhood, various sights and attractions conducive to an ethnic experience have been distilled as a cultural resource for the city. The most prominent purveyor of local ethnicity is the old Italian church with its annual *festa Italiana,* Christmas display and relics belonging to the shrine. Pastors have deliberately cultivated this "touristy" dimension, with the aid of sophisticated public relations, as the number of parishioners has dwindled. Emulating the success of Little Italy, businessmen have given patrons Italian atmosphere. Thus, a neighborhood luncheonette and a corner bar installed facilities

---

[1] Neighborhood Italians were uncomfortable with the assertive style and ideology of the "new ethnicity. Historically, Italian American ethnicity has been taken for granted, reserved, ambivalent. Low status ethnic groups like Italian Americans have sought to cultivate a low profile in order to deflect attention from themselves. Ethnic assertion has taken ethnic identification and solidarity in new directions (Congress of Italian American Organizations, 1975; Novak, 1973).

for the *al fresco* trade. Neighborhood Italians have become part of the attraction. Tourists come to see animated cornerbovs. old women in black coats and loquacious shopkeepers, in addition to salamis and cheese hanging in shop windows.

5) Besides having a touristic value, the South Village has had an appeal for the middle class students and artists as a *gemeinschaft* community in the midst of an impersonal, bureaucratic society. The Problem Center enlisted the support of a number of post-Woodstock young people from affluent backgrounds who were impressed with ethnic localism. A nostalgic article in *The New Yorker* portrayed the South Village not only as "a nice place to live", but as the embodiment of fundamental national values. In particular, its citizens did not rely on bureaucrats for solutions to their problems. The article focused attention on the Problem Center as an example of "community self help". although it missed the point that the Center was establishing a precedent by trying to integrate the South Village with city agencies and federal programs. There was also approbation for the physical neighborhood. Professional urban planners waxed enthusiastic about the historic storefronts and patterns of street use ("pedestrianization"), and urged preservation of the existing local scale as opposed to clearance and high-rise development. It was ironic that the larger society was extolling the tenement neighborhood and ethnic community now that few Italians were left; hitherto, they were regarded as constraints which had to be transcended if one was to be considered an American and possess a respectable status.

6) At the present time, the South Village Italian population includes a significant number of people whose membership in the community is defined by some setback or constraint rather than choice (Pahl, 1970:105). This includes the elderly and/or persons in poor health, individuals who are widowed or divorced, children whose duty it is to look after aging and infirm parents, and those who gamble or drink too much. There are also the so-called "characters" who affect socially deviant life-styles.

Neighborhood Italians are sometimes accused by mobile relatives and friends of not wanting to better themselves, often because they do not think they're worthy of something better. Mobile Italians "escaped" from the neighborhood and tend to relate to the old neighborhood as a measure of how far they have come. With the elderly as possible exceptions, many people are uncomfortable with the knowledge that they are the last ones in the neighborhood. Their situation has become more precarious now that the neighborhood has fewer redeeming qualities with the ero-

162

sion of social frameworks, crime, "strangers", etc.

7) Although SoHo has brought the physical benefits of gentrification to the neighborhood, it has made many Italians even more conscious of being "left behind". Newcomers have thrown their lower socioeconomic status into relief; Italians are aware of disparities in income, education, experience, diction and housing, although Italians claim a moral superiority. Invidious status distinctions have intensified the resentment felt toward the newcomers for "taking over the neighborhood". Immigrants from Portugal evoke feelings of this sort only when there is word that one of them has bought a house out of the city or has started a small business—their success is typically rationalized by imputing to the immigrants frugal living habits and a propensity for working "like dogs".

8) Many South Village Italians assign the blame for the decline of their neighborhood to "outsiders". An articulate second generation attorney and civic leader bitterly suggested that the process started with "the first guitar player who came down here to play in the sixties"; the bohemians were followed by "rowdies and drunks and addicts" who were identified as being predominantly black. When this happened, according to the proprietor of a local grocery store, "the old families got fed up and moved out". Italian politicians like to point out that this process was abetted by "liberal non-Italians", in particular, the reform club that gained power in the early sixties. They adopted a permissive attitude toward these intruders at the expense of the Italian community. Liberals called Italians racists when the latter defended their neighborhood against intrusions like the welfare hotels. SoHo is perceived as one of a long line of encroachments—urban renewal, the expressway, drug treatment centers, coffee houses, etc.—which has expropriated the South Village on behalf of outside interests. One civic leader saw this as a final insult since American society had segregated Italians in slum neighborhoods and now the latter were being dispossessed.

While there is considerable truth in this scenario, it deflects attention from the principal cause of neighborhood decline: the preference of Italian Americans themselves for other lifestyles and settings. Moreover, mobile Italians have tended to escape from criticism because leaving the neighborhood has been accomplished in the name of "bettering yourself" and becoming American (*i.e.,* the rules laid down by the core culture). One civic leader did reach the conclusion that the neighborhood was disappearing because "second and third and fourth generation Italians are trying to become Americans", opting for the suburbs and consumerism. However, he was quick to shift the blame

163

for the betrayal to the "media, mainly television, which has made them want to be like everybody else". As with other Italians, there is a reluctance to admit that the present situation has anything to do with limitations in neighborhood life; Italians wanted to stay, but gave up on the neighborhood as the outside world began closing in. In this interpretation, neighborhood Italians are stalwarts who have not abandoned an authentic way of life, although they are being overrun by external forces. Perhaps in this manner the "social- psychological dilemmas" (Vidich and Bensman.1960:293) of those who are left behind are made more palatable.

9) Nostalgia has assumed an important function for neighborhood Italians. Reminiscing about the old days recreates for the moment a time when, even though "things were rough", "families were close", "people had respect", and "our doors were always open". The feeling for the past has spawned several reunions. Several middle- aged cornerboys organized an "Old Timers' Affair" for a group of people who were neighbors before World War II. The reception in a Jersey City catering hall was attended by 529 people; approximately half were no longer living in the South Village. Harkening back to the old days reflects a preference for a time when everyone was still in the neighborhood and lived the same way. However, while nostalgia for a common past can furnish a basis for integration, a "community in the mind" (Pahl, 1970:102; Vidich and Bensman, 1960) obviously has its limits. This was driven home when less than 300 people attended the second annual "Old Timers' Affair"; people were curious about one another, but the neighborhood had been relegated to the past.

Rethinking Ethnic Community

The case of the South Village points up the shortcomings of a perspective that views the ethnic neighborhood from the standpoint of assimilation (and disorganization) and generally regards ethnic community as an artifact of the immigrant experience. A more fruitful approach would recognize ethnic community as capable of assuming new forms and shapes in response to the social-historical context.

The present period suggests that the neighborhood-based Italian American community, like the immigrant (paesani) colony, is an historically specific form of urban ethnic community. Notwithstanding the "new ethnicity" and hopes for a risorgimento of the old neighborhoods, third and fourth generation Italian Americans are moving further into the mainstream. This does not discount the possibility of predominantly Italian American areas such as Dyker Heights in Brooklyn. However, they have more in common with other middle class communities than neighborhoods like the South Village.

While the old neighborhood is in eclipse, certain institutions have managed to adjust to new settings. Most notably, core ethnic family patterns are still discernible in the suburbs; Mafia syndicates have penetrated legitimate enterprises far beyond the ethnic neighborhood. They are further transformed in the process. The family group is smaller, more conjugal and child- centered; the Mafia has adopted corporate practices and syndicate personnel commute from the suburbs.

At the same time, new forms of ethnic identification and association are evident outside the neighborhood. They are based on common interest, as well as the satisfaction of primordial or affective needs (Glazer and Moynihan, 1963). Thus there are associations of Italian American businessmen and professionals, advocacy groups, as well as symposiums on the ethnic experience; specialized ethnic networks are kept in touch by mass circulation techniques. A wider American subsociety is informed (and defined) by the magazine *Attenzione* with features on successful Italian American personalities, the Italian heritage and contemporary Italian society. It is a subsociety that is rather affluent and acculturated. In 1980, *Attenzione* subcribers had a median income of $37,300; 80 percent were homeowners (19% owned a second home); 58 percent had professional or managerial occupations; in their leisure, they attended the theater, visited art galleries, jogged and played tennis (*Attenzione* Subscriber and Subscriber *Household Profile,* 1980).

In contrast to the "24 hours a day" ethnicity (Ibson, 1981) of the urban village, these developments signify an ethnicity that is circumscribed by nonethnic roles and identities. The social and psychological investment in ethnicity is limited and 'situational' (Etzioni, 1959). Italian Americans featured in *Attenzione* are firmly embedded in the dominant culture; articles discuss matters such as energy, environment, medicine and feminism (although against the background of cherished ethnic tradition). Ethnic expression tends to focus on elements that are "abstracted" from the larger cultural pattern, like Renaissance art and traditional cooking, and transformed into "symbols"; to this extent, mainstream Italian Americans have evolved a "symbolic ethnicity" that is compatable with mainstream life-styles (Gans, 1979). Moreover, this "new" Italian American ethnicity would seem to be palatable to upwardly mobile Italian Americans or at least not pose any major status dilemmas at higher class levels (Tricarico, 1983). *Attenzione* depicts an affluent

165

standard of living beyond ethnicity (*e.g.*, advertisements for designer clothing) that leaves little room for working class Italian Americans. A middle class ethnicity also relies heavily on high Italian culture: that this is not rooted in the "actual and immediate background circumstances of Italian Americans" (Aversa, 1978) illustrates the ability of ethnic groups to engage in "collective impression management" (Lyman and Douglass, 1973) and even "fictitious accounts" (Shibutani and Kwan 1965:43) in the development of new cultural "styles" (Royce, 1982). These developments suggest that what is happening among Italian Americans (and other groups) may be viewed not as a resurgence or "gasp" of ethnic sentiment in the face of more complete assimilation (Steinberg, 1981; Crispino, 1980), but an aspect of their ongoing transformation.

Ironically, the old neighborhoods have acquired a significance for the new Italian American ethnicity. Hitherto, mobile Italian Americans have had to sever ties to the neighborhood to consolidate status gains and resist cultural backsliding. However, with the qualified acceptance of ethnicity in contemporary society, the search for ethnic roots has focused attention on the old Italian neighborhoods. As their population and communal base continue to contract, neighborhoods like the South Village provide a context for the situated public expression of Italian American ethnicity, as well as a "cultural scene" (Irwin, 1977) that enriches and entertains the cosmopolitan middle class in the manner of Chinatown and Lincoln Center (the enthusiasm of significant others has legitimated the Italian neighborhood as a symbol for upper status Italian Americans). As "Little Italy", the Mulberry Street/East Side neighborhood has become the symbolic homeland for the city's Italian Americans, although it could be argued that the restaurants and street festivals trivialize the ethnic heritage. Its official status has overshadowed other neighbohoods, including more vital Italian communities in Brooklyn and the Bronx (the East Side had an effective political lobby and offered a Manhattan location). Notwithstanding Little Italy and the new SoHo scene (*i.e.*, modern art and trendy sophistication), the South Village has maintained credible links to the Italian American experience with attractions like the annual *festa Italiana.*

Although a powerful focus of ethnic identification and expression, the old neighborhood may not be indispensable. The principal "*festa* from the heart of Little Italy in New York" now has an out-of-town run in a New Jersey suburb. Although the parking lot of a sprawling shopping center that served as the site lacked the ambiance of Mulberry Street, the movable feast points to the changing, nonspatial character of Italian American life. This is important if only because the old neighborhoods have new residents; even Little Italy is predominantly Chinese.

166

The Italian South Village cannot rival Mulberry Street as an ethnic quarter; its cultural and symbolic value for a larger audience remains limited (of course, for those who have never left the ethnic neighborhood, the latter has more than symbolic and situational significance). At the same time, SoHo has successfully introduced an entirely different cultural "scene" (Irwin, 1977), virtually erasing a distinctive Italian neighborhood. While the Italian American population has retained a foothold, the future of the area belongs to the art galleries, co-ops, boutiques, and fern bars.

Bibliography

Abrahamson, H. 1973. *Ethnic Diversity in Catholic America.* New York: John Wiley.

Adams, C. 1881. "Italian Life in New York", *Harpers Monthly.* Pp. 666 - 684. April.

Albini, J. 1971. *The American Mafia: Genesis of a Legend.* New York: Appleton- Century- Crofts.

Aversa, A. 1978. "Italian Neo- Ethnicity: The Search for Self- Identity", *The Journal of Ethnic Studies,* 6(2):49- 56. Summer.

Banfield, E.C. 1958 *The Moral Basis of a Backward Society.* New York: Free Press

Banfield, E.C. and J.Q. Wilson. 1966. *City Politics.* New York: Vintage.

Barth, F. 1969. *Ethnic Groups and Boundaries.* Boston: Little Brown.

Bayor, R. 1978. *Neighbors in Conflict.* Baltimore: Johns Hopkins University Press.

Bell, D. 1961. *The End of Ideology.* New York: Collier.

Bianco, C. 1974. *The Two Roseto's.* Bloomington: Indiana University Press.

Blauner, R. 1972. *Racial Oppression in America.* New York: Harper and Row.

Breton, R. 1964. "Institutional Completeness of Ethnic Communities and the Personal Relations of Immigrants", *The American Journal of Sociology.* 70:193- 205. September.

Campisi, P. 1948. "Ethnic Family Patterns: The Italian Family in the United States", *The American Journal of Sociology.* 53:443- 449. May.

Chapman, C.G. 1971. *Milocca: A Sicilian Village.* Cambridge: Schenkman Publishing Company.

Child, I. 1970. *Italian or American? The Second Generation in Conflict.* New York: Russell and Russell.

Cloward, R. and F.F. Piven. 1975. *The Politics of Turmoil.* New York: Vintage.

Congress of Italian American Organizations. 1975. *A Portrait of the Italian American Community in New York City.* Vol. 1.

169

Connable, A. and E. Silberfarb. 1967. *Tigers of Tammany.* New York: Holt, Rinehart and Winston.

Cordasco, F. and E. Bucchioni, eds. 1974. *The Italians: Social Backgrounds of an American Group.* Clifton, N.J.: Augustus M. Kelly.

Covello, L. 1967. *The Social Background of the Italo- American Schoolchild.* Leiden, Netherlands: E.J. Brill.

Cressey, P.F. 1938. "Population Succession in Chicago: 1898- 1930", *The American Journal of Sociology.* 44:59- 69.

Crispino, J. 1980. *The Assimilation of Ethnic Groups: The Italian Case.* Staten Island: Center for Migration Studies.

D'Alessandre, J. 1935. "Occupational Trends of Italians in New York City", *Italy- America Monthly.* 2:11- 21. February.

DeVos, G. and L. Romanucci- Ross eds. 1975. *Cultural Continuities and Change.* Palo Alto: Mayfield.

Ernst, R. 1949. *Immigrant Life in New York, 1823- 1863.* New York: Columbia University Press.

Etzioni, A. 1959. "The Ghetto: A Re- evaluation", *Social Forces.* 39:255- 262.

Feagin, J. 1974. "Community Disorganization: Some Critical Notes". In *The Community: Approach and Application.* Edited by M.P. Effrat. Pp. 124- 146. New York: Free Press.

Femminella, F.X. and J. Quadagno. 1976. "The Italian American Family". In *Ethnic Families in America.* Edited by C.H. Mindel and R.W. Habenstein. New York: Elsevier. Pp. 61- 88.

Fenton, E. 1975. *Immigrants and Unions, A Case Study: Italians and American Labor, 1870- 1920.* New York: Arno Press.

Firey, W. 1947. *Land Use in Central Boston.* Cambridge: Harvard University Press.

Fischer, C. 1975. "Toward a Subcultural Theory of Urbanism". *The American Journal of Sociology.* 80(6):1319- 1341. May.

Fitzpatrick, J. 1966. "The Importance of 'Community' in the Process of Immigrant Assimilation". *International Migration Review.* 1:5- 16. Fall.

Foerster, R. 1919. *The Italian Emigration of Our Times.* Cambridge: Harvard University Press.

Francis, E.K. 1976. *Interethnic Relations.* New York: Elsevier.

Fried, M. 1973. *The World of the Urban Working Class.* Cambridge: Harvard University Press.

_____ 1963. "Grieving for a Lost Home". In *The Urban Condition.* Edited by L. Duhl. New York: Simon and Schuster.

Gabriel, R. and P. Savage. 1976. "The Urban Italian: Patterns of Political Accommodation to Local Regimes". In *the Urban Experience of Italian Americans*. Edited by P. Gallo. New York: Center for Migration Studies.

Gallo, P. 1975. *Ethnic Alienation*. Rutherford, N.J.: Farleigh Dickinson University Press.

Gans, H. 1982. "Symbolic Ethnicity: The Future of Ethnic Groups and Cultures in America". In *Majority and Minority*. Edited by N.R. Yetman. Boston: Allyn and Bacon.

———— 1962. *The Urban Villagers*. New York: Free Press.

Glanz, R. 1971. *Jew and Italian*. New York: KTAV Publishing Company.

Gordon, M. 1978. *Human Nature, Class and Ethnicity*. New York: Oxford.

———— 1964. *Assimilation in American Life*. New York: Oxford.

Greeley, A. 1972. *Ethnicity in the United States*. New York: Wiley.

————. 1971. *Why Can't They Be Like Us?*. New York: E.P. Dutton.

Gutman, H. 1977. *The Black Family in Slavery and Freedom*. New York: Vintage.

Hall, P. 1966. *The World Cities*. New York: World University Library.

Harris, R. 1977. "A Nice Place to Live". *The New Yorker*. April 25.

Hemstreet, C. 1895. *Nooks and Corners of Old New York*. New York: Charles Scribner's Sons.

Hobsbawm, E. 1959. *Primitive Rebels*. New York: Norton.

Ianni, F. 1972. *A Family Business*. New York: Mentor.

————. 1971. "The Mafia and the Web of Kinship". *Public Interest*. 22. Winter.

Ibson, J. 1981. Virgin Land or Virgin Mary? Studying the Ethnicity of White Americans", *American Quarterly*. 33(3):284- 308.

Iorizzo, L. and S. Mondello. 1971. *The Italian Americans*. New York: Twayne.

Irwin, J. 1977. *Scenes*. New York: Russell Sage.

Italian American Center for Urban Affairs. 1974. *Preliminary Profile of Italian Americans Living in New York City.*

Jacobs, J. 1961. *The Death and Life of Great American Cities*. New York: Random House.

Janowitz, M. 1967. *The Community Press in an Urban Setting*. Chicago: University of Chicago Press.

Johnson, J.W. 1930. *Black Manhattan*. New York: Knopf.

171

Jones, H.D. 1933. The Evangelical Movement Among Italians in New York City. Community Committee of the Federation of Churches of Greater New York and the Brooklyn Churches and Missions Federation.

Judson Health Center. 1927. *Annual Report.*

Keller, S. 1968. *The Urban Neighborhood.* New York: Random House.

Kempton, S. 1966. "Beatitudes at Judson Church", *Esquire.* March.

Kessner, T. 1977. *The Golden Door.* New York: Oxford.

Kommaravosky, M. 1967. *Blue- Collar Marriage.* New York: Random House.

Kramer, J. and S. Leventman. 1969. *Children of the Gilded Ghetto.* New York: Archon Books.

Laidlaw, W.F. 1933. *Population of the City of New York, 1890- 1930.* New York. Cities Census Commission, Inc.

Lieberson, S. 1963. *Ethnic Patterns in American Cities.* New York: Free Press.

Lofland, L. 1973. *A World of Strangers.* New York: Basic Books.

Lopata, H. 1976. *Polish American Competition in an Ethnic Community.* Englewood Cliffs, N.J.: Prentice Hall.

Lopreato, J. 1970. *Italian Americans.* New York: Random House.

Lord, J. *et al.* 1905. *The Italians in America.* New York: B.F. Buck and Company.

Lyman, S. 1974. *Chinese Americans.* New York: Random House.

_____. 1972. *The Black American in Sociological Thought.* New York: Capricorn.

Lyman, S. and M. Scott. 1970. "Territorially: A Neglected Dimension". In *The Study of Society.* Edited by P. Rose. New York: Random House.

Lyman, S.M. and W. Douglass. 1973. "Ethnicity: Structure of Impression Management", *Social Research.* 40(2):344- 365. Summer.

MacDonald, J. and L. 1962. "Urbanization, Ethnic Groups, and Social Segmentation", *Social Research.* 29:433-448. Winter.

Mangano, A. 1915. *Religious Work for Italians in America: A Handbook for Leaders in Missionary Work.* New York: Immigrant Work Committee of the Home Missionary Council.

Mariano, J. 1921. *The Italian Contribution to America.* New York: The Christopher Publishing House.

Marraro, H. 1949. "Italians in New York in the 1850s". *New York History.* 30:181- 203. April.

Moquin, W. and C. VanDoren eds. 1974. *A Documentary History of the Italian Americans.* New York: Praeger.

Mumford, L. 1961. *The City in History.* New York: Harcourt, Brace and World.

Muraskin, W. 1974. "The Moral Basis of a Backward Sociologist: Edward Banfield, the Italians, and the Italian Americans". *The American Journal of Sociology.* 79(6):1484- 1496.

Nelli, H. 1970. *Italians in Chicago, 1880- 1930.* New York: Oxford.

New York City Department of City Planning. 1974. *Little Italy Risorgimento: Proposals for the Restoration of an Historic Community.*

Novak, M. 1973. *The Rise of the Unmeltable Ethnics.* New York: Macmillan.

Odencrantz, L.C. 1919. *Italian Women in Industry.* New York: Russell Sage.

Ottley, R. and C. Weathersby, eds. 1967. *The Negro in New York.* New York: New York Public Library.

Pahl, R.E. 1970. *Patterns of Urban Life.* London: Longman.

Park, R.E. 1952. *Human Communities.* New York: Free Press.

Park, R.E. and H. Miller. 1921. *Old World Traits Transplanted.* New York: Harper and Row.

Park, R.E. *et al.* 1925. *The City.* Chicago: University of Chicago Press.

Parsons, A. 1969. *Magic Belief, and Anomie.* New York: Free Press.

Parsons, T. 1954. *Essays in Sociological Theory.* New York: Free Press.

Patterson, O. 1977. *Ethnic Chauvinism: The Reactionary Impulse.* New York: Stein and Day.

Pecorini, A. 1974. "Italian Progress in the United States". In *A Documentary History of the Italian Americans.* Edited by W. Moquin and C. VanDoren. New York: Praeger. 89- 95.

Pleck, E. 1978. "A Mother's Wages: Income Earning Among Married Italian and Black Women, 1896- 1911". In *The American Family in Social- Historical Perspective.* Edited by M. Gordon. New York: St. Martin's. 490- 510.

Queen, S.A. and D.B. Carpenter. 1972. *The American City.* Westport, Conn.: Greenwood Press.

Riis, J. 1900. *A Ten Year's Wait.* New York: Houghton- Mifflin.

———. 1890. *How The Other Half Lives.* New York: Charles Scribner's Sons.

Royce, A.P. 1982. *Ethnic Identity: Strategies for Diversity.* Bloomington: Indiana University Press.

173

Sandberg, N. 1974. *Ethnic Identity and Assimilation: The Polish American Case.* New York: Praeger.

Schiavo, G. 1958. *Four Centuries of Italian American History.* New York: Vigo Press.

_____. 1947- 1949. *Italian American History* (2 volumes). New York: Vigo Press.

_____. 1924. *Italians in America Before the Civil War.* New York: G.P. Putnam's Sons.

Selvaggi, G. 1978. *The Rise of the Mafia in New York From 1896 Through World War II,* New York: Bobbs-Merrill.

Sennett, R. 1974. *Families Against the City.* New York: Vintage.

Sennett, R. and J. Cobb. 1972. *The Hidden Injuries of Class.* New York: Vintage.

Shibutani, T. and K.M. Kwan. 1965. *Ethnic Stratification: A Comparative Ap proach.* New York: Macmillan.

Shorter, E. 1975. *The Making of the Modern Family.* New York: Basic Books.

Simpson C. 1981. *SoHo: The Artist in the City.* Chicago: University of Chicago Press.

Sollors, W. 1981. "Theory of American Ethnicity, OR: ? Ethnic/TI and American/TI, De or United (W) States S SI and Theor?", American Quarterly, Vol. 33. No. 3 (Bibliography 1981), pp. 257- 283.

Sowell, T. 1975. *Race and Economics.* New York: Davis McKay Company.

Stack C. 1974. *All Our Kin.* New York: Harper and Row.

Stein, M. 1960. *The Eclipse of Community.* New York: Harper and Row.

Steinberg, S. 1981. *The Ethnic Myth: Race, Ethnicity and Class in America.* New York: Atheneum.

Suttles, G. 1972. *The Social Construction of Communities.* Chicago: University of Chicago Press.

_____. 1968. *The Social Order of the Slum.* Chicago: University of Chicago Press.

Tomasi, L. 1972. *The Italian American Family.* New York: Center for Migration Studies.

Tomasi, S. 1975. *Piety and Power.* New York: Center for Migration Studies.

Tomasi, S. and M. Engel, eds. 1970. *The Italian American Experience.* New York: Center for Migration Studies.

Tricarico, D. 1984. "The 'New' Italian American Ethnicity". *Journal of Ethnic Studies.*

Vecoli, R. 1978. "The Coming of Age of the Italian Americans: 1945-1974". *Ethnicity*. 4:119-147.

_____ 1972. "European Americans: From Immigrants to Ethnics". *International Migration Review*. 6:403-434. Winter.

_____. 1969. "Prelates and Peasants: Italian Immigration and the Catholic Church". *Journal of Social History*. (2):217-268. Spring.

Vidich, A. "Community Structures in World Perspective: Decline and Transfiguration", an unpublished paper.

Vidich. A.J. and J. Bensman. 1975. *Metropolitan Communities*. New York: The New York Times Company.

_____. 1960. *Small Town in Mass Society*. Garden City, Doubleday.

Wallace, S. 1980. *The Urban Environment*. Homewood, Illinois: The Dorsey Press.

Ward. D. 1971. *Immigrants and Cities: A Geography of Change in Nineteenth Century America*. New York: Oxford.

Ware, C. 1965. *Greenwich Village, 1920-1930*. New York: Harper and Row.

Weed, P. 1971. *The White Ethnic Movement and Ethnic Politics*. New York: Macmillan.

Whyte, W.F. 1943. *Streetcorner Society*. New York: The Free Press.

Williams, P. 1938. *Southern Italian Folkways in Europe and America*. New Haven: Yale University Press.

Wirth, L. 1964. *On Cities and Social Life*. Chicago: University of Chicago Press.

Works Project Administration. 1937. *Community Study of Greenwich Village*. No. 465-97-3-96.

Yancey, W. *et al.* 1976. "Emergent Ethnicity: A Review and Reformulation". *American Sociological Review*. 41:391-403. June.

Yans-Mclaughlin, V. 1971. "Patterns of Work and Family Organization: Buffalo's Italians". In *The Family in History*. Edited by T.K. Rabb and R.I. Rotberg. New York: Harper and Row.

Young, M. and P. Wilmott. 1957. *Family and Kinship in East London*. London: Routledge and Kegan Paul.

Index

178

179